Argumentative Writing in a Second Language

PERSPECTIVES ON RESEARCH AND PEDAGOGY

Argumentative Writing in a Second Language

PERSPECTIVES ON RESEARCH AND PEDAGOGY

Edited by

Alan Hirvela
Ohio State University

AND

Diane Belcher
Georgia State University

University of Michigan Press
Ann Arbor

Copyright © by the University of Michigan 2021
All rights reserved
Published in the United States of America
The University of Michigan Press
Printed and bound by CPI Group (UK) Ltd, Croydon, CR0 4YY

ISBN-13: 978-0-472-03867-1 (print)
ISBN-13: 978-0-472-12947-8 (ebook)

2024   2023   2022   2021   4   3   2   1

■ Acknowledgments

First, we want to thank the contributors to this volume for the valuable insights they have provided on L2 argumentative writing and for their deep commitment to this important area of teaching and research. We also want to thank, on yet another occasion, Kelly Sippell at the University of Michigan Press. We have had the great pleasure of working with Kelly on several volumes published by UMP, and she has always been immensely helpful and supportive. She's always there when we need her. She is also a long-time and important ally for the field of second language writing, as witnessed by the numerous books on L2 writing that the UMP has published under her guidance, and we want to note these extremely valuable contributions she has made. Finally, our love and appreciation go to our always patient and understanding spouses.

■ Contents

■ Introduction

ALAN HIRVELA AND DIANE BELCHER

Argumentative writing has been part of the landscape of the second language (L2) writing field since its emergence as a field in its own right in the 1980s. By argumentative writing we mean writing in which, at a minimum, an author states a claim, uses some form of evidence—data, reasons, examples, etc.—to support the claim, and shows how the evidence supports the claim, i.e., engages in what is called warranting. In more elaborate forms, such writing may also include backing—statements which elaborate on the authority underlying the warrants—as well as rebuttals challenging the argument being made, and counterarguments which refute the rebuttals. Collectively, these elements form the core architecture of what is known as the "Toulmin model" introduced by Stephen Toulmin in 1958 and widely considered the dominant approach to argument used in argumentative writing instruction.

As noted by Silva (1993) in his major review of L2 writing research across different topics, early argumentative work focused on identifying the structures used by L2 writers in their argumentative essays. Another major topic in this earlier period was the issue of how to assess L2 argumentative essays. This was especially true in a series of important articles, book chapters, and conference presentations by Ulla Connor that involved looking at native language (L1) and L2 influences and relationships.

Argumentative writing was also one of the topics explored in two major international studies (1988, 1992) of writing conducted by the International Association for the Evaluation of Educational Achievement (IEA). Here, too, there was an emphasis on the characteristics and assessment of such writing. The scope began to widen in the 1990s (e.g., Belcher, 1997, focusing on models of argument, and Johns, 1993, looking at audience-related issues). In the current century, there has been a gradual increase in argumentatively oriented L2 scholarship, and it has continued to move beyond the foci of earlier argumentative work.

However, the situation on the whole is less than satisfactory. This point was brought home forcefully in a 2017 "Disciplinary Dialogues" section of the

Journal of Second Language Writing that addressed the current state of L2 argumentative writing scholarship. In his lead piece that initiated the dialogue, Hirvela raised a question as to whether L2 writing scholars are "missing the boat" in this area and commented on a number of specific shortcomings that he felt needed to be addressed. The authors of six commentaries written in response to his contribution (including some who appear in this edited collection: Ann Johns, Amanda Kibler, Silvia Pessoa, and Lia Plakans) shared a core belief in the importance of argumentative writing and offered important recommendations for how to move the field forward in this domain. This edited collection, *Argumentative Writing in a Second Language: Perspectives on Research and Pedagogy,* is in part a follow-up to this "Disciplinary Dialogues" conversation. That is, we have sought to explore, in greater depth, some of the questions and issues raised in that 2017 collection of papers, as well as other published work on this topic. We have also drawn upon our own experiences and knowledge as L2 writing scholars and teachers. We have witnessed firsthand the challenges that both teachers and students encounter as they engage this important but complex type of writing.

Another perspective guiding us in assembling this volume is how little L2 argumentative scholarship there is compared to the L1 domain as relates to both the teaching and learning of argumentative writing. This is a significant gap that needs to be filled. As Hirvela observed in his 2017 essay, in the L1 field there is what he called an "argument industry." In the L1 field, for example, there are numerous textbooks devoted *solely* to argumentative writing, many published in more than one edition due to their popularity. The same cannot be said about the L2 writing field. Indeed, there are no textbooks of that kind. Furthermore, when argument is addressed in L2 writing textbooks, it appears as just one type (or mode) of writing to be taught in a writing class. Even if L2 textbook writers note its importance as a kind of writing that students need to acquire, its significance is diminished by the fact that it is surrounded by so much information about other essay types (or modes) and other areas of writing. The argumentative essay is just one more face in the writing crowd.

Also noteworthy in the L1 field is the publication of teacher resource books that help prepare teachers to teach argumentative writing. Here, again, there are entire *books* devoted to argument, and they provide what might be called mainstream teachers with a wealth of pedagogical information and guidance. And here, too, we do not see an equivalent situation in the L2 field. Nor do we see edited collections focused on L2 argumentative writing. A number of such collections focusing on argumentative writing have been published, but L2-related work is almost non-existent in them.

This situation leaves L2 writing teachers with difficult choices to make. One option is to depend on the L1 textbooks and resource books and then attempt to adjust and transfer that input to the L2 writing classroom. While this effort may work to some degree, a challenge to overcome is that the L1 material is aimed at native speakers/writers of the target language (i.e., English in this case) and thus does not account for characteristics, nuances, and needs specific to L2 writers. Another choice is to draw upon the small supply of individual L2 articles that offer pedagogical suggestions and recommendations. However, despite the quality of that work, this is a still vastly underdeveloped body of pedagogical scholarship that is not likely to fully meet the needs of teachers, especially those lacking experience. Meanwhile, and as suggested earlier, L2 writing textbooks that include coverage of argumentation tend to allocate only a small amount of space to it due to the need to cover other essay types and topics. Furthermore, they are likely to present it in more formulaic ways that lead to superficial understanding and treatment of the argumentative essay. Thus, textbook treatment of argumentation, depending on the textbook, may not be the best option for many teachers. Finally, L2 writing teachers can also choose to rely strictly on their own instincts and beliefs, and for experienced L2 writing teachers, with their accumulation of experience and insight, this approach may work, but what about those who lack such a background?

In the final analysis, there is, at present, no place where L2 writing teachers can consult a larger body of L2 argumentative work instead of relying on fragments of argumentative scholarship that, however good it is, does not present a comprehensive and deeply informed picture of L2 argumentative writing. Our intention in this edited volume is to begin filling that gap in the L2 writing field by offering a wide-ranging collection of chapters that can serve as a first critical mass of L2 argumentative writing scholarship—that is, one thorough place where teachers and scholars can take an in-depth look at L2 argumentative writing.

Mitchell (2000, p. 146) points out that "a defining characteristic of a good student at the undergraduate level is success in argumentative writing." Along these same lines, Miller, Mitchell, and Pessoa (2016, p. 11) explain that "argumentative writing is a vital but challenging genre for university students, particularly second language writers." These same observations can apply to some L2 students at earlier points in their educational lives. This overall situation, together with the lack of sustained explorations of L2 argumentative writing, is what we sought to address in compiling this collection. Our hope is that this volume will also inspire the creation of other more substantial bodies of work that give teachers and researchers more extensive food for thought and more substantial supplies of pedagogical guidance.

While we have arranged the book so that it contains material that will appeal to teachers and researchers, we do not see these as separate groups of readers. Indeed, those chapters that view argumentative writing through a research lens focus on the L2 writing classroom and offer information as well as insights that can feed into classroom practice. Thus, while the book features separate sections that provide information, ideas, and insights concerning how we conceptualize argumentative writing for L2 writers (Part 1) and the results of classroom-based explorations of argumentative writing instruction (Part 2), we see the two parts as having reciprocal or bidirectional relationships with each other.

Another introductory point we want to draw attention to is a well-known distinction between two core orientations to argumentative pedagogy—*learning to argue* and *arguing to learn*—that directly or indirectly inform the chapters appearing in the two parts of the book. *Learning to argue* is an approach in which the primary intention is to help students build or construct arguments. In other words, they learn the commonly used ways of arranging or organizing an argumentative essay, as well as the reasoning underlying the content of their essay. In that respect, argumentation is an end or product. By contrast, *arguing to learn* is a pedagogical option in which the main purpose is to help students understand how to use argumentation as a tool of inquiry or learning, that is, as a process or means, not a product. The argumentative process leads them to deeper understanding of a topic or situation of interest to them. Our hope is that this book sheds useful light on these two different ways of treating argumentative writing.

Overview of Contents

This book features two parts, each comprising seven chapters. Part 1 is more discussion-oriented, with its authors offering analyses, perspectives, and suggestions that explore argumentative writing from a wide range of angles. Part 2 shifts the focus to argumentative writing in action via classroom-based research, as well as illustrations of what can be attempted and achieved in pedagogy. Through this arrangement, the book allows readers to view L2 argumentation in multiple ways and to triangulate their own understanding of and practices concerning L2 argumentative writing relative to the contexts in which they operate. This opportunity to engage L2 argumentation from numerous vantage points at the same time has been missing in the L2 writing field, save for the handful of short commentaries in the 2017 "Disciplinary Dialogues" section of the *Journal of Second Language Writing*. Therefore, the transition from Part 1 to Part 2 in this volume takes readers through a journey into L2 argumentation that we hope will generate new ideas, new research, and new pedagogy. We now provide brief highlights of the book's chapters.

Part 1: Conceptualizing Argumentative Writing Instruction and Research

This opening section of the volume addresses several different topics. The first chapter, "Situated Argumentation as a Rhetorical Act," written by Ann Johns, views argumentative writing instruction through the broader lens of *rhetoric*. Johns begins with the construct of argumentation as a complicated and context-dependent type of writing involving a number of rhetorical acts and encourages teachers to approach it from the perspective of what she calls "rhetorical flexibility." She cautions against viewing the argumentative essay as a rigid rhetorical structure to be imitated and discusses a number of aspects of argumentative writing that need to be accounted for in the creation of full, well-rounded argumentative essays. There are, she says, various rhetorical acts to be performed while composing an argumentative essay; she looks in particular at the language that is appropriate for the performance of these rhetorical acts. Also, as in other work she has published over the years, Johns promotes the idea of students studying the argumentative writing of experts and of teachers helping them, as novices, learn how to apply what experts do in their own L2 writing.

Amanda Kibler, Christine Hardigree, and Fares Karam, in "Online Resources for L2 Argumentative Writing in Secondary Schools: A View from the Field," shift the focus to *resources* available to teachers—more specifically, online resources that would be of interest and value to high school teachers. Working from the premise that these resources operate as "defacto conceptualizations of argumentation," they stress the need to carefully critique these resources. Their chapter then analyzes many of the activities and lesson plans in these resources. Next, in "Using the 3x3 Toolkit to Support Argumentative Writing across Disciplines," Tom Mitchell and Silvia Pessoa introduce another angle, *discipline-based writing* and argument as a *genre*, while also working from a pedagogical resources framework. Drawing on insights from systemic functional linguistics, they introduce a pedagogical device, the "3X3 toolkit," that they have developed to help students and teachers analyze and isolate genre features of argumentative writing as an important step toward students being able to meet the genre-based expectations for argumentative writing in three specific disciplinary settings (history, organizational behavior, and information systems).

Another transition in focus occurs in "Source-Based Argumentative Writing Assessment," where Lia Plakans and Renka Ohta discuss the *assessment* of argumentative writing involving the use of source texts and offer insights on how teachers can assess student performance through integrated reading-writing tasks that perform an argumentative function. Then, in "An Analysis of the Chinese Way of Arguing: Creating a Hybrid Model to Teach Argument as an Inquiry Process," Weier Ye and Lan Wang-Hiles bring an *intercultural rhetoric* lens to the volume as they explore the philosophical values that help shape Chinese students' understanding of argumentation and the challenges that arise for many Chinese writers as they transition to argumentative writing in English. Alan Hirvela then uses his chapter, "Expertise and the Teaching of Argumentative Writing," to focus on the notion of *writing teacher expertise* and to propose a model of expertise that can be used to study writing teachers' involvement in teaching argumentative writing. Noting the heavy emphasis in L2 argumentative writing research on students and their written performance—that is, student expertise—he discusses why it is equally important to study writing teachers and to foreground a notion of writing teacher expertise.

Part 1 concludes with "A Multilingual Orientation to Preparing Teaching Assistants to Teach Argumentation in First-Year Writing," where Parva Panahi takes up the topic of *teacher preparation*, and more specifically, that of graduate teaching associates who teach first year writing (FYW) courses that include both L1 and L2 writers. Panahi writes about the value of having a notion of "difference" in such courses and wants teachers to have what she calls an "understanding of difference as a resource." She describes a version of an FYW course for multilingual writers that could serve as a pedagogical model to be used in preparing FYW graduate teaching assistants.

Part 2: Applications and Research in the Classroom

In this part, we move into L2 classrooms where there are innovative approaches to teaching argumentation that researchers/teachers have closely examined the effectiveness of. The first two chapters, by Joel Bloch and Nugrahenny Zacharias, based in English as a second language (ESL) tertiary settings in the U.S., explore the affordances for teaching and learning argumentation in a digital multimodal environment, where the semiotic resources extend far beyond monomodal words on a page (or screen).

In "The New Bricolage: Assembling and Remixing Voice and Images in a Multimodal Argumentative Text," Bloch examines how digital storytelling presents an alternative approach to argumentation capable of increasing novice authorial autonomy by enabling L2 composers to become *bricoleurs* who transformatively assemble found images with their personal argumentative narratives. By offering expanded means of developing and expressing authorial voice and engaging with audience, digital storytelling, as analyzed by Bloch, facilitates use of rhetorical strategies potentially of value in both multi- and monomodal argumentation. Similarly, in her chapter, "Remediating L2 Students' Argumentation in an ESL Composition Class: From Print to Digital Argumentation," Zacharias looks at how an L2 student's remediation of a written argument in a website allows for the use of multiple visual modes with a variety of design options and intermodal relationship possibilities that greatly diversify the means of support for argumentative claims. Zacharias is realistic, however, about the disadvantages as well as the advantages of this digital approach to enlarging learners' argumentative repertoires.

English as a foreign language (EFL) settings, where English language learners may have limited opportunities for exposure to and use of their target language, can present significant challenges to teachers of L2 argumentative writing. In the next three chapters, the authors explicate how they have productively addressed these challenges in EFL settings. In "Blending Learning to Argue and Arguing to Learn in EFL Writing Instruction: A Classroom Inquiry," set in China at the university level, Min Zou, Xiaohui Li, and Icy Lee examine how a sequence of nine argument-focused activities designed to internalize argument schema and provide experience with inquiry helped students learn to argue and argue to learn. Through engagement with inquiry into intriguing easy-to-relate-to problems, Zou, Li, and Lee's approach appears to offer the possibility of heightening both cognition and motivation at the same time. Also in China, but in a high school setting, Qiling Wu and Zehang Chen's chapter ("An Action Research Study Aimed at Improving Chinese High School Students' Argumentation in EFL Writing") looks at the value of a two-phased series of classroom activities focused on learning to reason and then learning to argue, in other words, teaching reasoning, or logic, first, followed by written argument construction. The outcome of their action research has persuaded Wu and Chen that high school is not too soon to introduce Chinese students to L2 argumentation, and even as challenging a concept as counterargument can be effectively taught. At a university in Argentina, Natalia Dalla Costa addressed the particular challenges that source-based argumentative writing poses to even advanced language learners in "The Argumentative Essay from Multiple

Sources: Genre-Based Instruction to Foster Autonomy in EFL Academic Literacy." These challenges were met with a systemic functional linguistics (SFL) genre-based approach, using the SFL scaffolded teaching-learning cycle of guided, collaborative, and increasingly more independent activities, which was found to have quite positive effects not only on writing performance but also on student attitudes and confidence in their abilities.

The final two chapters in Part Two, and this volume, both present promising ways forward to developing L2 argumentation abilities by offering learners innovative opportunities for increased learner autonomy. In their chapter on undergraduate English for academic purposes instruction (EAP) at an EMI (English medium of instruction) university in Hong Kong ("Argumentative Writing at the Tertiary Level: Students' and Teachers' Perceptions of a Hybrid Approach"), Lucas Kohnke and Frankie Har describe an integrated five-input hybrid approach to teaching argumentation consisting of videos, quizzes, reflections, peer review, and face-to-face instruction. According to Kohnke and Har, especially effective were the short out-of-class online activities, a menu of videos on argumentative-writing-related topics for just-in-time learning accompanied by online quizzes for self-testing, which together motivated learners to do the activities multiple times to deepen their understanding. In a quite different setting, undergraduate L2 writing classes for foreign language education majors in Turkey ("Analysis of Pre-service Teachers' Reflective Journals: Learning-to-argue through Writing about Writing"), Lisya Seloni and Nur Yiğitoğlu Aptoula found another means of heightening learner autonomy and, hence, consolidating L2 argumentation learning—namely, with writing-about-writing journals. By reflecting on themselves as developing L2 argumentative writers, the journal writers were able to increase their metacognition and sense of themselves as maturing critical thinkers, while at the same time providing their instructors with a window on their struggles and progress. Pre-service language teachers such as those described by Seloni and Yiğitoğlu Aptoula, trained to be reflective on their own practice as L2 writers, may be especially well poised to help new generations of novice L2 writers meet the challenges of argumentation.

Closing Comments

Our hope in assembling this collection is that it helps lend coherence to the L2 writing field's treatment of argumentative writing. Quality scholarship on L2 argumentative writing is not lacking. Valuable articles and conference presentations have been appearing with increasing frequency. However, as noted earlier, such writing—the teaching and learning of it—has not been addressed in any collective sense, and if argumentation in the L2 writing field is to gain the momentum it needs to move forward in meaningful ways, we need occasions where there is a gathering together of insights from research and practice, especially as we engage a new multimodal turn in academic literacy through which argumentation can be approached. The contributors to this volume have enabled us to view L2 argumentative writing instruction from multiple vantage points while also enabling us to provide a sustained focus on argumentation that has been missing in L2 scholarship up to now. We see the authors' combined efforts as a starting point in a more comprehensive and cohesive treatment of argumentation that we believe the L2 writing field needs at this point in its own development.

REFERENCES

Belcher, D. D. (1997). An argument for nonadversarial argumentation: On the relevance of the feminist critique of academic discourse for L2 writing pedagogy. *Journal of Second Language Writing, 6*, 1–21.

Hirvela, A. (2017). Argumentation & second language: Are we missing the boat? *Journal of Second Language Writing, 36*, 69–74.

Johns, A. M. (1993). Written argumentation for real audiences: Suggestions for teacher research and classroom practices. *TESOL Quarterly, 27*, 74–90.

Mitchell, S. (2000). Putting argument into the mainstream. In S. Mitchell & R. Andrews (Eds.), *Learning to argue in higher education* (pp. 146–154). Portsmouth, NH: Boynton/Cook Publishers.

Miller, R. T., Mitchell, T. D., & Pessoa, S. (2016), Impact of source texts and prompts on students' genre uptake. *Journal of Second Language Writing, 31*, 11–24.

Silva, T. (1993). Toward an understanding of the distinct nature of L2 writing: The ESL research and its implications. *TESOL Quarterly, 27*, 657–677.

Toulmin, S. (1958). *The uses of argument.* Cambridge: Cambridge University Press.

Part 1

Conceptualizing Argumentative
Writing Instruction and Research

1

Situated Argumentation as a Rhetorical Act

ANN M. JOHNS

Abstract

This chapter addresses challenges that argumentative writing poses for multilingual students and their instructors in English-dominant settings. The proposed approach to these challenges involves teaching learners to be rhetorically flexible in the face of a broad range of argumentative tasks, as well as to use linguistic strategies commonly found in expert argumentative writing.

The EAL community is indebted to Alan Hirvela (2017) for pointing out the relative absence of argumentation in the teaching of second/foreign language writing. This is certainly a problem, one of several that we face as practitioners (see, e.g., Caplan and Johns, 2019). The questions that can be raised regarding this gap then become: How do we teach argument to students whose first-language education has included texts that present argument in different ways (see Connor & Ene, 2019)?

n   How do we teach argument to students whose only experience with argumentation has been with the templated five-paragraph-essay (Caplan, 2019)?
n   How do we teach argument to those who have had little experience with academic or professional writing in any language?

In this chapter, I will point out some issues that we face regarding argumentation in first language environments. Then I will suggest that, like all rhetorical actions in writing, argumentation is complex and context-dependent—and we should teach it with these characteristics in mind, particularly in novice, introductory EAL classes where, unfortunately, predicting the texts students will be assigned and on which they will be assessed in their academic and professional careers is difficult if not impossible (Johns, 2019, p. 134; Melzer, 2014). Of particular concern and focus will be issues of establishing *rhetorical flexibility* and what research tells us about the differences in language use between experts' and novices' argumentation texts.

Argumentation as (Often) Taught in L1

In contrast to the EAL classes described by Hirvela (2017), the first-year composition class (FYC) in the United States, an almost universally required course, often makes argumentation, particularly argument essays, the centerpiece of writing. One only needs to conduct a search for FYC textbooks on Amazon or Google to realize how important argument essays are to many FYC classrooms across the country and perhaps in many other parts of the world as well. One of the most popular of the FYC textbooks focusing on argument is *Everything's an Argument* (Lunsford, Ruszkiewiecz, & Walters, 2019). It is visually attractive and includes readings on topics designed to be motivating, such as internet privacy, popular culture, and the Me Too Movement. Although the term *essay* predominates in this textbook, writing assignments include a variety of texts—print, visual, and online. Its longevity is likely due to the fact that teachers have become comfortable with it (the first edition was published in 1998) and have continued to order the newer editions.

Another very popular volume, often paired with the Lunsford et al. textbook, is *They Say/I Say: Moves That Matter in Academic Writing* (Graff, Birkenstein, & Durst, 2018). This short textbook provides various templates, particularly for essays, that are designed for students to effectively present their arguments.

However, these volumes only encourage the production of certain kinds of academic prose and take on limited writer purposes. What we find when researching situated academic assignments is that there are a variety of actions beyond argumentation required of students in writing prompts that they may not recognize. Three of these actions are description, explanation, analysis (see Pessoa & Mitchell, 2019, and Caplan & Johns, 2021). In their study of assignments in the information systems major, for example, Pessoa and Mitchell (2019, p. 161) often discovered writing prompts that required

Table 1.1

Sample Writing Prompts

Three-Part Prompt	How to Respond
What is mobile payment? How has mobile payment evolved over time?	Description
Research, identify, and explain four critical challenges facing the mobile payment industry.	Analysis
For each challenge, identify and justify situations in which information systems could provide an innovative solution.	Argument

academic actions separate from, or leading up to, argument, as shown in the first two of these assignment sections in Table 1.1.

When teaching each of these actions in Table 1.1 to student writers, these researchers argue, *appropriate language* should be taught along with the action itself—not only specialized vocabulary, but the language of stance, certainty, and scope and other linguistic features that play a role in successful texts.

Therefore, learning to write in actions beyond argumentation is crucial, as well. Students at all levels can be asked, for example, to *explain*, an action "used for the purposes of informing, organizing, identifying, or describing" (de Oliveira & Smith, 2019) but not to argue. Explanations often involve writing about how things work or why they happen; they may involve definitions, both extended and contested, or glosses internal to text. Caplan identifies defining verbs, relative clauses, and in-text glosses for student practice as they write assigned explanation texts (Caplan & Johns, 2021).

Two points that have been made so far that need to be highlighted. The first is that not every assigned text focuses on argument—or argument alone. Instead, students can be asked to explain, analyze, and inform in their writing without taking sides. Sometimes this is because instructors want students to display their knowledge through explanation, showing that they understand the material they have been taught. At other times, mere display is insufficient: students must transform their knowledge (Scardamalia & Bereiter, 1987) through analysis, "reorganizing materials in an original way" but not for the purposes of argumentation (Pessoa & Mitchell, 2019, p. 155).

The second major point to be made here is that as instructors of diverse learners, we always need to teach the language appropriate to the actions that writers are taking in texts. We need to ask: What language do expert writers use as they explain, define, or analyze? How do we help students to notice this language? What components of language should we be emphasizing and asking the students to practice as they take on various academic actions?

Promoting Rhetorical Flexibility: The Common Core

Of course, there are many teachers who do not fall into the "everything's an argument" trap. In literacy programs throughout the world, variation in assigned text types is taking place, assisting students to develop a "rhetorical flexibility" that will enable them to face new, unpredictable writing tasks (Connor & Ene, 2019; Johns, 2019). A major effort in this direction can be found in the establishment of the Common Core Standards in the United States, adopted for K–12 classrooms by 43 of the 50 states when the standards were introduced in 2014 (Johns, 2016). The Common Core (CCSS) does not stipulate which genres should be produced (or read); instead, vertically across the curricula, certain abilities (e.g., summarizing, using appropriate language, solving a problem) are to be perfected and assessed, depending on the nature and requirements of content area classes in which the students are enrolled. In the CCSS, then, all teachers are expected to be literacy instructors, as they assign reading and writing while developing the prescribed abilities appropriate to their content areas.

Writing texts subsumed in the CCSS Anchor Standards (www.corestandards.org) are divided into the general categories of "informational, narrative, and persuasive," with increasing emphasis on the informational and persuasive as students advance in school. Students are to be exposed to readings, video and audio clips, graphs, charts, or pictures on a topic and then asked to respond to a "constructed response question"—that is, a timed, in-class writing common to many secondary and college classes in the disciplines (see Melzer, 2014). Or they may be asked to write a story, report, or script under other conditions, enabling a more leisurely and thoughtful writing process.

Of course, the success of the Common Core or any set of standards depends on the teachers themselves; and as is the case in many parts of the world, U.S. K–12 content teachers are often untrained to do the kinds of literacy work that would ideally take place in the CCSS classroom and on the assessments. This lack of training for effective teaching and assessment, whatever the standards, is also true among college and university instructors, not only in the United States but in Great Britain as well, an issue discussed by Nesi and Gardner in their extensive study of U.K. university writing assignments (2012).

Viewing Argumentation as Situated (and thus, Rhetorical)

One of my principal goals so far in this text has been to demonstrate that there is more to writing than argumentation, a point that some students find difficult to understand or accept. Nonetheless, I must acknowledge that argumentation is crucial in the teaching of academic and professional writing. Unfortunately, however, the "essay" approaches to argumentation in FYC and the secondary schools tend to limit students' understanding of the remarkable variety of ways in which arguments are made in the many genres to which they may be exposed in their future academic or professional lives. Secondary content instructors, having been trained for the most part by English teachers, may assign argument essays even if they are teaching biology or sociology where other genres are more highly valued. High-stakes secondary assessments in many countries also emphasize argument essays, therefore making these pedagogical texts central to teaching (Crusan, Plakans, & Gebril, 2016). These tendencies are undoubtedly problematic because students seemingly can produce only one form with confidence: the five-paragraph essay, with the claim ("thesis statement") always appearing at the end of the first paragraph, a few internal paragraphs developing the claim, and a conclusion restating it. When asked to prepare an argument, or even a text in another action, students tend to revert to what they know from secondary school and FYC instruction: this one specific and rigid form. Beyond the United States and countries that use textbooks published in the United States, it is difficult to generalize about the rigidity of essays. Connor and Ene (2019) found that the five-paragraph-essay is non-existent in some countries; nevertheless, even in other countries, particularly those with strict national testing, it has become the norm.

Teaching or assessing argumentation writing using a rigid structure like the five-paragraph essay is thus problematic. Tardy (2019b) notes that writers "argue" through many genres; and in any given situation, they should "choose the genre that will be most effective" (p. 32). In some cases, of course, what is often referred to as an *essay* (Melzer, 2014) is selected as the task for the students by the instructor, so the expectations are that an argument is to be made in that way. When I directed the Teaching and Learning Center for several years at my university, I collected assignments from outstanding faculty in a variety of disciplines to determine what their student writing tasks might be. Not surprisingly, I found that the kinds of argument writing tasks found in the Department of Recreation and Tourism were considerably different from those in chemistry or other sciences, in history, and in the business classes. In what ways did they differ? They differed in the types of claims made, in the uses of evidence, and, of course, in the structure and language of the texts themselves. Even the so-called "essays" in these classes contained multiple traces of disciplinary practices because, for many faculty across the disciplines, "essay" merely means written in prose using paragraphs, which is also a confusing use of a term in the writing lives of our students (Melzer, 2014).

From the very beginning of their university education, and even in secondary school, students need to think of an argument as a situated, rhetorical act, not as a rigid form drawn from students' previous writing experiences. To prepare students for their tasks, I would argue, it is our responsibility to encourage them to ask questions about their writing assignments of their writing teachers and of their content instructors as well, so that they can determine how to contextualize their work for a specific classroom (see Johns, 2019). Some questions I encourage my students to ask of instructors are: "When you use *essay* in this assignment, what does that term mean?" or "May I see an example of a good student paper?" (Johns, 2019).

We need to create curricula that encourage this type of questioning, not only in their classes but among the professions within which students may work. As I draft this chapter, my grandson is designing support documents for untrained volunteers who will be observing the immigration courts in San Diego. He must develop and pose appropriate questions for the lawyers and professionals with whom he works—and then "translate" this information into language that will be both revealing and accessible for those who will be observing in courts but who have not been educated in the law. Without a doubt, this is a situated series of rhetorical acts, ones that need to satisfy the experts while still becoming comprehensible for the volunteer observers, and the use of questions about this situation pays off.

By the same token, our students need to become the researchers in their classrooms (see Johns, 1997) to study what types of texts are most appropriate for the tasks assigned. They can draw from prior experience, but in selective ways. For example, they need to continue to apply their knowledge of coherence in writing in relation to new texts, but what coherence is and how it is achieved will vary from task to task.

Some Pedagogical Implications

How, then, can we assist students to view their writing, wherever it takes place, as a rhetorical act and help them to recognize argument and other actions in their various forms? Here, I will focus on instruction for students "in the interstices"—that is, those students studying in the two- or three-year gap between their test-heavy experiences in secondary school and the points at which they should become serious initiates in their disciplines. This gap is most noticeable in the United States, though it exists in other countries as well (Connor & Ene, 2019). Wherever the students are located, a thorough initiation into the genres of the disciplines often does not take place until students are advanced undergraduates or graduate students; however, many of us are teaching students writing before they have reached the advanced level.

Encouraging "Rhetorical Flexibility:" Drawing from Macro-Genres

For a number of years, I have been guided in my curriculum planning by Carter's (2007) work in which he identifies what he calls "macro-genres" across the curriculum: four categories of discipline-oriented texts that respond to prompts calling for certain text structures, purposes, and the placement of claims. One of these response types, the "*quintessential research paper*," is typical of many writing and humanities classes at universities. This paper type, typically using the MLA referencing style, requires the critical evaluation of written or online sources. The thesis/claim generally appears in the introductory paragraph, often in a sentence that includes language such as: *In this paper, I will argue that . . .*

Perhaps even more common than the "quintessential research paper" described briefly, is the "argument essay" (Aull, 2015, pp. 56-81), with a prompt that asks students to agree or disagree with the author of a print text, drawing from the text itself or from their personal experience. These essays are, in many cases, in the typical five-paragraph organization with the thesis (claim) appearing at the end of the introductory paragraph. Since students are comfortable with and often controlled by this form, I do not assign "argument essay" papers in my class, although we do discuss this pedagogical genre when they present their literacy histories.

Much more relevant to many of our students' future lives are two other response types mentioned by Carter (2007) that I frequently assign. The first of these is the **problem-solution** assignment, which appears in genres from a variety of disciplines: business, social work, engineering, and nursing, among others. In texts of this type, a problem is identified, defined, and perhaps analyzed; causes for the problem are discussed; and then solutions using evidence appropriate to the discipline and task are applied in an attempt to solve the problem. The claim for this type of text appears in the proposed solution or suggested alternative solutions. The claim is sometimes tentative and multi-faceted depending on the complexity of the problem and other factors. Often unmentioned but important to many problem-solution texts is the author's evaluation of proposed solutions, thus suggesting which of the proposed solutions is most viable and why.

What types of problem-solution assignments do I make in novice classes? In a recent content-based instruction class where students were studying homelessness, they were asked to use expert interviews and assigned sources to work through the problem-solution process. In the student papers, the proposed solutions provided opportunities to make hedged claims based on the evidence they had collected throughout the class. For this assignment, I require the use of the APA referencing system, with headings, much more common across the disciplines than the MLA. Why use headings? This assists students to write their paper in sections: an introduction including a purpose statement, the problem and its causes, and proposed solutions (evaluated). With a topic like homelessness, which is very broad, students are encouraged to use their sources to narrow and dig deeper into certain aspects of the problem. For example, some of my students studied problems related to collaboration among concerned agencies, financing services, and the variety of homeless people and their needs. Assigning a problem-solution paper and the writing process are presented at some length in Caplan & Johns, 2021).

A second response type that I assign, one common in the sciences, engineering, and the social sciences, is the **IMRaD** (introduction, methodology, results, discussion), which generally requires APA referencing, as well. Made famous by Swales (1981, 1990) and further examined in Swales and Feak (2012), this response-type in its various manifestations may be most important for most of my students. At the interstices levels, I ask students to design and conduct a short survey and then prepare a headed text based on the IMRaD. In this text type, with the Swalesian moves (Swales & Feak, 2012), the claim, often hedged, appears in the discussion after the results have been analyzed. Because this type of research paper is so important, an entire chapter has been devoted to it in Caplan & Johns, 2021).

As is the case in all of my teaching, transfer to other classes and contexts is my aim (Nowacek, 2011). In the problem/solution and IMRaD projects, students become accustomed to using headings, to preparing a common introduction type (Swales, 1981), to completing data commentaries in their results, and to making claims in the discussion or solution section that are carefully hedged. After the classes have been completed, students have written to me about how important these writing experiences have been for other academic classes.

Figure 1.1

The Rhetorical Planning Wheel

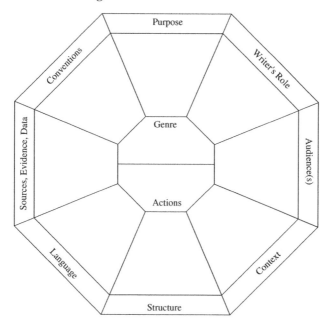

Student Planning for and Analyzing Arguments:
Using the Rhetorical Planning Wheel (RPW)

At all levels of instruction, but particularly in the interstices, students need to be literacy researchers (Johns, 1997), asking questions of instructors or other audiences, of writing prompts, of texts, of the context, and of themselves as writers as they attempt to craft a text that responds to a particular task in a specific context (see also Tardy, 2019a; Johns, 2019, p. 149). The Rhetorical Planning Wheel (Caplan & Johns, 2021) presented in Figure 1.1 covers the major topics/components that should be addressed as students plan their writing or analyze example texts based on the tasks and contexts at hand.

Using the components from the RPW and, if possible, writing prompts and exemplars of the text types that have been assigned, students can ask questions like these, discussed at greater length in Tardy (2019a) and Johns (2019):

❐ What is the genre of the texts we are analyzing or assigned? More specifically, what does a successful text in this context do and look like?

❏ How is a successful text structured? Why is it structured in this way?

❏ If the principal "action" is to argue: Where in the text does the claim tend to appear? How is argument generally constructed? What is the language of a claim? Is it hedged, for example? What types of evidence are appropriate? What are the sources of this evidence?

❏ Who are the audiences for this text? What are their assumptions, their values and expectations?

❏ Who am I as a writer in this writing task? Student? Expert? Reader?

❏ If I am a student, how should I approach the argument linguistically?

❏ How and where are sources cited (if any?). What is the referencing style (e.g., APA, MLA . . .)?

As students study their prompts/tasks and the context in which their writing is to be produced, including the audience, the content of the course, and other factors, they practice **noticing**, an important move on the road to developing rhetorical flexibility.

Student Writing Processes

In *Genre-Based Writing: What Every ESL Teacher Needs to Know* (2019a), Tardy devotes one chapter to designing genre-based writing activities, including selecting the genres of focus and sample texts. I recommend this short e-book for details about genre and text selection and other classroom activities involved in writing processes. There are a number of other volumes that discuss the richness and depth of writing processes. Two of my favorites are by Hjortshoj (2009) and Murray (2001). Suffice it to say here that our purposes as writing teachers include enhancing for transfer, and there is evidence that the development of genre analysis skills in the writing process is an important move in achieving these ends (Ferris & Hayes, 2019, p. 127)

The Language of Argumentation: Metadiscourse

Metadiscourse is "an umbrella term for words used by a writer to mark the direction or purpose of a text" (Nordquist, 2020). In undergraduate textbooks, this signaling is generally taught through text connectives such as *however, in addition, and in conclusion,* terms that move the reader from one topic or section to another in a variety of ways. These *transition markers* are certainly important to text coherence and are discussed later in this section.

However, there are other linguistic features, fully as important to a successful text, that "allow writers to specify the inferences that they want their readers to make" (Barton, 1995, p. 219). These inferencing features are addressed in some popular graduate-level textbooks that are designed to assist students to distinguish among texts in their chosen disciplines and identify features of metadiscourse with which claims are modified. Other features include: using evaluative language (Swales & Feak, 2012, p. 242), expressing a degree of certainty (Swales & Feak, 2012, p. 161), or hedging and boosting ideas and points of view (Caplan, 2019, pp. 111–131; Swales and Feak, 2012, p. 239). Among these discourse features are those employed by experts in their argumentation, often to avoid overstating claims or committing to claims that might not be supportable. Unfortunately, these more subtle features are often absent from textbooks for novices in the interstices.

Hedges and Boosters

Laura Aull's (2015) corpus-based work, contrasting linguistic choices found in published, professional texts across the disciplines and argument essays of first year university students, is valuable in this regard: it is student misuse of the more subtle linguistic features of an argument are often what annoy instructors and other expert readers the most. In her volume, Aull compares data from the Contemporary Corpus of American Academic English (COCAA), 91 million words of published academic writing, with a large first-year corpus of argument essays written at two U.S. institutions between 2009–2013 as part of the universities' first-year self-placement process. The prompts for these novices were "designed to simulate evidence-based argumentative essays which require engagement with source texts, involving drafting and revising over several days" (Aull, 2015, p. 53). Although, as Swales (2002) points out, corpus-based data use for research has its limitations, this comparison between expert and novice writing provides practitioners with the opportunity to make generalizations about how language at the sentence level might be approached when teaching argumentation.

Aull (2015) notes that one important difference between the expert and novice writers is found in interpersonal metadiscourse, particularly in the use of hedges and boosters. **Hedges**, often realized through modal verbs (*may, might*), approximate adverbs (*generally, likely, possibly*), or minimizers (*almost, nearly, somewhat*) open the possibility that the claims made by the writer may be risky, at the very least, or that there may be alternative views to be considered. Hedging is found quite commonly in expert discourses, especially when writers are drawing conclusions about their findings presented in their results or discussion sections (Hyland, 2005). **Boosters** are the opposite of hedges; they indicate that the writers are quite certain of their claims. These features are marked by intensifying adverbs (*absolutely, clearly*), directive verbs (*should, must*), intensifiers (*always, never*) and directive verbs (*should, must*).

Aull's (2015) findings indicate that novice writers more frequently "err heavily on the side of certainty" when attempting to use these features in their writing, resulting in texts that are inappropriate for novices (p. 96). On the other hand, she says, "While the FY writers tend to use many boosters [rather than hedges] and construct less measured claims, the expert academic writers use more hedges, constructing more delimited claims, [for] an authoritative argument in academic writing shows caution" (p. 97).

Why do novice writers overuse the languages of certainly? This tendency probably can be traced to the writing they have been assigned in secondary school or on which they have been assessed—prompts that require them to argue that an idea or personal opinion is true rather than open to debate and possible revision. There are other reasons, as well. When I asked one novice student why she employed so much language of certainty, she said, "If I don't, my teachers will think I don't care enough about the subject or I don't know enough about it." She resisted my encouragement to tone her language down until her political science instructor scolded her after reading one of her papers, saying "Who do you think you are?" It should be noted that the languages of certainty and caution are not exclusively academic; they appear in many types of professional texts as well. Seema Yasim (2020), a former member of the U.S. Epidemic Intelligence Service, an agency charged with hunting down diseases and proposing responses to them, created texts in the past in which strict "certainty" directives were given to government agencies about responding to viruses, including phrases like "You must provide respirators . . ." or "Residents of the area should be tested." However, for political reasons during the 2020 pandemic, only "weak and evasive" language could be used in their recommendations. Comments in 2020 reports are couched in language such as this: "These steps are discretionary and not required or mandated by the EIS" and "If feasible, employees should wear face coverings." Since the 2020 November election, steps are being taken to mandate masks on public transit. In addition, a White House Office of COVID-19 response will be producing a number of clear mandates designed to combat the pandemic (https://www.healthcarefinancenews.com/news/president-joe-biden-will-begin-his-plan-control-covid-19-pandemic-day-one). All language use is situated—and, of course, it is sometimes politically motivated.

Like Caplan (2019) and Caplan and Johns (2021), Aull suggests that students have the opportunity to analyze accessible expert prose for its use of hedges and boosters by completing noticing exercises that distinguish between claims that are hedged and those that are boosted. Then, students might explore questions such as these:

1. Why do expert academic writers use hedges? What in their writer roles, the audience, the genre from the context might indicate this use?

2. Where are examples of hedging in the expert texts you have been studying? Where do they appear in the expert texts—at the beginning or the end? Why do you think this is?

3. Find examples of boosting in the expert academic writing samples. Where do they appear in the texts–toward the end or the beginning? Why do you think they use boosters in these cases?

4. Examine your own writing. Which claims could benefit from a hedge? What hedges might you use?

5. Which claims in your own writing would benefit from a boost? Why? What boosting terms might you use? (adaptedfrom Aull, 2015, p. 118)

Constructing the Scope of the Argument

Another linguistic difference between experts and novices, Aull (2015, p. 221) found, is in "constructing argumentative scope." Her research indicates that novice students tend to surround topics with broad, sometimes limitless, text-external scope words, creating claims such as "Everyone loves pizza," "Throughout the world, human beings are anxious about the future," or in a number of cases, referring to themselves as participants in the claims, "In our world. . . ." Sentences like these may appear initially in students' introductions without evidence to support their claims. Experts, on the other hand, limit the scope of their claims to the data or topic at hand. They tend to use phrases such as "In this study . . ." or "In this regard," metadiscourse that refers to text-internal rather than text-external ideas and topics.

In the pedagogical chapter of her volume, Aull suggests that writers again examine expert academic texts (p. 126). I have adapted and augmented her suggestions for students:

1. Why do expert academic writers use less personal evidence than novice writers?

2. Why do novice writers tend to use more text-external claims or claims based on personal evidence in their academic writing?

3. Why do expert academic writers make fewer statements that relate to large groups of people ("the world") or phenomena?

4. Find a scope-creating sentence in the expert data. Why is the writer using this language? What does the sentence do for the reader? Where does it appear?

5. Select one of your sentences relating to scope in your draft. How might it be revised to be more limited and text-internal?

6. You have been looking at published academic writing in which text-internal scope statements are generally favored. In what types of writing would text-external scope, particularly writing from personal experience, be acceptable?

Reformulation Markers

A third area of Aull's study of the differences between expert academic writers and novice writers of argument essays relates to "reformulation markers." These linguistic features "signal that a writer is restating reported information in their own words" (2015, p. 135). In expert texts, these markers, often summarizing the sources cited, may begin with phrases such as *meaning that* or *to be precise*. What these phrases show is that the writer understands the source cited and considers it to be important enough to paraphrase to make an argument.

Aull identifies three formulation marker types:

1. **Elucidation**, during which the preceding information is summarized, using words like "in other words" to initiate the summary.

2. **Emphasis**, during which writers emphasize certain topics or ideas that have been presented in a source, using phrases like "put another way." Or

3. To indicate **counter-expectancy,** pointing out a contrast to views that have been expressed in the source, involving phrases like *in fact*, as in *in fact, this does not appear to be the case.*

As in the case of the hedges, boosters, and the scope markers, there were considerable differences between the two corpora: experts included more than twice as many formulation markers of each of the three types than did novice essay writers (2015, p. 137).

In studying reformulation markers, rather than asking questions of students regarding what they see in expert texts, it would be useful to provide students with short passages from their textbooks or other sources and then ask them to work in groups to create reformulations of the material they have read.

Transition Markers

As mentioned earlier, transition markers showing the logical relationships between ideas are very important to the coherence or "flow" of a text. In contrast to the other features studied by Aull, transition discussions and practice are often presented in novice textbooks, organized according to their functions (e.g., additive, adversative, internal temporal). What is interesting about the Aull research are, again, the differences between expert and novice use. She found that experts use a greater variety of transitions than novices, demonstrating that they have a broader command of textual relationships and a more subtle understanding of the individual meanings and uses of markers.

Predominant in novice texts were "countering" transitions like *however*, making the writers sound aggressive in intent and quick to draw hasty conclusions about a particular issue being discussed. On the other hand, experts used a variety of transitions showing contrast, sequencing, addition, comparison, and illustration, making their texts more nuanced and cautious than those of the novice writers (Aull, 2015, p. 141).

When Aull teaches transitions, she asks a broad question about "flow" in a text, for example, how lexical cohesion is achieved (see also Caplan, 2019, pp. 148-161). Another way to capture and discuss text flow is found in Caplan and Johns (2021). It's called **text charting of a source**, and an example is shown in Table 1.2 where various cohesive items, including transition, contribute to the flow. Table 1.2 provides the sample text and then the charting. Sentences have been numbered for analysis.

Asking students to analyze sentences in groups while focusing on one aspect of text, in this case, flow, is a useful way to promote noticing, an important element in their metacognitive awareness of texts and eventual rhetorical flexibility.

Final Comments

In this chapter, I have contended that the creation of academic arguments requires a considerable amount of thought about text type, writing processes, and language employed. I have discussed two of several considerations in creating written arguments: the response types most common in certain disciplines (Carter, 2007) and the language of argumentation and coherence

Table 1.2

Charting the Paragraph of a Sample Text

(1) *Different transition words have different rhetorical functions, so writers have many options for displaying how their ideas fit together. 92) For example, academic writers can show textual relationships like causation, comparison, contrasting or countering. (3) The distinction between the last two categories, contrasting and counters, is that while contrasting transitions may show similarity between two ideas, countering transitions show disagreement (Aull, 2015, p. 141).*

Sentence #	What Is the writer DOING in This Sentence?	What Language Is Used to Show the "Doing"?
1	Framing the paragraph in terms of topic and cause and effect claim	*different, so*
2	Providing an example of the topic/point in the first sentence	*for example*
3	Comparing the functions of two transition words.	the distinction

that separates novices from expert academic writers (Aull, 2015). There is much more to be considered, of course, but this relatively short discussion will, I hope, assist teachers to take additional responsibility for preparing students for the rhetorical flexibility necessary to examine a context and a task and respond appropriately. I can say with some certainty that we cannot continue to teach argumentation as if it is enclosed in a rigid essay form, nor can we continue to focus on personal opinion and experience when much of academic argumentation relates to discipline-specific evidence. Note that these claims are intentionally unhedged because there is considerable evidence to support them (Caplan & Johns, 2019).

REFERENCES

Aull, L. (2015). *First-year university writing: A corpus-based study with implications for pedagogy.* London: Palgrave Macmillan.

Barton, E. (1995). Contrastive and non-contrastive connectives: Metadiscourse functions in argumentation. *Written Communication, 12*(2), 219–239.

Caplan, N.A. (2019). *Grammar choices for graduate and professional writers* (2nd Edition). Ann Arbor: University of Michigan Press.

Caplan, N. A. (2019). Have we always taught the five-paragraph essay? In N. A. Caplan & A. M. Johns (Eds.), *Changing practices for the L2 writing classroom: Moving beyond the five-paragraph essay* (pp. 2–23). Ann Arbor: University of Michigan Press.

Caplan, N. A., & Johns, A. M. (2021). *Essential actions in academic writing.* Ann Arbor: University of Michigan Press.

Caplan, N. A., & Johns, A. M. (Eds.) (2019). *Changing practices for the L2 writing classroom: Moving beyond the five-paragraph essay.* Ann Arbor: University of Michigan Press.

Carter, M. (2007). Ways of knowing, doing, and writing in the disciplines. *College Composition and Communication, 58,* 385–418.

Connor, U. M., & Ene. E. (2019). Does everyone write the five-paragraph essay? In N. A. Caplan & A. M. Johns (Eds.), *Changing practices for the L2 writing classroom: Moving beyond the five-paragraph essay* (pp. 42–63). Ann Arbor: University of Michigan Press.

Crusan, D., Plakans, L, & Gebril, A. (2016) Writing assessment literacy: Surveying second language teachers' knowledge, beliefs, and practices. *Assessing Writing, 28,* 43–56.

de Oliveira, L. C., & Smith, S. L. (2019). Interacting with and around texts: Writing in elementary schools. In N. A. Caplan & A. M. Johns (Eds.), *Changing practices for the L2 writing classroom: Moving beyond the five-paragraph essay* (pp. 65–88). Ann Arbor: University of Michigan Press.

Ferris, D., & Hayes, H. (2019). Transferable principles and processes in undergraduate writing. In N. A. Caplan & A. M. Johns (Eds.), *Changing practices for the L2 writing classroom: Moving beyond the five-paragraph essay* (pp. 116–132). Ann Arbor: University of Michigan Press.

Graff, G., Birkenstein, C., & Durst, R. (2018). *They say/I say: With readings.* (4th ed). New York: W. W. Norton and Company.

Hirvela, A. (2017). Argumentation in second language writing: Are we missing the boat? *Journal of Second Language Writing, 36,* 69–74.

Hjorshoj, K. (2009). *The transition to college writing* (2nd ed). Boston: Bedford: St. Martin's.

Hyland, K. (2005). *Exploring interaction in writing.* London: Bloomsbury Classics.

Johns, A. M. (1997). *Text, role and context: Developing academic literacies.* Cambridge, England: Cambridge University Press.

Johns, A.M. (2008). Genre awareness for the novice academic student: An ongoing quest. *Language Teaching, 41,* 237–252.

Johns, A.M. (2016). The Common Core in the United States: A major shift in standards and assessment. In K. Hyland & P. Shaw (Eds.), *The Routledge handbook of English for Academic Purposes* (pp. 461–476). London: Routledge.

Johns, A.M. (2019). Writing in the interstices: Assisting novice undergraduates in analyzing authentic writing tasks. In N. A. Caplan & A.M. Johns [Eds.], *Changing practices for the L2 writing classroom: Moving beyond the five-paragraph essay* (pp. 133–149). Ann Arbor: University of Michigan Press.

Lunsford, A. A., Ruszkiewicz, J. J., & Walters, K. (2019). *Everything's an argument: With readings* (8th ed.). Boston: Bedford/St. Martins.

Melzer, D. (2014). *Assignments across the disciplines: A national study of college writing.* Logan: Utah State University Press.

Murray, D. (2001). *The craft of revision.* Ft. Worth, TX: Harcourt.

Nesi, H., & Gardner, S. (2012). *Genres across the disciplines: Student writing in higher education.* New York: Cambridge University Press.

Nordquist, R. (Feb. 11, 2020). What is metadiscourse? Retrieved from thoughtco.com/metadiscourse-writing-and-speech-1691381.

Nowacek, R. S. (2011). *Agents of integration: Understanding transfer as a rhetorical act.* Carbondale: Southern Illinois University Press.

Pessoa, S., & Mitchell, T. D. (2019). Preparing students to write in the disciplines. In N. A. Caplan & A. M. Johns (Eds.), *Changing practices for the L2 writing classroom: Moving beyond the five-paragraph essay* (pp. 150–177). Ann Arbor: University of Michigan Press.

Scardamalia, M., & Bereiter, C. (1987). Knowledge telling and knowledge transforming in written composition. In S. Rosenberg [Ed.]. *Advances in applied psychologists: Vol. 2. Reading, writing, and language learning* (pp. 142–175). Cambridge, England: Cambridge University Press.

Swales, J. M. (1981/2011). *Aspects of article introductions.* Ann Arbor: University of Michigan Press.

Swales, J. M. (1990). *Genre analysis: English in academic and research settings.* Cambridge, England: Cambridge University Press.

Swales, J. M. (2002). Integrated and fragmented worlds: EAP materials and corpus linguistics. In J. Flowerdew (Ed.), *Academic discourse* (pp. 150–164). London: Longman.

Swales, J.M., & Feak, C.B. (2012). *Academic writing for graduate students: Essential tasks and skills* (3rd ed.). Ann Arbor: University of Michigan Press.

Tardy, C. (2019a). *Genre-based instruction: What every ESL teacher needs to know.* Ann Arbor: University of Michigan Press.

Tardy, C. (2019b). Is the five-paragraph-essay a genre? In N. A. Caplan & A. M. Johns (Eds.), *Changing practices for the L2 writing classroom: Moving beyond the five-paragraph essay* (pp. 24–41). Ann Arbor: University of Michigan Press.

Yasim, S. (24 May 2020). Disease detectives meet the politicians. *New York Times (Sunday Review),* p. 2.

2

Online Resources for L2 Argumentative Writing in Secondary Schools: A View from the Field

AMANDA KIBLER, CHRISTINE HARDIGREE, AND FARES KARAM

Abstract

This chapter analyzes freely available online activities and lesson plans related to argumentative writing for teachers of L2 high school writers. Despite the need for these resources due to an increased reliance on distance learning models during the pandemic, we found that such pre-pandemic resources were rare. Those that did exist operate from multiple different definitions of argumentation, tend to portray L2 writers and argumentation differently, and propose a range of instructional strategies. We call for further research and scholarly involvement in the development of free online pedagogical materials.

Argumentative writing holds significant prestige in secondary and post-secondary institutions worldwide, and an emphasis on teaching and learning argumentation continues to grow. We focus this analysis on the case of the United States, where the teaching of argumentative writing has never been more important in secondary schools (Grades 6–12), given the emphasis on argumentation in recent standards-based reform (Valdés, Kibler, & Walqui, 2014) and in calls for greater attention to critical thinking and writing that can support an increasingly diverse student population's civic participation and improve college and career readiness (Newell, VanDerHeide,

& Wynhoff Olsen, 2014). Moreover, argumentative writing is challenging for most pre-college students and second language writers in particular because they are in the process of developing their academic reading and writing expertise—a situation that has been documented in the U.S. (Hirvela, 2013) and globally (Horverak, 2017). Although writing pedagogies in U.S. secondary schools have in general become more sophisticated over time according to national survey data (Applebee et al., 2013), several aspects of teachers' professional training remain under-developed. Notably, although professional development efforts into argumentative writing instruction for pre- and in-service secondary teachers have grown in recent years (e.g., Newell et al., 2014; O'Hallaron, 2014), attention to L2 writing issues of any kind continue to be limited (Gilliland, 2018). In the context of an increasing focus on argumentation, the lack of attention paid to L2 writing pedagogy is ever-more concerning.

Although many L2 writing textbooks address argumentation, teacher education programs rarely offer coursework that addresses L2 writing issues in general and argumentation in particular. Then once in the field, where do teachers turn to for resources for teaching argumentative writing to multilingual writers? Although professional development initiatives provide a range of resources for teachers, online materials are an increasingly common source for teachers as they plan instruction (Kaufman et al., 2018). To understand implications of this trend for secondary L2 argumentative writing, this chapter analyzes curriculum resources, tools, and guidance readily available to high school teachers of L2 writers through various free and open-access materials as of January 2020. Although this analysis predates the COVID-19 pandemic, it serves as a critical reference point because these were the references available just as many schools and teachers turned to online learning platforms, which necessitated development of new and revised curricula. As teachers went online to seek resources to develop those curricula, these would have been the ones they found.

With a particular focus on high schools (Grades 9–12), where argumentative writing instruction is arguably most critical to preparing students for post-secondary schooling and careers, our research questions are: (1) Which sites provide resources on teaching argumentative writing for teachers of L2 high school writers? (2) How do these resources define *argumentation, L2 writers,* and "appropriate" instructional strategies to support L2 argumentative writing? We argue that it is critical to understand the materials that are available and used by teachers because they create de-facto conceptualizations of argumentation, and in particular, of L2 writers and their expertise.

Background and Relevant Literature

We base this analysis on theoretical understandings of argumentation as a social practice (Newell, Bloome, & Hirvela, 2015), one that is enacted in various ways through teachers' and students' engagement with curricular materials and each other. Further, while instructional resources are only one piece of a complex instructional ecology, they play an important role— they "curricularize" (Kibler & Valdés, 2016; Valdés, 2015) language and literacy in ways that implicitly define what argumentation is and is not, as well as who L2 writers are and what literacy expertise they are assumed to have.

According to Applebee et al. (2013), writing pedagogy in secondary schools—in English Language Arts classrooms in particular—has changed notably in the last 40 years and is now frequently characterized by a process approach, the use of models and rubrics to guide and assess students, and the provision of organizational guidance. They found, however, that the assignment of extended writing is still rare and that teacher-led activities and those that prepare students for high-stakes testing dominate secondary classrooms.

Accountability and standardized testing pressures, in combination with limited instructional time and teacher expertise, are some of the many factors that may restrict robust writing pedagogies and tend to lead to prescriptivist writing approaches, notably the "five-paragraph essay" (Crusan & Ruecker, 2019). Such structural approaches to writing instruction remain common in secondary schools and elsewhere (Caplan, 2019), despite the fact that the Common Core Standards emphasize rhetorical *mode* rather than structure. Argumentation, for example, is a "text type and purpose" (National Governors Association, 2010, p. 8), and individual standards emphasize arguments, claims, reasons, evidence, echoing if not prescribing an approach to argumentation based on the work of Toulmin (Prior, 2005). Critics have noted limitations to the current focus on argumentation (DeStigter, 2015) and to a focus on discourse structure or rhetorical mode (e.g., compare/contrast; argue) rather than genre (e.g., defined by specific social and communicative purposes) in writing instruction (Tardy, 2019). However, new standards have placed an undeniably greater emphasis on the teaching and learning of argumentative writing in secondary schools, and in particular in high schools, where writing often serves a gatekeeping function for passing courses and standardized assessments required for graduation (Kibler, 2019; Valdés, 2004).

Such trends are present, though with different nuances, in secondary schools across the globe. And while "argumentation" is an increasingly common feature of L2 writing instruction worldwide, the purposes of argumentative writing can vary notably across cultures and literate traditions (e.g., Høegh-Omdal, 2018).

Methodology

Even prior to the COVID-19 pandemic, teachers were increasingly reliant on online resources for teaching materials (Kauffman et al., 2018). This need has likely increased with the recent switch to distance learning models of instruction. As such, data for this study include activities and lesson plans freely available online. Our initial plan was to explore three popular websites for each type of materials: pinterest.com (educator-sourced and posted materials), readwritethink.org (National Council of Teachers of English: professional organization), and EngageNY.org (New York Department of Education: state organization). We searched each website using combinations of search terms and selection criteria of "argumentative writing," "grades 9–12/high school" and "ELL/L2/ESL/bilingual," but quickly found that no freely available material from these sites met our specific criteria. We then expanded our search to a wide range of websites and a broad Google search using the same criteria.

In analyzing activities and lesson plans, we adopted a content analysis approach (Krippendorff, 2003). In reading each resource, we identified instances in which argumentation and L2 writers were defined, implicitly or explicitly, or when instructional strategies were mentioned. We also noted when and how authors cited research or theory to support their choices. We completed analyses of each resource individually and then compared them with each other, using discussion to reach consensus when any differences were noted. We then developed summaries of each resource to contextualize the analysis.

Findings

Through our search, we found that freely available lesson plans and activities for high school teachers focused on L2 argumentative writing were exceedingly rare at the time of our analysis. Those that do exist operate from multiple different definitions of argumentation, tend to portray L2 writers and argumentation very differently, and propose a range of instructional strategies.

Freely Available Teaching Resources: Where Are They?

Once we shifted from an initial search of three prominent websites to a broader search of online materials, we found only two websites with freely available resources meeting all our criteria: the TESOL International Association's Resource Center, containing two member-generated and posted lesson plans, and an online article from the Association for Supervision and Curriculum Development (ASCD)'s practitioner journal, *Educational Leadership*, highlighting activities for teaching L2 argumentative writing in high school. A third website, EngageNY.org (New York State Department of Education), contained the most extensive treatment of L2 argumentative writing, but the lesson plan that focused on this topic was aimed at Grade 7 rather than Grades 9–12. Because this website was designed to offer exemplar lessons (which is described later in the chapter) that invite teachers to apply pedagogies to other contexts, and because there were simply so few materials of any type, we decided to include it in our findings.[1]

For our discussion here, we have chosen to focus our analysis on the latter two sets of resources. We do so because lessons were posted to the TESOL website by individual members who may not have anticipated their resource would be the subject of subsequent analysis and critique. Further, it is not possible to describe the lessons in sufficient depth for analysis without making the plans (and their authors) locatable through an online search.

Conceptualizations of Argument, L2 writers, and Instructional Strategies

The ASCD and EngageNY instructional resources will be described, first summarizing the overall presentation of the materials before examining the explicit or implicit conceptualizations of argument, L2 writers, and appropriate instructional strategies that "curricularize" these language and literacy practices (Kibler & Valdés, 2016; Valdés, 2015).

A View from a Practitioner Journal: "Teaching Argument Writing to ELLs"

Our search on Google led us to "Teaching Argument Writing to ELLs" (Ferlazzo & Hull-Sypneiski, 2014) in *Educational Leadership,* written by teachers of English language learners (ELLs) in a public secondary school. This article is freely accessible on the ASCD website and describes three separate learning activities designed for students at different proficiency levels.

Presentation of the Materials

The authors note that to create this resource they drew from their professional experience as well as various "Resources of Note," which include three papers from the Council of Chief State School Officers, TESOL, and the New York State Education Department via EngageNY. (However, they do not cite these resources directly in the body of their article.) The authors do not explicitly claim a conceptual framework or learning theory, but they emphasize several "crucial elements" at the beginning of the article that they believe should inform the teaching of writing. While some of these elements are directly connected to argumentative writing, most are not connected to argumentation specifically. They divide their pedagogical suggestions into three sections, each of which includes a description of a learning activity they completed with their students. Following these sections is a concluding paragraph that echoes Newell et al.'s (2015) framing of writing as a social practice, in which the authors explain that their efforts focus on "read[ing] and listen[ing] to the claims and proposals of others, and . . . respond[ing] and join[ing] the conversation" (p. 49). At the end of the article is a set of instructional "Dos and Don'ts" subdivided by topic: close reading, argument, vocabulary, and grammar.

Different writing activities are prescribed for three proficiency levels: beginning, intermediate, and advanced. For beginners, students engage in what the authors claim is a Freirian problem-posing activity, which they cite from a Peace Corps instructional manual, by writing a problem-solution essay that emphasizes cause and effect from the narrative *Les Misérables*. The activity first involves identifying relevant vocabulary, watching clips of the movie with the English subtitles, and then discussing and clarifying various scenes. Then, the teachers ask students to identify the problems facing the characters and what they think the causes of the problems are by relating to their own experiences. Afterward, students write a paragraph with their solution, with the help of sentence starters (a term they use interchangeably with "sentences frames"). The writing activity, framed as argumentative, appears to blur genres between problem-solution and cause-and-effect text structures, which underscores Hirvela's (2017) point that argumentation is "difficult to define" (p. 69), resulting in conflicting classroom manifestations.

Intermediate students write a "persuasive essay" that uses evidence, including demographic information as well as their lived experiences "comparing their neighborhood" (where the authors' inner-city school is located) with a wealthier neighborhood (para. 17). The activity includes pre-teaching vocabulary, computer research, and a field trip to the wealthy community. Students write their essay with the help of discourse- and sentence-level supports, and grammar instruction is included based on errors students make in their writing. Similar to the assignment for beginning students, this one blurs distinctions among modes, referencing features of persuasion, argumentation, and comparison-contrast writing in this activity.

Advanced students analyze a written argument about whether smartphones belong in the classroom. First, teachers introduce the concepts of ethos, logos, and pathos, as well as the differences between claims and evidence. Then, students engage in a close reading of an article about smartphones using annotation and storyboarding to identify the author's position and the evidence used to support it; students also have an opportunity to consider their opinions on this. Students then use a graphic organizer with sentence starters to write their text. The emphasis on the elements of persuasion within this activity, as opposed to activities at the other designated proficiency levels, suggests an emphasis on logic, which aligns with the classic Toulmin model of **learning to argue** (Hirvela, 2017) in which students learn the building blocks of argumentation, versus the one of **arguing to learn,** in which students engage argumentation as a means to gain deeper understanding of a topic. Again, although the written text is framed as argumentative, it appears to be a hybrid genre that forefronts argumentative analysis while leaving some space for students to engage with their own position in relation to that of the mentor text.

Positioning L2 Writers and Argumentative Writing

By beginning the article with "How in the world are we supposed to apply the Common Core writing standards to teaching English language learners?" the authors frame teaching argumentative writing as a burden to teachers beholden to new standards. While this may have been intended to create camaraderie between authors and readers by decrying teachers' perceived lack of support, it can be interpreted as positioning L2 writers themselves as the challenge. Later in the article, lesson activities are assigned according to three proficiencies, which are not themselves linked to a specific assessment. This may have been an editorial choice, as *Educational Leadership* has a national readership, and states define ELLs differently. As a result, however, these students were conceptualized according to generalized proficiency levels (beginning/intermediate/advanced) that do not attend to domain-specific differences in language expertise across written, spoken, and other modalities, or differences between comprehension and production.

Regarding argument, it is viewed alternatively as encompassing cause-and-effect, problem-solution, persuasion, and argumentation, without clearly articulated differentiation between these text types. At the same time, the article forefronts the importance of teaching argumentative writing as a relevant real-life skill related to issues students care about and have experience with, such as their neighborhood. The article emphasizes the importance of teaching argument as connected to reading, grammar, and vocabulary, as well as honoring students' "everyday" knowledge, which encompasses students' funds of knowledge (Moll et al., 1992) in addition to evidence gleaned from written texts.

Instructional Strategies

Throughout the article, numerous instructional strategies are described. The activity for beginners includes a word chart to preview key vocabulary (e.g., *cause, effect*) and to make connections to students' other language(s). The use of a multimodal text (a video with subtitles) allows students to engage with multiple literacy domains. During the discussion of the film to review the material, students are given whiteboards to use to convey their meaning. They are also given sentence starters and models from the teacher to help them in their written response. In the intermediate activity, the students also complete a word chart to pre-teach vocabulary, complete a brainstorming activity, take guided notes during a field trip to a different community, and make annotations on their readings as they conduct computer-based research. During drafting, students use an outline with sentence starters and also engage in an inductive grammar-focused lesson. Advanced students complete a pre-teaching vocabulary activity using visual representations of word meanings alongside graphic organizers for understanding different persuasive techniques. To analyze the mentor text, students annotate the reading, receive teacher guidance for unknown words, and use storyboards to create a visual summary of the text. To draft their essays, students create their own graphic organizer based on a structure from the *They Say/I Say* (Graff & Birkenstein, 2007), a frequently used guide for argumentative writing.

Each of the activities described includes several instructional strategies to support ELL-classified high school writers, with a particular emphasis on pre-teaching key vocabulary, annotating texts, and using graphic organizers and sentence starters.[2] In this way, argument is positioned as something that is both holistic, intersecting with grammar, vocabulary, reading and background knowledge instruction, and something to be carefully differentiated along a supposed continuum of proficiency, where beginners are not ready to analyze persuasive strategies or evaluate evidence claims and where it is only at the advanced level that the effectiveness of claims and evidence are explored.

A View from a State Department of Education:
Lesson Exemplar from EngageNY

The second freely available online resource is a lesson plan designed to help Grade 7 students analyze a position paper and plan their own (New York State Education Department, 2018). This lesson is part of a complete Grade 7 language arts curriculum aligned with the New York State P–12 Common Core Learning Standards. More specifically, the focus lesson is part of an eight-week "Science and Society" module, which is comprised of three units, each of which contains 10–19 lessons (39 daily lessons total). The lesson described is the first in Unit 3, which covers the entire writing process (drafting, revising, editing, and submitting, etc.). We chose to focus on this first lesson because it is the only lesson that explicitly mentions ELLs and multilingual language learners (MLLs).

Presentation of the Materials

The entry task asks students to reflect on their strengths and challenges in writing a narrative essay (from a previous module) before reviewing this new lesson's focus on argumentative writing, with peers. Students transition to analyzing a model position paper by reading it and discussing it with peers. Then, they analyze a model position paper according to an expository writing rubric.[3] The rubric criteria are applied to the model position paper. Students discuss with peers how claims and reasons presented in the paper reflect (or not) insightful analysis or how counterclaims are acknowledged. Next, students reflect on potential challenges of writing their own position paper and then review the assigned homework where they were asked to identify three reasons they intend to use in their position paper, which will be based on independent research on the topic (the ways that the developing adolescent brain may be affected by screen time).

Positioning L2 Writers and Argumentative Writing

The lesson explicitly describes L2 writers as multilingual and differentiates instruction based on various levels of language proficiency: entering, emerging, transitioning, and expanding levels—the official designations from New York State. Thus, there is an acknowledgment that instructional approaches should respond to students' various levels of L2 development. Although this was the only lesson in the unit and module to include explicit differentiation techniques for ELLs/MLLs, a supplementary resource guide for scaffolding instruction across the year-long curriculum highlights the fact that all students have access to word banks throughout the lessons presented and encourages teachers to differentiate instruction using some of the various techniques demonstrated in this particular lesson plan. One of the subsequent lessons in the same unit states that any scaffolding provided in the unit as a whole also addresses the needs of students with special educational needs. This type of statement unfortunately positions L2 writers as having needs that are seen as similar to those identified as having "special educational needs," which then seems to argue for the use of the same instructional strategies that may (or may not) work for both groups of students.

Argumentative writing in this lesson is explicitly introduced and linked to evidence and reasons. In particular, teachers are instructed to use guiding questions to enhance students' background knowledge regarding claims, reasons, and evidence. As a result, students arrive at explicit definitions of these key terms, as stated in the lesson: "Reasons are the cause or explanation for an action, opinion, or event. Reasons support a claim. Evidence (also called reasoning) is the proof or facts that support a reason" (p. 11). Through use of a graphic organizer, argumentation is also conceptualized as a set of hierarchical relationships for the claim and the evidence and reasons that support the claim. Notable as well is the emphasis of having at least three pieces of evidence to support a claim—reflected both in the graphic organizer and the homework assignment that requires students to brainstorm three reasons to support a claim in their position paper. No rationale is provided as to why every claim might need three pieces of evidence (which is perhaps due to formatting issues, or mere convenience), and there was no space in the graphic organizer for students to incorporate or consider counter claims in the position paper.

Instructional Strategies

To help write this position paper, students read and analyze a mentor text. When deconstructing the model text, various scaffolding techniques are suggested to facilitate comprehension and aid in analysis of the text. For example, the lesson suggests using a glossary of key terms (e.g., "claim— something you believe to be true," p. 11) when reading. Teachers are also encouraged to preview the text with students (e.g., whole group discussion of the title), enhance background knowledge, build vocabulary (e.g., pre-teaching abstract words), and conduct a read-aloud and close reading of the text. Each of these strategies is supported with resources to facilitate students' understanding. For example, the close reading activity comes with a list of guiding questions, a glossary of key terms, a word bank, and sentence frames/sentence starters (differentiated according to the various levels of L2 development) to support students' ability to comprehend the text.

Relevant to analyzing the mentor text with the writing rubric, the lesson plan recommends translating the rubric into the students' home languages and adopting language and phrasing that is "student-friendly" (p. 26). Although L2 writers are described as multilingual in this lesson plan, limited attention is given to multilingualism beyond this recommendation. Throughout the lesson, other strategies are included but not explicitly highlighted. They include opportunities for peer discussions, metacognitive reflections, multiple readings, and using supplemental guiding questions to enhance comprehension.

In summary, this lesson plan positions students as multilingual, acknowledges their levels of L2 development, and includes various instructional strategies to address these differences. Reasons and evidence are central to argumentative writing from this lesson plan's perspective, and explicit definitions of these key terms are provided. The lesson provides opportunities to analyze a model of argumentative writing in the context of numerous instructional strategies that are designed to support this work. Despite the richness in scaffolding techniques, there is limited attention to multilingualism. In addition, students in this lesson are provided with a sole position paper, arguing that "Facebook is Not For Kids." While they will have engaged in reading about and researching multiple viewpoints on this topic prior to this lesson, providing a single mentor text within the context of this lesson may dissuade them from presenting a different argument that highlights the benefits of online interactions, perhaps on other social media platforms. Finally, while the reading aspect of the lesson is guided by the teacher and implemented collaboratively in class, drafting is assigned as homework.

Discussion and Implications

When we began our online search for freely available resources, we assumed that the primary challenge would be sifting through the vast array of materials available, but this was not the case. In all likelihood, teachers in the U.S. at that time who were seeking pedagogical resources on L2 argumentative writing online would not dedicate the many hours we did to scouring the internet; while it is possible that they might have come across the few resources we have identified here, it is just as likely that they would simply have stopped looking. Where they would go next—or if they would choose to just use curricula designed for monolingual writers "as-is"—is an open question, but what we have determined is that specialized guidance was not readily and freely available online at the time of our analysis. As a result, it is likely that L2 writers at the time were receiving instruction that did not account for their unique backgrounds, strengths, and needs as multilingual writers, which in turn limited their opportunities to learn to write in a school-valued genre often seen as a key to post-secondary success.

Further, the two primary resources we analyzed portray a less-than-unified understanding of argumentative writing, showing that it is being "curricularized" for teachers of L2 writers in different ways. There are important differences in how argumentation is defined: Ferlazzo and Hull-Sypnieski (2014) employ various modes under the guise of argumentation (problem-solution, cause-and-effect, persuasion) along with attention to the use of claims and evidence, while the New York Department of Education (2018) focuses specifically on claims, reasons, and evidence. It is notable that only the latter resource includes attention to reasons ("the cause or explanation for an action, opinion, or event. Reasons support a claim," p. 11), which serve to connect claims and relevant evidence. The College and Career Readiness Standards (National Governors Association, 2010) state that students will "write arguments to support claims in an analysis of substantive topics or texts, using valid reasoning and relevant and sufficient evidence" (p. 41). This three-part structure (claims, reasoning, evidence) is missing from Ferlazzo and Hull Sypnieski's (2014) activities.

The resources we examined also differ in how they frame the purpose of argumentation. Hirvela (2017) explains that argument as reasoning has the end-goal of writing a well-structured argument essay. Argument as inquiry, on the other hand, frames argument as a tool to gain deeper learning of a certain topic. EngageNY's emphasis on student research into a topic to develop a position and Ferlazzo and Hull-Sypnieski's (2014) activity involving inquiry into neighborhoods both focus on providing a deeper understanding of the topic, thereby framing **argument as inquiry**. On the other hand, Ferlazzo and Hull-Sypnieski's (2017) other activities more clearly support students' end-goal of writing an argument, thus framing **argument as reasoning**.

What both resources share, however, is that both hew closely to the CCSS notion of **argumentation as mode**, rather than a genre-based approach that focuses on writing as social action (Tardy, 2019). Further, neither resource attends substantively to counterclaims, which first appear in Grade 8 writing standards. Attention is not completely absent: the Grade 7 EngageNY unit mentions counterclaims one time as an aspect of analyzing a reading, which is notable given that counterclaims are not introduced in the standards until Grade 8. Ferlazzo and Hull-Sypnieski (2014) mention in a footnote to the article that they cover counterclaims through their use of the book *They Say/I Say* (2007) in class. Nonetheless, ignoring possible objections to an argument—and also not tying the argumentative writing tasks to a genre with a specific social purpose—means that teachers are not exposed to models of pedagogy in which they and their L2 writers grapple with complex issues of audience or purpose.

In terms of these online resources' conceptualizations of L2 writers, both articulate an understanding that instructional efforts should be responsive to students' levels of development. The scales by which they based these learner labels (Kibler & Valdés, 2016) differ, however, with one that remains abstract—beginning, intermediate, advanced (Ferlazzo & Hull-Sypnieski, 2014)—and the other tied to state-level descriptors (entering, emerging, transitioning, and expanding, as used in New York State). This type of variation may be confusing for teachers but is perhaps unsurprising, given a lack of consistency across states in defining K–12 English language proficiency (Linquanti & Cook, 2013) and even broader discussions over time in applied linguistics about defining levels of development (Kibler & Valdés, 2016). One important distinction was EngageNY's (2018) explicit recognition of students as multilingual through use of the acronym MLL and through suggesting home language translations for rubrics. It is important to note the singularity of this suggestion, though, and to question the extent to which it addresses larger calls in the field for a consideration of learners' full multilingual repertoires throughout the learning process (e.g., Velasco & García, 2014). A final point relevant to our analysis of these instructional materials is that resources tended to conceptualize students across language modalities, as ELLs or ELLs/MLLs, and not as L2 writers specifically. There are certainly advantages of this holistic treatment, given the interconnectedness of all modalities in literacy, but there may also be a danger of underspecifying L2 writers in particular, and the ways in which writing may be unique, especially when working across languages and cultures.

Finally, the instructional strategies largely reflect Applebee et al.'s (2013) assessment of writing pedagogy in many regards, such as analyzing mentor texts, engaging in a multistep writing process, and, in one of the two cases, using rubrics to guide writing. They also share the use of other strategies that are commonly (though not universally supported, theoretically or empirically: see Grapin et al., 2020) proposed for L2 writers and students classified as English learners, like graphic organizers, vocabulary previews, and sentence starters to guide some students' writing. Both online resources also veered into a flattening of L2 teaching expertise to "generic good teaching practices" (Harper & de Jong, 2009, p. 137), but in different ways, either through not calling out particular strategies that would be uniquely important to EL-classified students or by generalizing strategies as being likely just as useful for multilingual students as for those with a learning disability. Where these two sources differ most strongly instructionally is their approach to differentiation: Ferlazzo and Hull-Sypnieski (2014) conceptualize differentiation as completely **different** writing tasks (and even modes) to be undertaken separately with learners grouped by levels of proficiency; whereas EngageNY (2018) employs graduated strategies to support various students within a single curriculum and classroom.

And so, what is the "view from the field" in L2 argumentative writing instruction for high school teachers in the U.S.? It is clear that at the time we conducted our analysis, freely available online materials, which are a frequent instructional resource for teachers, were providing little guidance about L2 writers, argumentation, and instruction. We hope that over time teachers will have access to additional local resources in their schools and districts or to commercially available resources such as student textbooks with L2-focused ancillary materials for teachers. Although we cannot speak to similar situations within other countries worldwide, it is clear that English as a Foreign Language (EFL) educators seeking to prepare high school students to enter U.S. post-secondary institutions will likewise struggle to locate resources to guide them.

Fieldwork would be necessary to understand how teachers locate and use materials in "real time," and this is an important area for future research (see also Hirvela, 2017). Further, given the limited resources we analyzed, it is not possible to fully articulate what high-quality freely available resources would look like. What is clear, however, is that this analysis provides a call for L2 writing scholars to play a more active role in materials development, with hopes of developing a robust and openly accessible community of researchers and practitioners engaging in this work together.

NOTES

1. It should be noted that the unit published by Stanford University's Understanding Language Initiative entitled "Persuasion Across Time and

Space" is similar to the EngageNY resource: it is designed for 7th grade and addresses CCSS standards on argumentation. However, we chose not to explore this resource because it is *not* designed as an exemplar within a larger set of materials designed for broad use, and because persuasion and argumentation are not differentiated in these materials. Given ongoing ambiguities in defining these terms, we chose to focus only on materials that foregrounded "argumentation" in their framing and title.

2. It is worthwhile to mention that two of these common instructional strategies—pre-teaching vocabulary and using sentence frames—recently have been critiqued (Grapin et al., 2020).

3. It is not clear why an expository rubric is mentioned in the lesson plan but an explanatory writing rubric is included in the materials package at the end of the lesson: we assume this was simply a formatting error.

REFERENCES

Applebee, A.N., Langer, J.A., Campbell Wilcox, K., Nachowitz, M., Mastroianni, M.P., & Dawson, C. (2013). *Writing instruction that works: Proven methods for middle and high school classrooms.* New York: Teachers College Press.

Caplan, N. A. (2019). Have we always taught the five-paragraph essay? In N.A. Caplan & A.M. Johns (Eds.), *Changing practices for the L2 writing classroom: Moving beyond the five-paragraph essay* (pp. 2–23). Ann Arbor: University of Michigan Press.

Crusan, D., & Ruecker, T. (2019). Standardized testing pressures and the temptation of the five-paragraph essay. In N. A. Caplan & A.M. Johns (Eds.), *Changing practices for the L2 writing classroom: Moving beyond the five-paragraph essay* (pp. 201–220). Ann Arbor: University of Michigan Press.

DeStigter, T. (2015). On the ascendance of argument: A critique of the assumption of academe's dominant form. *Research in the Teaching of English, 50*(1), 11–34. https://www.jstor.org/stable/24889903

Ferlazzo, L., & Hull-Sypnieski, K. (2014). Teaching argument writing to ELLs. *Educational Leadership, 71*(7), 46–52. http://www.ascd.org/publications/educational-leadership/apr14/vol71/num07/Teaching-Argument-Writing-to-ELLs.aspx

Graff, G., & Birkenstein, C. (2007). *They say/I say: The moves that matter in academic writing with readings* (3rd ed.). New York: W.W. Norton and Company.

Grapin, S. E., Llosa, L., Haas, A., & Lee, O. (2020). Rethinking instructional strategies with English learners in the content areas. *TESOL Journal, 00*:e557. https://doi.org/ 10.1002.tesj.557

Gilliland, B. (2018). Teacher preparation for writing in kindergarten to 12th grade. In Liontas, J.I. (Ed.), *The TESOL Encyclopedia of English Language Teaching*, Volume IV. Hoboken, NJ: Wiley Blackwell.

Harper, C. A., & deJong, E. J. (2009). English language teachers' expertise: The elephant in the room. *Language & Education, 23(2)*, 137–151. https://doi.org/10.1080/ 09500780802152788

Hirvela, A. (2013). Preparing English language learners for argumentative writing. In T. Silva & L. de Oliveira (Eds.), *Second language writing in the secondary classroom* (pp. 1–31). New York: Routledge.

Hirvela, A., (2017). Argumentation & second language writing: Are we missing the boat? *Journal of Second Language Writing, 36*, 69–74. http:// dx.doi.org/10.1016/ j.jslw.2017.05.002

Horverak, M. O. (2017). A survey of students' perceptions of how English writing instruction is carried out in Norwegian upper secondary schools. *Journal of Second Language Teaching and Research, 5*(1), 120–144. http:// pops.uclan.ac.uk/index.php /jsltr/article/view/438

Høegh-Omdal, L. (2018). English argumentative writing in Norwegian lower secondary school: Are year 10 lower secondary students sufficiently prepared for L2 argumentative writing in upper secondary? Master's thesis, Universitetet i Agder; University of Agder).

Kaufman, J. A., Opfer, V. D., Bongard, M. & Pane, J.D. (2018). *Changes in what teachers know and do in the Common Core Era: American teacher panel findings from 2015 to 2017.* Santa Monica, CA: RAND Corporation. https:// www.rand.org/pubs/research_reports/ RR2658.html

Kibler, A. K. (2019). *Longitudinal interactional histories: Bilingual and biliterate journeys of Mexican immigrant-origin youth.* London: Palgrave Macmillan.

Kibler, A. K., & Valdés, G. (2016). Conceptualizing language learners: Socio-institutional mechanisms and their consequences. *Modern Language Journal, 100*, 96–116. https://doi.10.1111/modl.12310

Krippendorff, K. (2003). *Content analysis: An introduction to its methodology.* Thousand Oaks, CA: Sage.

Linquanti, R., and Cook, H.G. (2013). *Toward a "common definition of English learner": A brief defining policy and technical issues and opportunities for state assessment consortia.* Washington, DC: Council of Chief State School Officers.

Moll, L. C., Amanti, C., Neff, D., & Gonzalez, N. (1992). Funds of knowledge for teaching: Using a qualitative approach to connect homes and classrooms. *Theory into Practice, 31*(2), 132–141.

National Governors Association Center for Best Practices, Council of Chief State School Officers. (2010). *Common Core State Standards for English*

Language arts & literacy in history/social studies, science, and technical subjects. www.corestandards.org

New York State Department of Education, with August, D., Staehr-Fenner, D., & Synder, S. (2018). *Lesson exemplar for English language learners/multilingual language learners: Grade 7 module 4A, unit 3, lesson 1: Facebook: Not for kids*. Albany: State Department of Education. https://www.engageny .org/resource/grade-7-ela-module-4a-unit-3-lesson-1-lesson-exemplar -ells-mlls/file/156576

Newell, G. E., Bloome, D., & Hirvela, A. (2015). *Teaching and learning argumentative writing in high school language arts classrooms*. New York: Routledge.

Newell, G. E., VanDerHeide, J., & Wynhoff Olsen, A. (2014). High school English language arts teachers' argumentative epistemologies for teaching writing. *Research in the Teaching of English, 49*, 95–118. www. jstor.org/stable/24398670

O'Hallaron, C. L. (2014). supporting fifth-grade ELLs' argumentative writing development. *Written Communication, 31*(3), 304–331. https://doi .org/10.1177/0741088314536524

Prior, P. (2005). Toward the ethnography of argumentation: A response to Richard Andrews' "Models of argumentation in educational discourse." *Text & Talk, 25*, 129–144. https://doi.org/10.1515/text.2005.25.1.129

Tardy, C. (2019). Is the five-paragraph essay a genre? In N.A. Caplan & A.M. Johns (Eds.), *Changing practices for the L2 writing classroom: Moving beyond the five-paragraph essay* (pp. 24–41). Ann Arbor: University of Michigan Press.

Valdés, G. (2004). Between support and marginalisation: The development of academic language in linguistic minority children. *International Journal of Bilingual Education and Bilingualism, 7*, 102-132. https://doi .org/10.1080/13670050408667804

Valdés, G. (2015). Spanish, Latinas and intergenerational continuity: The challenges of curricularizing language. *International Multilingual Research Journal, 9*, 253–273. https://doi.org/10.1080/19313152.201 5.1086625

Valdés, G., Kibler, A., & Walqui, A. (2014). *Changes in the expertise of ESL professionals: Knowledge and action in an era of new standards*. Alexandria, VA: TESOL International.

Velasco, P., & García, O. (2014). Translanguaging and the writing of bilingual learners, *Bilingual Research Journal, 37*(1), 6–23. https://doi.org/10.10 80/15235882.2014.893270

3

Using the 3x3 Toolkit to Support Argumentative Writing across Disciplines

THOMAS D. MITCHELL AND SILVIA PESSOA

Abstract

This chapter discusses our use of the SFL-based 3x3 professional learning toolkit (Humphrey, Martin, Dreyfus, & Mahboob, 2010) to conceptualize, analyze, and model argumentative writing in three genres in three disciplines. We argue that 3x3–based analysis of student writing is particularly useful for understanding where to focus students' attention to help them meet genre expectations. By applying the 3x3 to analyze and model particular argumentative genres, we can help disciplinary instructors and students isolate the linguistic features that are most valued in particular contexts.

Across the disciplines, a one-size-fits-all approach to writing argumentatively is inadequate. Different genres within and across disciplines require particular ways of representing knowledge, aligning readers, and organizing texts. However, disciplinary instructors do not always have explicit awareness of the nuances of argumentative writing in the genres they assign or how argument in their discipline differs from argument in others. All students, but particularly L2 learners, need explicit instruction about the language resources needed to meet genre expectations; without such support, students are likely to fall back on familiar approaches to writing tasks, regardless of the demands of the assignment at hand, which can result in writing that does not meet these expectations.

We present how we have used the 3x3 professional learning toolkit (Humphrey et al., 2010) as a way of unpacking the language resources needed to meet genre expectations in our collaborations with disciplinary faculty to scaffold argumentative writing. The 3x3 is a Systemic Functional Linguistics (SFL)–based toolkit for supporting instructors to frame the resources needed for a particular writing context and "inform[ing] the development of genre-specific frameworks for analyzing, modeling, and assessing texts in particular disciplines" (Humphrey et al., 2010, p. 186). The 3x3 helps focus analytical attention on the linguistic features of academic genres by considering the three meta-functions of language (ideational, interpersonal, and textual) at three levels of text (the whole text, its phases or parts, and its sentences). **Ideational meanings** are construed by resources for representing specialized and formal disciplinary knowledge, including resources for relating "information . . . in logical relationships (e.g., time, cause, consequence, comparison)" (p. 188). **Interpersonal meanings** are construed by resources for convincing the reader in critical yet authoritative ways. These include resources for incorporating source texts to further the writer's purpose and creating a consistent stance through evaluations. **Textual meanings** are construed by resources for organizing clearly scaffolded texts, including resources for cohesion and logical flow of information that moves from "more dense abstract terms in topic sentences to expanded concrete terms in subsequent sentences" (p. 188). Our analysis of student writing in this chapter provides further details about the 3x3 and its application for teaching and researching academic arguments.

We argue that 3x3–based analysis of student writing is particularly useful for understanding where to focus students' attention. We support this claim with findings from our 3x3–based analysis in different classroom contexts. Specifically, we show how control of particular *different* linguistic resources is vital to meeting genre expectations in three genres—historical argument, case analysis, and case development—in three disciplines—history, organizational behavior (OB), and information systems (IS). We suggest that this SFL-based approach is valuable for scaffolding argumentative writing because it puts the focus squarely on language, providing concrete, detailed descriptions of the language resources that make an argument effective. This focus—the *how-to-do-it-with-language* aspect of claims and support—is particularly important for L2 writers but commonly missing in descriptions of argumentative writing.

In our work supporting disciplinary writing, we follow an iterative, multi-pronged design-based research approach (Anderson & Shattuck, 2012) that involves: reviewing student texts to get a sense of the genre and its language expectations; testing these initial impressions in interviews with the disciplinary faculty and think-aloud protocols while they read student texts; reviewing literature on the genre to understand its linguistic demands according to the expectations of the social context; using this understanding to develop a 3x3 framework for the particular genre in the particular classroom context; and using our particularized 3x3 to undergird our subsequent analysis of student writing and development of scaffolding materials, which we refine with each iteration of the course based on our evolving understanding. We do not present the students with the 3x3, but our materials are based on our 3x3 analysis. We often opt for "bridging metalanguage" (Humphrey, 2016) in our interactions with students and disciplinary faculty.

In our 3x3–based **analysis of arguments in history**, we found that control of interpersonal resources was key: many students struggled with maintaining a consistent evaluative position and marshaling authoritative voices to advance the argument (e.g., Miller, Mitchell, & Pessoa, 2014). In our 3x3–based **analysis of case analyses in OB**, we found that control of ideational resources was key: less successful students wrote argumentative analyses that remained solely focused on ideational meaning by only stating what they "know" from the textbook (disciplinary knowledge) or only reporting what they "see" in the case data, rather than oscillating between what they "know" and what they "see" to draw meaningful conclusions (cf. Hao, 2015). In our 3x3–based **analysis of case developments in IS**, we found that control of textual resources was key: less effective case developments included individual parts that provided discrete answers to questions instead of creating cohesive connections across the text to facilitate its larger argumentative purpose.

The 3x3 learning toolkit provides a conceptualization of academic writing that can help L2 writers across the disciplines. Rather than conceiving of argumentative writing as monolithic, an approach based on 3x3 affords flexibility and facilitates adjustments to the expectations of the particular discipline and classroom where it is applied. Thus, by applying the 3x3 to analyze and model particular argumentative genres, we can help disciplinary instructors and students focus on what linguistic features are most valued in particular contexts.

We contrast prototypical examples of less and more effective student texts to emphasize the importance of controlling the resources of one metafunction in argumentative writing in each discipline. While focusing students' attention on the resources of one meta-function at one level of the text is not a panacea, this approach helps uncover the nuances of argumentative writing in different disciplines and provides an entry point for addressing the most pressing student needs.

Using the 3x3 to Highlight Interpersonal Resources for Writing Historical Arguments

In university history classes, students are often expected to write arguments by following certain genre stages as they select, interpret, and evaluate facts to transform knowledge and create meaning (Coffin, 2006). However, many L2 writers often struggle with knowledge transformation, presenting information as factual rather than something that needs to be argued for.

In our work in history classrooms, our 3x3–based analysis has shown that the most striking differences between less and more effective student texts stem from their control of interpersonal resources. To effectively write history arguments, students must use interpersonal resources to assert and defend a position, acknowledge source texts, show how evidence supports claims, and strategically manage multiple perspectives. Students may write non-arguments or ineffective arguments when (1) they do not understand that they need to take a position (Miller, Mitchell, & Pessoa, 2016), (2) they take a position but do not maintain it consistently (Miller et al., 2014), or (3) they take a position but do not integrate evidence effectively to support it (Pessoa, Mitchell, & Miller, 2017). Thus, the interpersonal resources from the 3x3 are pivotal for meeting genre expectations. With Excerpts 1 and 2, we present contrasting prototypical student texts to illustrate the importance of interpersonal resources for historical arguments.

Excerpt 1: Prototypical Historical Arguments Exhibiting Challenges Controlling Interpersonal Resources

Prompt: How would you characterize Babylonia's social structure?

Thesis: Hammurabi's Code indicates a distinct social hierarchy present in ancient Babylonia, and suggests that certain social classes were viewed superior to others as perceived in the different punishments and rewards based on social class.

Paragraph 1: The first social class in Babylonia is the free upper-class people. [. . .]

Paragraph 2: Below the free upper-class people in Ancient Babylonia are the class of freed men. The freed men were former slaves who became free or men from the upper class who committed mistakes and were punished by losing their status. People from this class received different treatment from people from the upper-class people. A doctor would receive 5 shekels for treating a freed man . . .

Excerpt 2: Prototypical Historical Argument
Effectively Controlling Interpersonal Resources

Prompt: How would you characterize Babylonia's social structure?

Thesis: Hammurabi's Code indicates a distinct social hierarchy present in ancient Babylonia, and suggests that certain social classes were viewed superior to others as perceived in the different punishments and rewards based on social class.

Paragraph 1: In Hammurabi's Code, laws that established punishments for certain crimes indicate that certain social classes are given preference over others. [. . .]

Paragraph 2: Laws that established rewards for certain actions indicate different levels of social class superiority in the ancient Babylonian social structure. This is evident in rewards offered to physicians for treating patients of different social classes. For example, Law 215 states that "if a physician saves the patient's eye, he shall receive ten shekels in money (215)." However, the subsequent laws add that "if the patient be a freed man, he (the physician) receives five shekels, and if the patient is a slave, the physician receives two shekels (216–217)." This is indicative of an attempt to assign a monetary value to an individual's health, and suggests that a free man's health is worth five times more than a slave's health. Thus, one can assume that a free man is superior than a freed man, and a freed man is superior than a slave, indicating a social hierarchy. Although some may view this law as fair because payment was based on the wealth of the patient, it actually promoted unequal health treatment as physicians first attended to the needs of upper-classmen while neglecting the needs of lower-class people.

Excerpts 1 and 2 include essentially the same information, and both set up the writer to make an argument in the thesis statement. Both thesis statements also effectively respond to the prompt's invitation to characterize and evaluate Babylonia's social structure (*a distinct social hierarchy*) and preview the supporting claims (*different punishments and rewards based on social class*). Each text follows this organization by first presenting one supporting claim and then the other. Thus, both texts exhibit similar control of ideational and textual resources. However, the two texts differ in how effectively they use interpersonal resources.

While Excerpt 1 has a thesis that takes a position that can be defended, the rest of the text falls back into knowledge display: the writer reports information from the source text without citing it directly or linking the information back to the thesis to show how it supports the overall position. There are no indications, apart from the thesis, that the writer anticipates a reader who might disagree with this interpretation of historical knowledge. In other words, after the thesis, Excerpt 1 presents historical information as factual, a characteristic of non-argument historical genres where the focus is on providing "relatively categorical explanations of historical phenomena" (Coffin, 2006, p. 77). This type of writing is reminiscent of high school history textbooks, where the rhetorical goal is not to persuade the readers that events happened in the way described or anticipate objections to a particular version of events, but to provide an uncontested account of history that the reader will take to be factual. When students are asked to write arguments based on a source text, the professor does not want to see the student writer explain its content as if it were unquestionably true. Student responses like Excerpt 1 reveal how challenging it can be for students to write arguments and indicate the importance of being explicit about the interpersonal resources needed to write arguments.

In Excerpt 2, the writer uses evidence and strategically manages multiple voices to support and advance the argument to persuade a potentially resistant reader. In contrast with mostly the "single-voiced" representation of history in Excerpt 1, Excerpt 2 is "multivoiced" in its representation of one possible interpretation of history articulated against a backdrop of other possibilities (cf. Martin & White, 2005). Multivoiced language either opens the dialogue between the writer and potential readers, inviting other perspectives, or narrows the dialogue, attempting to bring readers closer to the writer's perspective. Effective arguments use expanding and narrowing multivoiced language together strategically and in combination with single-voiced language. As exemplified in Excerpt 2, it is important to incorporate the source text, which expands the dialogue by incorporating an authoritative voice (*Law 215 states that*). The writer then narrows the dialogue by explaining the quotations as they relate to the argument (*This is indicative of*). This narrowing move restricts the possible interpretations of the evidence to that of the writer, thereby bringing the reader closer to the writer's perspective. Another way Excerpt 2 illustrates a strategic combination of expanding and narrowing resources is with a **concede-counter**, a move that can make resistant readers more receptive: *Although some may view this law as fair because. . . , it* *promoted unequal health treatment.* . . . By conceding that it is understandable that someone might interpret things one way, the writer expands the dialogue and gives up some ground to an alternative perspective. With the counter that follows, the writer narrows the dialogue toward their own position. Taken together, these strategic uses of interpersonal resources are vital for writing effective historical arguments.

Ideational Resources in Case Analyses in Organizational Behavior

In the case analysis genre, the writer applies disciplinary concepts, theory, and knowledge to identify problems in an organization and uses this analysis as support for recommendations to improve the organization (Gardner, 2012). This requires students to draw on ideational resources to represent the specialized knowledge of the discipline while also expanding that knowledge to make their own conclusions about the case that will be used as the basis for their recommendations.

Our 3x3–based analysis of student case analyses in an OB course shows that the most striking difference between less and more effective student texts stems from their control of ideational resources. Specifically, many students were challenged by the expectation that their writing strategically oscillate between disciplinary knowledge and case knowledge, so instead focused mostly on either representing disciplinary knowledge or information about the case. The more effective student texts were those that created effective patterns of logical connections between disciplinary and case knowledge to produce new knowledge from their analysis that could support the claims made in their recommendations. Thus, the 3x3 provided us the tools to determine that ideational resources were what the students needed to focus on first to effectively meet case analysis genre expectations. With Excerpts 3 and 4, we present contrasting prototypical student texts to illustrate the importance of ideational resources for case analyses in OB.

Excerpt 3 does not meet genre expectations because the writer provides an explanation of the disciplinary concept of motivation but does not expand that knowledge in connection to the actual company (the case) under analysis. In fact, the writer makes no reference to the company—the reader would never know that the student is doing a case analysis of Whole Foods® because the writer does not connect disciplinary knowledge to the case at all—and thus never makes conclusions about the case to create new meanings. In other instances (not shown), students mostly reported case information without making significant connections to disciplinary knowledge; for example, they might start with a sentence similar to the first one in Excerpt 3, defining the disciplinary concept, but then move immediately into a representation of details of the company under study with no return to the concept of motivation or analysis of those details using this concept to produce ideas that could lead to a recommendation.

Excerpt 3: Prototypical OB Case Analysis Exhibiting Challenges Controlling Ideational Resources

---

Motivation, according to Victor H. Vroom (as cited in Aworemi, Abdul-Azeez, & Durowojo, 2011), is prioritizing a choice among other "alternative forms of voluntary activities" (Martinus, H. & Ramadanty, S., 2016), and the individual has complete autonomy over it. People's motivation is highly dependent on their perception on the value of effort and the belief that the effort will help the individual achieve the goal [. . .] Having employees with different levels of motivations makes it harder for the organization to construct motivation strategies. Moreover, people are motivated by different factors. The motivation factors can be intrinsic factors, extrinsic factor, or a mixture of both. Having people with very different mentalities and backgrounds entails that each individual will have different motives [. . .], which makes the process of motivating employees very challenging.

To call students' attention to the ideational resources needed to meet case analysis genre expectations, we use the heuristic "I know; I see; I conclude" (Hao, 2015). We use this heuristic to help students implement patterns of reasoning to integrate what they *know* about the discipline with what they *see* in the case, eventually leading to *conclusions* about the case that form the basis of their recommendations, as represented in Excerpt 4.

Excerpt 4: Prototypical OB Case Analysis Effectively Controlling Ideational Resources

---

The leadership style of the new management at M University seems to be a primary point of friction. Leadership style, using Hersey-Blanchard's Situational Leadership Model (1988), depends on primarily three factors: follower readiness, relationship behavior, and task behavior. At M University, the leadership had developed a culture that made the faculty and staff "able and willing" to do their jobs and fulfill the university's mission, demonstrating that they had high follower readiness (Konopaske et al., 2018, p. 416). In such a situation, Hersey-Blanchard's model predicts an appropriate leadership style would have low task behavior, either leaving much of the direction of the faculty and staff to themselves or sharing in governance of the institution. In contrast, the new leadership at M University seems to have adopted a Telling Leadership style, with high task behavior and low relationship behavior. This style has been shown in the institution of monthly performance reviews and the proliferation of new and detailed policies and procedures at every level of the organization. The mismatch between the high readiness of the employees and the high task behavior of the leadership has created a tension between management and labor while also doing damage to the culture of high achievement that had already been established.

Excerpt 4 starts with a claim about fictional M University (MU) using a concept from organizational behavior: leadership style. Following from the claim, the writer first explains what they *know* about leadership style from the disciplinary knowledge (Hersey-Blanchard's Situational Leadership Model), then uses the move "At M University" to move to evidence of what the writer *sees* in the case in terms of leadership style practices prior to the establishment of the new leadership. The writer not only describes the past leadership style at MU but also connects it to the disciplinary knowledge of leadership by *concluding* that under the old leadership style, the university had "high follower readiness." The sentences that follow contrast the old leadership style with the new leadership style through a series of similar moves. These moves connect what the writer *knows* about the disciplinary knowledge (Telling Leadership Style) with what the writer *sees* at MU to *conclude* that there is tension between the management and the employees due to changes in the leadership style. With this conclusion, the writer creates new knowledge about MU, a negative evaluation ("mismatch") that can be addressed with a recommendation in a later section of the case analysis.

In our workshops, we presents students with annotated texts segmented into *know, see, and conclude* moves. We overlay a straight line over texts like Excerpt 3 to show students that when they focus only on what they *know* from disciplinary knowledge or only what they *see* in the case, their meaning "flatlines." We contrast such texts with ones like Excerpt 4, overlaid with "waves" depicting valued ways of oscillating between disciplinary knowledge and case knowledge. We also highlight the use of logical connections [e.g., cause (*"because,* consequence (*so*); comparison (*in contrast*)] to connect information presented. In sum, the heuristic "I know; I see; I conclude" is a useful tool to highlight the ideational resources needed to write effective case analyses.

Textual Resources in Case Developments in Information Systems

The case analysis is also a prominent genre in Information Systems (IS). In our university's IS program, students write case analyses across the four years, with differing expectations according to the professor and level of the course. In addition to challenges with moving between disciplinary knowledge and case information, the case analysis genre also poses challenges for students that result from "competing demands" (Gardner, 2012, p. 14) to perform both academic/learner and professional/mock-consultant roles within the same document. In other words, as an "apprenticeship" genre, the case analysis is training students for real workplace writing (such as consultant work) while also giving them practice learning and applying course concepts. We have argued (Mitchell, Pessoa, & Gomez-Laich, 2021) that the tension caused by these competing academic and professional demands is most acute in intermediate courses; in first-year courses, the focus is predominantly on the learner role, while in advanced courses, the focus is mostly on the professional role.

In a third-year (intermediate) IS class, we scaffolded a type of case analysis called *case development.* The case development requires students to generate the case themselves by writing a narrative of their visit to a local museum or library, analyze it using relevant disciplinary frameworks, and provide recommendations for enhancing the experience with technology. In this genre, students need to adopt a learner role to explicitly apply disciplinary knowledge in the analysis section, but then enact a professional role in the recommendations section. There needs to be a strong rhetorical relationship between these sections, with clear intertextual connections between them as the recommendations are supported by negative evaluations from the analysis. The professor provided students with guiding questions to help them craft the narrative and consider it in light of the disciplinary frameworks.

Our analysis of student writing using our 3x3 description of the genre revealed that the most striking difference between less and more effective student texts was their control of textual resources. Specifically, the organization of the less effective texts reflected an **exaggerated learner role** in both the analysis and recommendations sections: these students did not create connections across different parts of the analysis or create cohesive relationships between the analysis and recommendations sections; rather, they used the professor's guiding questions and structural guidance to produce a text that resembled separate short answer responses when a coherent, professional document was expected. By doing so, they neglected the necessary step of rearranging the text for their own analytical purposes. Effective texts, on the other hand, used textual resources to create connections among ideas within the analysis section and across sections to signal that the recommendations were grounded in the analysis. With Excerpts 5 and 6, we present contrasting prototypical student texts to illustrate the importance of textual resources for case developments in IS.

Excerpt 5: Prototypical IS Case Development Exhibiting Challenges Controlling Textual Resources

Analysis:

Spatio-temporal thread:

In the first half of the visit, I did feel rushed and completely lost the sense of time. I did not notice any clocks around to be able to even tell the time or judge how long it had been since I had figured out the answer to one of my questions. In the second half of the visit [. . . .]

Emotional Thread:

I felt. . . .

Recommendations:

#1 Motion Detectors for Light-up Displays
Processes: Anticipating
Threads: Sensual, Spatio-temporal
Expected to be able to see more information but I couldn't.
Wanted to experience museum in the dark but also see information when I got near the exhibits.
Museum adds technology to light up display information when someone moves close to exhibits.

In Excerpt 5, the writer uses the elements of the disciplinary framework (i.e., the threads of experience: *spatio-temporal, emotional*) as a macro structure for the section, but within each element, the focus of topic sentences is on evidence from the experience rather than on abstractions to be unpacked with this evidence. The writer organizes information by time (repeating the sequence of the narrative: *in the first half of the visit; in the second half of the visit*) in combination with answers to the guiding questions. Examples of the guiding questions include: What effects did space and time have on our experience? Did the technologies make you feel comfortable and you lost sense of time? Did you feel rushed? The phrasing *I* did *feel rushed* is the clearest indication that the questions are being answered directly.

The recommendations section of Excerpt 5 provides shorthand responses to information solicited in the guidelines. It is not always written in complete sentences, but instead lists the processes (i.e., the elements of the disciplinary framework) that relate to the recommendation and provides some notes that the reader must infer are reasons for the recommendation. Thus, there is a lack of control of textual resources that undermines the mock-professional role that is expected in this section. Even when the less effective recommendations were written in paragraphs, they often lacked intertextual links to the analysis section, leaving the two sections apparently disconnected and independent of each other.

In Excerpt 6, on the other hand, textual resources are used to create coherence by signposting and scaffolding ideas, both within and across phases. While the macro-structure of the analysis section is similar to Excerpt 5, in Excerpt 6 the information subsumed under each element of the disciplinary framework is organized by nominal expressions to bundle information that is then unpacked with details from the narrative as evidence. For example, after defining an element of the disciplinary framework—the compositional thread—the paragraph's ideas move from general to specific, as abstractions (e.g., *"insufficient explanatory information," "unconventional layout"*) are unpacked with concrete details from the experience that illustrate each evaluation. Each part ends by repackaging the analysis into a rough sketch of a technological solution (i.e., the lack of coherence of the floor plan could be mitigated by a wayfinding system). Thus, the organization moves from packed up assessment of the experience (*"the experience is not very coherent"*) to unpacked details from the case (*"a main room breaks off into many rooms and there are even rooms within rooms"*) to a repackaged articulation of what the original assessment means for the future of the museum (*"needs a more coherent experience for the user"*).

Excerpt 6: Prototypical IS Case Development
Effectively Controlling Textual Resources

Analysis:

<u>Compositional Thread:</u>

In McCarthy's framework, the compositional thread refers to how each part of the experience relates to the whole experience. Although there are many interesting objects at the museum (from old fancy cars to money from all over the world), the overall experience is not very coherent because of the unconventional layout and noticeable lack of signage. Specifically, the overall floor plan and flow from room to room makes it difficult to navigate through the museum. There is a main room that breaks off into many rooms and there are even rooms within rooms. Thus, the visitor does not have a sense for the overall size of the museum, or when the visit is at the halfway point. This makes it difficult to piece together the whole experience, especially considering there is no signage indicating the visitor's location and how to get to specific exhibits. Adding to this lack of coherence is the apparently random grouping of the objects. When objects are not grouped chronologically or thematically, the relationship between rooms is difficult to determine. The museum clearly needs to create a more coherent experience for the user by rearranging the spaces and the objects in a more meaningful way. Once this is done, technology can be used to create a wayfinding system to help the user navigate through the museum more smoothly.

Recommendations:

The museum clearly has an impressive collection and unique space that provides a rich experience for visitors. Even so, technology can provide opportunities to further enhance the visitor experience.
We recommend the following technology enhancements:

1. **A smart digital wayfinding system** that uses lights on the ceiling to project arrows and exhibit names on the floor. The museum's current lack of wayfinding system may confuse visitors who are not accompanied by a tour guide and make their experience less enjoyable. Adding the digital wayfinding system would allow visitors to more easily navigate the space.
2. **A phone application** that provides an overview of the contents of each room [. . . .]

The recommendations section of Excerpt 6 uses a recommendations-justification macro-structure and textual resources are controlled to help enact a mock-professional role. Each recommendation is numbered and key words are bolded to facilitate skimming for a busy professional reader. There are clear intertextual links between the analysis (e.g., *"lack of signal,"* *"difficult to navigate through the museum"*) and recommendations sections (e.g., *"smart digital wayfinding system," "allow visitors to more easily navigate the space"*), which are vital textual resources for signaling that the negative evaluations from the analysis are being recontextualized as justifications for the recommendations. In short, a focus on the role of textual resources from the 3x3 is important for writing cohesive and professional case developments.

Closing Thoughts

This chapter illustrated how the 3x3 learning toolkit can be used to conceptualize, analyze, and model argumentative writing across the disciplines. The three meta-functions of language represented in the 3x3 are inseparable in practice and work together in complex ways. Furthermore, all argumentative genres require students to control resources for representing specialized knowledge, aligning readers, and organizing texts. Nevertheless, different writing contexts present different challenges for students. Thus, this chapter has emphasized the importance of focusing on the resources of one meta-function to uncover the nuances of argumentative writing in particular disciplines as an entry point for addressing the most pressing student needs for meeting genre expectations.

Specifically, in our work scaffolding arguments in a history class, our 3x3–based analysis showed that students' most pressing need was with controlling interpersonal resources to incorporate outside voices and guide an imagined reader toward a consistent evaluative position. In our work scaffolding case analyses in an OB class, our 3x3–based analysis showed that students' most pressing need was with controlling ideational resources to connect their claims and support by articulating logical relationships between disciplinary knowledge and information from the case. In our work scaffolding case developments (a particular case analysis genre) in an IS class, we found that students' most pressing need was with controlling textual resources to signal the rhetorical relationship between the analysis and recommendations sections. Despite important differences in argumentative writing across disciplines, there are commonalities, too. Arguments are always grounded in evaluative claims, supported by evidence that is grounded in information that writers repackage and rearrange for the purposes of the text (Humphrey & Economou, 2015; Pessoa & Mitchell, 2019).

The examples presented in each section are based on real activities used in writing workshops with students. Teachers could implement similar approaches in their own classrooms. We frequently present students with pairs of texts to consider which is more effective in meeting the assignment requirements, asking them to look for differences that help explain why, inductively, and then building a technical vocabulary with them to describe these differences. Once we identify the valued resources used in mentor texts, we co-construct revisions to the texts that are less effective in controlling these resources.

Building a 3x3 for a particular genre requires time, time to gain familiarity through analysis of student writing, expertise by reading research literature, and local understanding by learning the particular expectations of individual instructors. Although we have spent substantial time talking with disciplinary faculty and analyzing student texts, our own understanding of the genres discussed in this chapter is still evolving, refined with each iteration of our collaborations in these courses. Analysis can begin with a sketch of a 3x1, considering the valued features of the genre at the level of the whole text, and build from there. It is important to get a sense of the stages of a genre, how specialized knowledge is built across them, and how the relationship with the reader is negotiated across them before delving into more detailed descriptions of what is happening within these stages at the paragraph or sentence level. As writing specialists engaged in collaborations with disciplinary faculty, we can work together to learn about the discipline and make the linguistic resources needed to meet genre expectations explicit for faculty and students.

REFERENCES

Anderson, T., & Shattuck, J. (2012). Design-based research: A decade of progress in education research? *Educational Researcher, 41*(1), 16–25.

Coffin, C. (2006). *Historical discourse: The language of time, cause and evaluation.* New York: Continuum.

Gardner, S. (2012). A pedagogical and professional case study genre and register continuum in business and medicine. *Journal of Applied Linguistics and Professional Practice, 9*(1), 13–35.

Hao, J. (2015). Construing biology: An ideational perspective. Unpublished PhD thesis, The University of Sydney, Australia.

Humphrey, S. (2016). *Academic literacies in the middle years: A framework for enhancing teacher knowledge and student achievement.* New York: Routledge/ Taylor & Francis.

Humphrey, S. L., & Economou, D. (2015). Peeling the onion–A textual model of critical analysis. *Journal of English for Academic Purposes, 17,* 37–50.

Humphrey, S., Martin, J. R., Dreyfus, S., Mahboob, A. (2010). The 3x3: Setting up a linguistic toolkit for teaching academic writing. In A. Mahboob and N. K. Knight (Eds.), *Appliable linguistics* (pp. 185–199). New York: Continuum.

Martin, J.R. & White, P.R.R. (2005). *The language of evaluation: Appraisal in English.* New York: Palgrave Macmillan.

Miller, R.T., Mitchell, T.D., & Pessoa, S. (2014). Valued voices: Students' use of engagement in argumentative history writing. *Linguistics and Education, 28,* 107–120.

Miller, R.T., Mitchell, T.D., & Pessoa, S. (2016). Impact of source texts and prompts on students' genre uptake. *Journal of Second Language Writing, 31,* 11–24.

Mitchell, T. D., Pessoa, S., & Gomez-Laich, M. P. (2021). Know your roles: Alleviating the academic-professional tension in the case analysis genre. *Journal of English for Academic Purposes, 61,* 117–131.

Pessoa, S. & Mitchell, T.D. (2019). Preparing students to write in the disciplines. In Caplan, N.A. and A.M. Johns (Eds.). *Changing practices for the L2 writing classroom: Moving beyond the five-paragraph essay* (pp. 150–177) Ann Arbor: University of Michigan Press.

Pessoa, S., Mitchell, T.D., & Miller, R.T. (2017). Emergent arguments: A functional approach to analyzing student challenges with the argument genre. *Journal of Second Language Writing, 38,* 42–55.

4

Source-based Argumentative Writing Assessment

LIA PLAKANS AND RENKA OHTA

Abstract

In completing academic writing tasks, L2 learners use source materials to support their thesis, argument, or position. Thus, source-based argumentative writing tasks have been increasingly used as assessment tasks in and outside of the classroom. This chapter first reviews literature on source-based writing from the construct validity perspective. It then discusses practical applications of source-based argumentative writing tasks for the purpose of classroom pedagogy, including how such tasks can be developed, incorporated into teaching and learning, scored using a rating scale, and used as a tool for providing effective feedback.

The assessment of writing has evolved and expanded over the past several decades. At one time, writing was tested through the display of language knowledge using indirect assessments such as multiple choice questions about sentence structure (Crusan, 2010). At present, writing assessments prompt students to use language directly in performance-based tasks such as extemporaneous essays positing an opinion or narrating a significant event. With "language use" as a central construct, teachers and test developers have explored what writing looks like in the domains of academic language use, finding that in these settings, writing is often framed as an argument (Hirvela, 2017). Studies have also shown that academic assignments routinely expect students to draw from source material such as books, articles, or other written texts (Cumming, 2013). Leki and Carson (1994, 1997) found that the most popular types of writing assignments that ESL students encounter in credit-bearing university classes include writing about and responding to reading input, explaining something, and arguing for and against a topic. This evidence has led to the popularity of assessing writing through integrated source-based argumentative writing tasks.

As we delve into argumentative source-based writing assessment in this chapter, it is important to mention context and to give some definitions. In educational assessment, there has long been a divide or distinction between *classroom-based* and *standardized* assessment. This difference can impact the purpose of an assessment, the resources available, and the level of attention to certain "test" qualities (validity, reliability, feasibility). For this chapter, the focus will lean toward contexts in which assessments are used in pedagogy for classroom purposes; however, some research cited will be drawn from studies of standardized assessments.

Three terms appearing throughout the chapter deserve definition: *source-based, integrated skills assessment,* and *construct.* In the field of writing, **source-based** refers to writing that draws on other texts—written, oral, visual—as content for writing. For example, for a literature review, writers read books, articles, and other documents that they summarize and synthesize to produce an original text. How much source material is drawn upon and how it is used in one's writing varies across genres and per assignment. **Integrated skills assessment** refers to tasks that require more than one of the four language skills: reading, writing, listening, and speaking (Knoch & Sitajalabahorn, 2013). They have experienced increasing popularity as they reflect the domain of academic writing. Source-based writing, as an assessment task, would fall under the umbrella of an integrated assessment task. Source-based integrated skills writing is common in assignments that require argumentation and those that are summaries. The former requires writers to select ideas, points, or arguments from source texts to support their thesis. Note that source-based argumentative essays require the use of source materials "as support for a particular point of view, but the examinee's own experience and knowledge may also be included in the written response" (Weigle & Parker, 2012, p. 119). Argumentation may include summarization of source material, but there are also assessment tasks that require summary in isolation, when the skill of selecting main ideas or capturing the gist of a source text is the skill being assessed.

Last, the term **construct** has important implications in assessment. By definition, a construct is the conceptualization of an ability or process; it is a theory or model of the abilities one is trying to assess. Defining the construct for an assessment assures us that we have thought through what we understand as language or language use, which represents a blueprint on which to develop an assessment task and a meaningful scheme for scoring. For example, a construct of source-based writing would entail various aspects of writing, components of reading, as well as abilities needed to draw ideas from sources and paraphrase/cite appropriately in original writing.

Research on Source-Based Writing

This section reviews research on source-based writing in the field of L2 writing assessment while focusing on *construct validity*, a term used to refer to evidence that is required for the proper interpretation and use of assessment scores in relation to a construct. Evidence for construct validity has been sought by conducting studies on (1) the major skills contributing to source-based writing performance; (2) the comprehension and productive processes and strategies that are used by L2 writers; (3) source text use; (4) discourse features across English proficiency levels; and (5) rating criteria and score reliability. As previously mentioned, some source-based writing tasks involve argumentation, while others require summarizing or comparing and contrasting information from one or more source materials. This section reviews literature that includes both argumentative and summary source-based writing.

Skills Contributing to Source-Based Writing Performance

Previous research has assessed the weight of contributing skills in successful performances on source-based writing tasks, with mixed findings reported on which skills are more important. In an early study, Watanabe (2001) used regression analyses to examine the relationship between (1) reading-to-write scores, (2) vocabulary and reading comprehension, and (3) writing scores. As the writing-only score was a significant predictor of read-to-write scores, he concluded that "the read-to-write task was primarily a measure of writing ability rather than that of reading ability" (pp. 97–98). Shin and Ewert's (2015) study revealed a moderate correlation between writers' reading-writing scores and reading comprehension scores ($r=.68$) and with independent writing scores ($r=.65$). Sawaki, Quinlan, and Lee (2013) conducted factor analyses to examine the abilities elicited by the TOEFL® iBT integrated reading-listening-writing task. They found that comprehension of reading and listening materials was an important predictor for the coverage and accuracy of source information in integrated writing. They also found that vocabulary knowledge was significantly correlated with all three skills involved (i.e., reading, listening, and writing), suggesting that it is critical knowledge for such a writing task. The overall findings across the studies indicate that writing skills as well as other related skills play a critical role in written performance on an integrated writing task.

Comprehension and Productive Processes and Strategies

Studies have also investigated the reading and composing processes and strategies elicited by source-based writing tasks. Researchers have collected evidence for L2 writers' **discourse synthesis** (Spivey & King, 1989), or the "process in which readers (writers) read multiple texts on a topic and synthesize them" (p. 11). Using think-aloud and interview data, Plakans (2009) confirmed that reading-to-write argumentative assessment tasks elicited discourse synthesis subprocesses, specifically connecting, selecting, and organizing texts. Throughout the *connecting* stage, writers establish the relationship between their experience, the text, the topic, and their essay. When *selecting*, writers scan and reread a particular part of the text and check for proper citation. In the *organizing* processes, writers comprehend the texts and structure their essay by arranging the source content to support their writing. Plakans noted that connecting and organizing processes appeared more frequently than selecting.

In another study of process, Yang and Plakans (2012) used structural equation modeling to examine the relationship between strategy use and integrated writing scores. The researchers found that selecting, connecting, and organizing strategies improved ratings in content, organization, and language use. In a similar vein, Yang (2014) focused on an argumentative summary essay using two reading texts, after which the participants were asked about the strategies that they used while writing. The test takers reported that the task engaged their comprehension and construction strategies, such as planning, evaluating, using sources, and synthesizing discourse.

Source Text Use

Source-based writing assessment typically requires L2 writers to integrate information from source texts in their compositions. Yet, using source materials appropriately is complex and challenging for L2 writers. Research has illuminated issues such as the direct copying of language from the source texts. For example, L2 writers may copy a string of words or phrases directly from the source texts because they experience difficulty in interpreting the content of source texts and/or expressing their understanding of such texts in paraphrase.

L2 writers' English proficiency level affects how directly or indirectly they use language from the source texts in their compositions. Indeed, researchers have found more instances of direct copying phrases from source texts in compositions written by lower-proficiency writers than their high-proficiency counterparts (Cumming et al., 2005, 2006; Johns & Mayes, 1990; Plakans & Gebril, 2013). Cumming et al. (2005, 2006) claimed that source-based writing uncovers not only the relationship between writers' proficiency levels and integration style but also the more complex picture of how multiple factors affect source use, such as input medium (reading vs. listening). They found that higher- proficiency examinees exhibited fewer instances of direct verbatim source use from the reading materials but more instances of such practice from the listening materials. The opposite phenomena occurred for lower-proficiency examinees, however, who used strings of words from the reading materials but not so much from the listening materials.

Related to indirect use of source texts, research has indicated that English proficiency level affects the ability to paraphrase, summarize, and synthesize input materials. Cumming et al. (2005, 2006), for instance, revealed that compositions by the most proficient students included more summaries of source input compared to their lower-proficiency counterparts. In examining the use of two reading passages in argumentative essays across three proficiency levels, Gebril and Plakans (2009) found that the two higher-proficiency groups exhibited more instances of source use, including direct source use with or without quoting, paraphrasing, and summarizing. They conclude that "there is a proficiency threshold that students should pass before successfully integrating reading sources in their writing" (p. 69). In terms of reading-listening-writing tasks, Burstein et al. (2012) also found that almost any type of paraphrase positively affected the scores; indeed, there was a particularly significant positive correlation between the number of paraphrases from the listening input and integrated scores.

Discourse Features across English Proficiency Levels

Another area of research that has received scholarly attention involves describing discourse features in the written products from source-based writing tasks. These features distinguish L2 writers' proficiency levels and provide insight into the underlying abilities that are required by such tasks. Fluency in text production (i.e., text length) is by far the strongest predictor of successful performance on source-based writing (Cumming et al., 2005;

Gebril & Plakans, 2013; Guo, Crossley, & McNamara, 2013; Watanabe, 2001). In examining the differences in discourse features across reading-writing and listening-writing essays, Cumming et al. (2005, 2006) found that higher-proficiency examinees were more likely to "write longer compositions, to use more different words, to write longer and more clauses, to demonstrate greater grammatical accuracy, to have better quality propositions and claims in their arguments, and to make more summaries of source evidence" (p.45). However, Gebril and Plakans (2013), in focusing on reading-to-write tasks, did not find systematic differences across the three proficiency levels in terms of lexical sophistication, syntactic complexity, and grammatical accuracy (though grammatical accuracy differentiated the lowest proficiency level). Guo, Crossley, and McNamara (2013) revealed that high-scoring essays exhibited frequent use of past participle verbs, often presented in passive voice constructions. In addition, the use of "less frequent and less familiar words" (p. 231) positively impacted the TOEFL® iBT integrated writing scores.

Scoring of Source-Based Writing Scores

Performance-based assessments, including source-based writing, often employ a rating scale to assign a score to a performance. Researchers have investigated this process to answer questions on what criteria are used, how raters make scoring decisions, and to what extent the resulting scores are accurate or reliable. All of these factors have a direct impact on score interpretation and use by test users. Source-based writing tasks have suffered from their scoring complexity, because when rating these tasks, one must attend to both the aspects of language use and to accurate integration of source materials.

One strand of research compares the reliability of scoring independent and integrated writing scores. For example, using a holistic scale and three raters, Gebril (2009, 2010) found that integrated and independent scores were equally reliable. Yet, rater variability was larger for integrated writing scores than for the independent writing tasks, suggesting that aspects of source use might cloud rater judgment of text quality.

A number of studies have addressed rater decision-making processes in source-based writing assessments. Using think-aloud, interview, and questionnaire data from raters who evaluated prototype TOEFL® essays, Cumming, Kantor, and Powers (2001) developed a framework for rater decision-making processes. In so doing, they found two major rating strategies: **interpretation** (i.e., reading essays for comprehension purposes) and **judgment** (i.e., evaluation of essay quality to assign a score). The raters in their study engaged more heavily in *judgment* strategies than in *interpretation* strategies. They also classified the raters' focus of attention into three categories: *self-monitoring*, *rhetorical and ideational*, and *language*. In evaluating integrated essays, raters paid more attention to rhetorical and ideational aspects than language, suggesting that their focus was on the integration of source information. Additionally, the raters' focus shifted depending on the writers' proficiency levels. When scoring essays at a lower-proficiency level, for instance, the raters attended more to language issues. At a higher- proficiency level, rhetorical and ideational aspects were considered more important to raters than language use.

In other research, Gebril and Plakans' (2014) raters who scored reading-to-write tasks using a holistic scale first looked for content derived from the reading passages, then checked for citation mechanics, and finally evaluated the quality of source use (particularly in terms of the accuracy and relevancy of source information). Judging the quality of source integration across different proficiency levels was challenging to the raters. Other researchers have also stated that L2 writers' source text use, including the quality of paraphrasing, direct copying of language in source materials, and citation mechanics affects how raters score source-based compositions (e.g., Chan, Inoue, & Taylor, 2015; Weigle & Montee, 2012).

Using Source-Based Argumentative Writing Assessment

The assessment of students' argumentative writing has posed challenges to teachers. First of all, it is more difficult to effectively develop a source-based argumentative writing task than one that is source-free, especially developing an appropriate prompt and setting the task requirements. In addition, there is an ongoing debate over how such writing should be accurately assessed to provide effective feedback to students. Given that argumentative writing involves a multitude of components, such as claims, evidence, warrants, counterarguments, or rebuttal, it is vital to have a clear link between students' performance and scoring criteria related to these components. Furthermore, rating needs to address the effective use of source texts, which makes scoring even more complicated. Next we offer suggestions for writing teachers on approaches to the assessment of students' source-based argumentative writing. Given the breadth of research on this type of assessment, we can draw evidence-centered applications for teaching and learning. This section outlines considerations in task development, incorporation of these tasks into learning, and approaches to giving feedback or scoring.

Developing Source-Based Argumentative Writing Assessments

In developing these types of tasks, instructors have critical choices to make. These decisions depend on clearly articulating the purpose and use of the assessment and the construct that is the focus of learning and measurement. The first step is to write the task prompt and detail the parameters for the performance, such as length, audience, and topic. The choice of genre is also important, and even with a narrowed focus on argumentative writing, there is still variety to consider. All of these prompt dimensions have been found to impact students' performance in source-based writing (Cho, Rijmen, & Novák, 2013). For example, in a study of audience, Cho and Choi (2018) compared writing from an integrated skills task with no specified audience and writing with instructions to report to classmates who have not heard or read the texts. Writing for classmates helped students understand their purpose in writing specifically and their writing has more contextual background, communicated ideas accurately, and provided more complete summaries.

Example 1 in Figure 4.1 illustrates a prompt that includes details to support writers in understanding and completing a source-based task that requires development of an argument. The goal is for a prompt to elicit the best possible performance and not be impacted by students' misunderstanding expectations or making faulty assumptions. Carefully written instructions can guide students through the task successfully and give them confidence about such writing.

Figure 4.1

Example 1, Source-Based Argumentative Writing Prompt

Read the question below, then, read the two passages to get more information about the topic. Write an essay on the topic giving your opinion in response to the question. Typically, an effective response will contain a minimum of 300 words. Your writing will be scored based on how well:

- your **ideas** are explained
- the **readings** support your argument
- you **organize** your essay
- you **choose words**

- you **use grammar**
- you **spell** and **punctuate**

> Some people believe that global warming is damaging our planet. Others believe that global warming is not a serious problem. Which point of view do you agree with? Why?
>
> Give reasons and support your writing with examples.

IMPORTANT! PLEASE READ CAREFULLY BEFORE WORKING ON THE TASK:

- The two passages should help you get some ideas about the topic.
- You may go back to the passages to check information while writing.
- You can borrow ideas and examples from the text. However, you should mention the author's name if you do so.
- Also, if you take exactly the same phrases or sentences mentioned in the passage, put them between two inverted commas ("").

Source: From Gebril & Plakans, 2009, p. 77.

This example prompt would be appropriate for students at high-intermediate to advanced proficiencies; for students at lower-proficiency levels, however, this task would be overwhelming. To write prompts for lower-proficiency levels, tasks should entail fewer steps and involve less text-heavy sources, such as resumes, agendas, or menus. It might even be preferable to have the instructions in the students' first language for clarity. A prompt might ask for simpler responses, like asking writers to "choose the best and give two reasons," which still gives the advantages of drawing on sources and moves students into argumentation, but with a lower demand on language comprehension and production. Example 2 in Figure 4.2 shows a very concise prompt for lower proficiency writers.

Figure 4.2

Example 2, Source-Based Argumentative Writing Prompt

> Review the three resumes for a job in a health care office. Write 5–6 sentences about the person who you would interview for this job and give two reasons for your choice.

The second or concurrent step in designing an argumentatively oriented source-based task is to decide on the source texts. For argumentative writing, sources usually serve the purpose of supporting a writer's argument or providing a counterargument. For higher- proficiency students, using sources that come from academic publications or other published media is common practice, as authentic materials can be motivating to students due to the close resemblance to real-life academic tasks. However, for students at lower-proficiency levels, the complexity of these texts can undermine their ability to use the sources in writing, and thus teachers could modify the language of sources or create original source material that makes the argumentative task more manageable. Researchers have identified characteristics of source-based prompts that can significantly affect students' writing—specifically, linguistic difficulty and the clarity or distinctiveness of key points made in the source text (Cho et al., 2013). Having multiple sources can make for a more authentic academic writing task but presents some additional challenges to consider. Some questions to guide the selection of source materials for argumentative writing are:

❏ Is the topic familiar and interesting to students?

❏ How many sources and at what length can writers feasibly read and integrate given time constraints and proficiency?

❏ Is the source material at a level of difficulty that will not limit students' ability to use it in their writing?

❏ Is the source material engaging and well-written?

❏ Are the key ideas clear and do they provide information on the topic that students can use in their writing?

❏ Does it cite other sources and is it attributable?

Integrating Source-Based Argumentative Writing Assessments into Learning

While assessments are often perceived as tests used for grading or in high-stakes decision-making, education scholars have advocated for incorporating assessment coherently into the learning process (Black et al., 2003; Jones & Saville, 2016; Purpura & Turner, 2014; Shepard, 2000; Stiggins, 1997). Two frameworks for this approach have received a good deal of attention in language learning: *Assessment for Learning* and *Learner-Oriented Assessment*.

Assessment for Learning (AfL) is a broad umbrella term for assessment that focuses on learning (process) rather than assessment of learning (product). This approach includes students in this process so they gain an understanding of their learning goals and how to work toward them (Stiggins, 1997). Students are encouraged to monitor, inquire, re-learn, and proceed with their learning. Five main activities have been cited for frequent use in AfL classrooms: (1) sharing criteria for success with learners, (2) using scaffolded questioning, (3) giving feedback without scoring, (4) providing peer- and self-assessment, and (5) using summative assessments for formative uses such as using a prompt similar to the final test to practice writing thesis statements and critiquing or revising them through class discussion (Black et al., 2003).

While peer- and self-assessment activities are fairly common in writing classrooms, with AfL, teachers invest considerable time in preparing students for giving feedback and creating opportunities for them to reflect on their learning. This would include presenting examples of writing that meet certain quality criteria and modeling how to give useful feedback. In addition, students reflect after a peer- or self-assessment on the process and what they learned from it. These practices surrounding peer- or self-review extend its value beyond the single activity and promote students' awareness of their learning processes and language development. AfL with source-based argumentative writing might include building students' understanding of source integration through exemplar student work showing appropriate paraphrasing and the selection of useful ideas to argue a point. Then the teacher would model a self-assessment of his/her own writing that focuses on these two criteria for good source integration. Students would then assess their own writing, followed by revision based on this assessment. AfL is especially important for argumentative writing given that it is known to be difficult for many L2 writers to learn how to make arguments using claim and evidence; assessments can support and scaffold learning at many stages in this learning cycle.

Learner-Oriented Assessment (LOA) is closely related to AfL but focuses more on the classroom learning cycle and where assessment is positioned (Jones & Saville, 2016; Purpura & Turner, 2014). It focuses on three key components:

1. utilizing assessments as learning tasks
2. involving students in self- and peer evaluation
3. giving feedback as feed-forward`

In thinking about the application of LOA to source-based argumentative writing assessments, all of these components could be applied. Focusing on assessments as learning tasks, an instructor might use the source-based argumentative writing task to teach source integration by breaking the task into multiple steps. The first step might entail understanding what source integration looks like, perhaps mapping some samples of student writing from sources. Another step would be reading-for-writing, including practicing comprehension strategies, reviewing text for relevant content, and identifying ideas to use in one's argument. Subsequent steps could include articulating a thesis, outlining an argument, considering counterarguments, paraphrasing, making citations, and performing other parts of the process. As students learn these steps in source-based argumentative writing, they would have opportunities to practice integration, receive feedback from peers and their instructor, and revise. Centering the task in the learning process allows an assessment to become a tool for teaching and can thus enrich learning how to write argumentative essays.

Feedback: Rubric and Scoring In the framework of LOA with source-based writing, teachers, peers, and students all provide L2 writers with constructive feedback on both language and content, especially on how to better use source texts in their essays as they build arguments (Kim & Kim, 2017). Rating scales reflect how test users (e.g., teachers, students) conceptualize and operationalize the skills that are measured in source-based argumentative writing.

For large-scale source-based writing assessments, the rating scales used to evaluate essay quality affect the kind of inferences test users can make based on the resulting score(s) (Bachman & Palmer, 1996). Holistic scales involve "a fast, impressionistic reading" (Hamp-Lyons, 1995, p. 759) on the part of raters and generate a single score that reflects the overall writing performance. In classroom-based assessments, on the other hand, teachers, peers, and writers can use a rating scale not only to judge the quality of essays but also to provide targeted feedback on strengths and areas for improvement. For the purpose of using assessments as learning, analytic scales that score writing relative to individual features (e.g., content, organization, language use, use of evidence) are particularly useful since they capture the multidimensionality of writing profiles that are common among L2 writers.

An analytic rating scale to be used in classrooms should explicitly state the criteria against which essay quality is assessed; performance descriptors for multiple aspects of writing with varying performance levels or degrees are particularly useful in such scales. Rating scales used for source-based argumentative essays typically include aspects of language and content that place particular importance on how students use source materials in their arguments. Research that has used analytic scales to score this type of writing has included four common dimensions, summarized in Table 4.1: (1) source use, (2) content/argument/idea development, (3) organization, and (4) language use.

The first row of Table 4.1 shows the analytic dimensions used in research studies to score source-based writing with a range of performance levels (score

Table 4.1

Analytic Scale Dimensions in Source-Based Argumentative Writing Assessments

	Score Range	Source Use	Content/Argument/Idea Development	Organization	Language	Others
Chan, Inoue, & Taylor (2015)	0-4	Reading for writing	Organization and structure		Language control	Task fulfillment
Ohta, Plakans & Gebril (2018)	1-5	Source use	Development of ideas	Organization	Language use	Authorial voice
Shin & Ewert (2015)	1-5	• Viewpoint recognition • Text engagement	Development	Organization	Language use	
Watanabe (2001)	1-4	Content	Content	Organization	Language use	
Weigle & Montee (2012)	1-10	• Content • Language: range and complexity	Content	Organization	• Language: accuracy • Language: range and complexity	• Vocabulary • Mechanics

range). In some studies, several dimensions were collapsed into one dimension. As indicated in Table 4.1, the label for the source use dimension differs across studies. Regardless of how it is labeled, this dimension assesses how well L2 writers demonstrated their understanding of the content of source texts, how effectively and accurately they used source materials to support their thesis, how well they paraphrased, whether quotations were overused, and the degree to which they used words directly from the original source text (textual borrowing). Some studies, such as Shin and Ewert (2015), created two dimensions to assess how source materials are used by L2 writers: *viewpoint recognition* and *text engagement*. **Viewpoint recognition** mainly assesses the writers' understanding of the two texts as well as the position the writers take, while the **text engagement** dimension focuses on the appropriate use of source texts, which is "the degree of copying and reference to texts" (p. 279). In addition, in Chan, Inoue, and Taylor's (2015) study, content and organization dimensions are assessed under one analytic criterion, "organization and structure."

Another important dimension in the assessment of source-based argumentative essays is the quality of arguments. Table 4.2 shows Ohta, Plakans, and Gebril's (2018) descriptors for each of the performance levels on the development of ideas dimension, which assesses the extent to which arguments are supported by details from source texts.

In summary, teachers and students can provide useful feedback on strengths and weaknesses by using analytic scales such as those described in Table 4.1 and performance descriptors for each score band on the target dimension. Students can revise and refine their source-based argumentative essays based on the feedback on their language ability and the accurate and effective use of source materials to support their arguments.

Table 4.2

Descriptors that Specify the Performance Level for the *Development of Ideas* Dimension

5—Full development of ideas using different types of details provided by the student and support from the source texts.

4—Development is adequate. Details provided by the writer or adapted from the source texts are generally used to support the argument.

3—Development is emerging, and few details support the argument are provided by the student or adapted from the source texts.

2—Little development in the essay, with hardly any details to support the argument.

1—No development of the topic; the argument is not supported with any details.

Closing Thoughts

Source-based argumentative writing assessments have several benefits, particularly in comparison to writing tasks without source material. As previously mentioned, these tasks parallel the writing found in academic settings. Second, after writing from sources and writing without, writers have reported a preference for the support of content from the sources; they express feeling less anxiety (Huang & Hung, 2013) and find the sources useful, not just for content, but also key words, organization, and for pushing them to think more deeply on a topic (Plakans & Gebril, 2012). For instructors of L2 writing, source-based writing tasks provide practice and diagnostic information on students' skill with the integration of reading and writing, including paraphrasing, finding main ideas, and citation.

A number of future directions in research and teaching should provide continued interest in source-based argumentative writing tasks. One area for more attention is specific to argumentation in these tasks. The construct cited for source-based writing has not fully accounted for aspects of argumentative writing but treated writing more generally. In some cases, it has conflated summary writing with argumentative writing, which deserves critical review. With the construct underspecified in this area, scoring rubrics also have not fully captured this dimension. While some scales have included "authorial voice," which can be considered a feature of argumentation, other elements of such writing like intent, interaction with the reader, accountability, or relevance have not been explored in research or teaching with these tasks.

Another area worthy of further consideration is introducing these tasks with lower- proficiency writers. Most research has been with advanced L2 writers who are close to entering or already admitted to an English-speaking institute of higher education. This level of proficiency is not representative of the broader population of English learners in the U.S. or globally, and thus creative and language appropriate task development and research is needed. This may include non-text sources, such as pictures or images, and it may require a streamlined concept of an argument; however, the opportunity to practice source-based argumentative writing across proficiency levels would support gradual development of the highly complex language use required by academic argumentative writing. While there are certainly more areas requiring work concerning source-based argumentative writing assessment, these tasks have clearly become a fixture in L2 writing classrooms and assessments over the past two decades. They have provided language teachers and learners with an alternative to essay writing dependent solely on students' experiences and ideas, with an assessment that taps into academic writing skills required in writing arguments supported by sources.

REFERENCES

Bachman, L. F., & Palmer, A. S. (1996). *Language testing in practice.* Oxford, England: Oxford University Press.

Black, P., Harrison, C., Lee, C., Marshall, B., & William, D. (2003). *Assessment for learning: Putting it into practice.* Maidenhead, England: Open University Press.

Burstein, J., Flor, M., Tetreault, J., Madnani, N., & Holtzman, S. (2012). *Examining linguistic characteristics of paraphrase in test-taker summaries.* (ETS Research Report No. RR-12-18). Princeton, NJ: Educational Testing Service.

Chan, S., Inoue, C., & Taylor, L. (2015). Developing rubrics to assess the reading-into-writing skills: A case study. *Assessing Writing, 26,* 20–37.

Cho, Y., & Choi, I. (2018). Writing from sources: Does audience matter? *Assessing Writing, 37,* 25–38.

Cho, Y., Rijmen, F., & Novák, J. (2013). Investigating the effect of prompt characteristics on the comparability of TOEFL iBT integrated writing tasks. *Language Testing, 30(4),* 513–534.

Crusan, D. (2010). *Assessment in the second language writing classroom.* Ann Arbor: University of Michigan Press.

Cumming, A. (2013). Assessing integrated writing tasks for academic purposes: Promises and perils. *Language Assessment Quarterly, 10*(1), 1–8.

Cumming, A., Kantor, R., & Powers, D. E. (2001). *Scoring TOEFL essays and TOEFL 2000 prototype writing tasks: An investigation into raters' decision-making and development of a preliminary analytic framework* (TOEFL Monograph No. MS-22). Princeton, NJ: Educational Testing Service.

Cumming, A., Kantor, R., Baba, K., Erdosy, U., Eouanzoui, K., & James, M. (2005). Differences in written discourse in independent and integrated prototype tasks for next generation TOEFL. *Assessing Writing, 10*(1), 5–43.

Cumming, A., Kantor, R., Baba, K., Erdosy, U., Eouanzoui, K., & James, M. (2006). *Analysis of discourse features and verification of scoring levels for independent and integrated tasks for the new TOEFL.* (TOEFL Monograph No. MS-30 Rm 05–13). Princeton, NJ: ETS.

Gebril, A. (2009). Score generalizability of academic writing tasks: Does one test method fit it all? *Language Testing, 26*(4), 507–531.

Gebril, A. (2010). Bringing reading-to-write and writing-only assessment tasks together: A generalizability analysis. *Assessing Writing, 15*(2), 100–117.

Gebril, A., & Plakans, L. (2009). Investigating source use, discourse features, and process in integrated writing tests. In *Spaan Fellow Working Papers in Second/ Foreign Language Assessment*, 7, (pp. 47–84). Ann Arbor: The University of Michigan.

Gebril, A., & Plakans, L. (2013). Toward a transparent construct of reading-to-write tasks: The interface between discourse features and proficiency. *Language Assessment Quarterly, 10*(1), 9–27.

Gebril, A., & Plakans, L. (2014). Assembling validity evidence for assessing academic writing: Rater reactions to integrated tasks. *Assessing Writing, 21*, 56–73.

Guo, L., Crossley, S., & McNamara, D. (2013). Predicting human judgments of essay quality in both integrated and independent second language writing samples: A comparison study. *Assessing Writing, 18*(3), 218–238.

Hamp-Lyons, L. (1995). Rating nonnative writing: The trouble with holistic scoring. *TESOL Quarterly, 29*, 759–762.

Hirvela, A. (2017). Argumentation and second language writing: Are we missing the boat? *Journal of Second Language Writing, 36*, 69–74.

Huang, H.-T., & Hung, S.-T. (2013). Comparing the effects of test anxiety on independent and integrated speaking performance. *TESOL Quarterly, 47*, 444–449.

Johns, A. M., & Mayes, P. (1990). An analysis of summary protocols of university ESL students. *Applied Linguistics, 11*(3), 253–271.

Jones, N., & Saville, N. (2016). *Learning oriented assessment: A systematic approach.* Studies in Language Testing (Vol. 45). Cambridge, England: Cambridge University Press.

Kim, A.-Y. A., & Kim, H. J. (2017). The effectiveness of instructor feedback for learning-oriented language assessment: Using an integrated reading-to-write task for English for academic purposes. *Assessing Writing, 32*, 57–71.

Knoch, U., & Sitajalabhorn, W. (2013). A closer look at integrated writing tasks: Towards a more focused definition for assessment purposes. *Assessing Writing, 18*(4), 300–308.

Lee Y.-W., & Kantor, R. (2005). *Dependability of new ESL writing test scores: Evaluating prototype tasks and alternative rating schemes* (TOEFL Monograph No. TOEFL-MS-31). Princeton, NJ: Educational Testing Service.

Leki, I., & Carson, J. (1994). Students' perceptions of EAP writing instruction and writing needs across the disciplines. *TESOL Quarterly, 28*, 81–101.

Leki, I., & Carson, J. (1997). "Completely different worlds": EAP and the writing experiences of ESL students in university courses. *TESOL Quarterly, 31*(1), 39–69.

Ohta, R., Plakans, L., & Gebril, A. (2018). Integrated writing scores based on holistic and multi-trait scales: A generalizability analysis. *Assessing Writing, 38,* 21–36.

Plakans, L. (2009). Discourse synthesis in integrated second language writing assessment. *Language Testing, 26*(4), 561–587.

Plakans, L., & Gebril, A. (2012). A close investigation into source use in integrated second language writing tasks. *Assessing Writing, 17*(1), 18–34.

Plakans, L., & Gebril, A. (2013). Using multiple texts in an integrated writing assessment: Source text use as a predictor of score. *Journal of Second Language Writing, 22,* 217–230.

Purpura, J. E., & Turner, C. E. (2014). *Learning-oriented assessment in language classrooms: Using assessment to gauge and promote language learning.* New York: Routledge.

Sawaki, Y., Quinlan, T., & Lee, Y.-W. (2013). Understanding learner strengths and weaknesses: Assessing performance on an integrated writing task. *Language Assessment Quarterly, 10,* 73–95.

Shepard, L. A. (2000). The role of assessment in a learning culture. *Educational Researcher, 29*(7), 4–14.

Shin, S.-Y., & Ewert, D. (2015). What accounts for integrated reading-to-write task scores? *Language Testing, 32*(2), 259–281.

Spivey, N., & King, J. (1989). Readers as writers composing from sources. *Reading Research Quarterly, 24*(1), 7–26.

Stiggins, R. J. (1997). *Student-centered classroom assessment* (2nd ed.). Upper Saddle River, NJ: Prentice Hall.

Watanabe, Y. (2001). *Read-to-write tasks for the assessment of second language academic writing skills: Investigating text features and rater reactions.* Unpublished doctoral diss., University of Hawaii-Manoa, Honolulu.

Weigle, S. C., & Montee, M. (2012). Raters' perceptions of textual borrowing in integrated writing tasks. In E. V. Steendam, M. Tilemma, G. Rijlaarsdam, & H. V. D. Bergh (Eds.), *Measuring writing: Recent insights into theory, methodology and practice* (pp. 117–151). Boston: Brill.

Weigle, S. C., & Parker, K. (2012). Source text borrowing in an integrated reading/writing assessment. *Journal of Second Language Writing, 21*(2), 118–133.

Yang, H.-C. (2014). Toward a model of strategies and summary writing performance. *Language Assessment Quarterly, 11*(4), 403–431.

Yang, H.-C., & Plakans, L. (2012). Second language writers' strategy use and performance on an integrated reading-listening-writing task. *TESOL Quarterly, 46*(1), 80–103.

5

An Analysis of the Chinese Way of Arguing: Creating a Hybrid Model to Teach Argument as an Inquiry Process

WEIER YE AND LAN WANG-HILES

Abstract

This chapter examines how Chinese social and philosophical values affect the way that Chinese English learners craft argumentative writing and discusses what Chinese rhetorical values have been expressed in argumentative writing. It also investigates how the differences between those Chinese rhetorical values contributing to argumentation and those used by U.S. students may account for many Chinese students' struggles in the U.S. English classroom. Preparing Chinese students to adapt to Western norms of argumentation and enhance their analytical thinking skills, this chapter proposes a hybrid model of "learning to argue through arguing to learn" to teach argument as an inquiry process.

In many English-speaking countries, such as the USA, the UK, Canada, Australia, and New Zealand, native English speakers have been taught to follow the claim-justification-conclusion pattern to construct an argumentative essay, with an emphasis on critical thinking and persuasion. By taking one side of a contentious issue, a native English speaker will make a claim that usually comes early in the essay. This gives readers a reason to think critically about the author's position, allowing them to understand the essay within a larger context. However, for many native speakers of East Asian languages, such as Chinese, instead of taking a direct or overt stance on an issue, the writer may provide instructive points for both sides and then leave it to readers to arrive at their own conclusion. This approach could leave many teachers in Western academic settings vulnerable to blind spots when working with students from East Asia, particularly Chinese students (Brett, Behfar, & Sanchez-Burks, 2013). That is, these teachers may not be well prepared for argumentative essays lacking an explicit claim or conclusion and thus regard the essays as unfinished or pointless (Abrams, 2000). At a broader level, they may be unprepared for a deeper cultural clash represented by different Chinese and Western approaches to argumentation.

With respect to argumentation, where writing in a L2 for Chinese students at English universities poses some serious challenges for them, what can their writing instructors do to acculturate Chinese learners of English into the practices associated with argumentation in the U.S. English classroom? In his article, Hirvela (2017) has provided us with an important framework that may address this situation: a socially oriented "**arguing to learn**" model that shifts attention from the more common "**learning to argue**" approach.

Drawing on the "learning to argue/arguing to learn" distinction, this chapter examines how Chinese social and philosophical values may affect the way some Chinese learners of English craft argumentative writing and explores what Chinese rhetorical values have been expressed concerning argumentation. Then, with the goal of assisting Chinese learners of English in adapting to Western norms of argumentation, this chapter proposes a hybrid model of "learning to argue through arguing to learn" to teach argument as a process.

The Impact of Chinese Social and Philosophical Values on Argumentation

Chinese argumentation differs from Western logic and rhetoric in that it has been greatly influenced by Chinese philosophy. Ancient Chinese philosophy is the intellectual tradition of Chinese culture; its major topics are primarily about human interactions and relationships. As a result of the profound influence of Chinese social and philosophical values, China developed its own way to argue in the Chinese cultural context. Of the many different and competing schools of thought in ancient China, we tend to think that the three systems of *Confucianism, Taoism, and Buddhism,* with Confucianism at the center supported by Daoism and Buddhism, seem to stand in the most influential position concerning argumentation skills.

The Influence of Confucianism

To understand the Chinese mind, one can start with Confucius (551–479 BCE), who established the Chinese past as an infallible model for the present. Modern Chinese argumentation is influenced by *Zhongyong*, a core idea of Confucianism. *Zhongyong*, often translated as the "Doctrine of the Mean," is considered a way of avoiding an embarrassing confrontation. Under *Zhongyong*, a central value of Chinese communication is thereby to achieve the ideal state of harmony and preserve relationships with other human beings.

In ancient China's hierarchical society, it was dangerous to present different views, particularly on sensitive social and political topics. To survive, it was critically important for one to develop implicit and non-linear thinking when building an argument. In many cases, authors would heavily employ methods such as metaphors, fables, maxims, quotes from influential people, inductive reasoning, suggestive expressions, metonymy, and even deliberate digression from the main topic out of fear of retribution (Chen, 2005; Kirkpatrick & Xu, 2012; Liu, 2007). Additionally, indirectness emerged as a face-saving strategy used to avoid conflict, simultaneously allowing for unforeseen circumstances (Chen & Chung, 1994; Liu, 2007).

As a result of this historical background, in contrast to many English-speaking people from the countries in the western part of the world who tend to appreciate directness and honesty, Chinese people tend to "beat about the bush and avoid speaking out the truth straightforwardly when expressing an idea" (Qin, 2009, p. 093). Confucian culture still matters today in many ways. When the Chinese write about a controversial topic, *Zhongyong* thinking may often guide them to seek common ground and avoid leaning to either side so as to be free from bias (Chen, 2007; Lian, 2010; Qin, 2009).

The Influence of Taoism

Along with Confucianism, Taoism, another prominent Chinese philosophical school, founded by Laozi, an extraordinary thinker who flourished during the sixth century BCE, has exercised an enormous impact on Chinese argumentation throughout Chinese history. Laozi presented a worldview of Chinese dialectical thinking characterized by accepting the harmonious unity of opposites rather than treating contradiction as antagonistic (Peng, Spencer-Rodgers, & Nian, 2006), thus considering the path of non-contention as a virtuous basis for speech and argumentation (Lu, 1998). Furthermore, this dialectical thinking is well manifested in the Taoist *Yin* and *Yang* principles, which state that all things exist as inseparable and contradictory opposites.

Consequently, many Chinese tend to balance the *Yin* and *Yang* with reference to argumentation, avoiding taking a decidedly one-sided view.

The Influence of Buddhist Principles

Buddhism, which initially came to China from India in 64 ACE, has some similarities with Confucian principles. The Buddhist teachings promote harmony and establish guiding principles for people to love each other as brothers or sisters, abide by the congruent precepts such as refraining from the misuse of the senses or sexual misconduct, share similar views, and not quarrel with each other. According to Guang (2013), Buddhism has influenced Chinese culture in a wide variety of areas, including Chinese philosophy, Chinese language, and the argumentative strategies of Chinese people.

In addition, it is important to stress that the Chinese way of thinking seems to be significantly affected by the Buddhist concept of *Wuxing*, the ability to understand or know something by using one's feelings without applying analytic reasoning. Ancient Chinese books, for example, are very difficult to understand if one lacks *Wuxing* because they are full of obscurities, consisting of implicit expressions and unconnected sentences. Only those among the few who have *Wuxing* are capable of grasping the essentials (Yun, 2005).

As *Wuxing* emphasizes intuition, inspiration, and associative thinking, the Chinese have come to associate *Wuxing* with intuition, which is greatly valued in Chinese academic and daily life (Lian, 2006; Yuan & Yang, 2010). For Chinese writing, therefore, understanding a writer's point of view is often achieved via readers' *Wuxing*. Within this framework, as the point is not always stated explicitly, readers need to decipher the implied message. In this sense, Chinese writing is highly **reader responsible** in orientation, as opposed to the **writer-responsible** orientation found in much of Western writing (Hinds, 1987).

The Impact of Chinese Social and Philosophical Values on Argumentative Writing

When it comes to EFL or ESL argumentative writing, some, perhaps many, Chinese students might take a neutral position in the argument because they are considerably influenced by these Chinese cultural backgrounds and unfamiliar with the Western rhetorical tradition (Liu & Fan, 2014). Or, at the very least, many students may not be aware of how linear and critical thinking is applied in argumentative writing in U.S. classrooms. Critics may argue that when Chinese students write essays for the TOEFL® test, they seem to have little trouble taking a position on an issue and supporting it with evidence, but that is only half the story, particularly in the Chinese cultural context. Many Chinese students will take a TOEFL® Test Preparation course offered by China's TOEFL® training or "cram" schools, where writing trainers work hard to summarize and present what are thought to be universal templates for TOEFL writing prompts. These students will be encouraged to follow the "models" the trainers provide. It might be possible that after memorizing such templates, which showcase a deductive approach to presenting and supporting a thesis or claim, Chinese students could boost their TOEFL® scores, but they may not clearly understand why they have to write the way they do.

Under these circumstances, many new arrivals in the U.S. need appropriate guidance regarding argumentative writing. In their research, Wang and Li (1993) and Liu (2009) found that many Chinese EFL university students, without being aware of how their writing was influenced by the deep-rooted Chinese social and philosophical values, adopted an inductive pattern in English writing with claims implied rather than stated explicitly early in the essay, even though they have already learned English for many years. In other words, they continued to be align themselves with a Middle Way type of thinking and writing.

Rhetorical Preference

While many Chinese students may prefer using the Middle Way to stating an explicit position, seeking the middle ground does not mean that the Chinese choose to reach a compromise instead of taking a firm position. As an argument still exists in the text, it is likely up to the reader to decide which side to follow. The interpretation of an argumentative essay seems to require readers' *Wuxing*, or intuition, to construct meaning from the text. The significance of Buddhism's *Wuxing* would suggest that readers are able to read between the lines while arriving at their own position after considering input from the writer.

With entrenched cultural traditions in mind, Chinese students may possibly transfer their values to the English context. Consider, for example, the following sample student essay taken from Liu's (2007) article in which he briefly analyzed the essay. It was written for a nation-wide basic college English writing test in China. Instead of taking an overt position, the writer offers a typical example of following the Doctrine of the Mean from the perspective of agreeing with both sides in Figure 5.1.

Figure 5.1

Essay title: Do "Lucky Numbers" Really Bring Good Luck?

Some people think that certian [certain] numbers will bring good luck to them. Numbers such as six, eight, sixteen and eighteen are regarded as lucky numbers. There are also people who think that their success is related to certain numbers.

However, some other people think numbers have nothing to do with their luck. They believe in their own rather than "lucky numbers." They don't do things according to certain numbers.

As far as I am concerned, I think it is a person's own business whether he believes in a certain number or not. The most important thing is that he has done the work by himself and has done it quite well. As to the belief in numbers, it is their [his] personal choice. (p.1)

This sample essay, which can be retrieved in a number of venues online, received a score of 14 out of a total score of 15, reflecting the three evaluative domains of the analytic rubric (expression of ideas, passage organization, and language use). Since the essay received a nearly full score on the test, the Writing Test Committee that designed the test distributed this sample essay across China as a writing assessment scoring model (Liu, 2007). As a result, this essay's inductive, or non-direct, approach became the one that many students may have imitated in their own writing.

To summarize briefly, many Chinese students' argumentative texts in English, like the one shown in Figure 5.1, may reflect the influences of Chinese philosophical ideas and rhetorical preferences—seeking harmony, taking no clear position on an issue, and leaving readers to draw their own conclusion, at least as perceived by a native English reader. These features in argumentative writing can challenge the writing instructors who teach Chinese learners of English in English-dominant countries. At the same time, the Chinese students, influenced by their cultural background, may unconsciously or consciously mount stiff resistance to changing how they think and write. Hence, it is critical to teach Chinese L2 students to understand the Western concept of argumentation and train them to be able to read, think, and write in a way that would be more successful in the English classroom.

In response to this situation, the chapter now moves to describe a "learning to argue through arguing to learn" approach to argumentative writing instruction that would address these issues. This model can offer some hands-on assistance to L2 writing instructors in teaching Chinese L2 learners, as well as others who may also struggle in argumentative writing.

A Hybrid Model of "Learning to Argue Through Arguing to Learn"

Inspired by the arguing to learn concept while also valuing learning to argue, we propose an instructional model that begins with arguing to learn as preparation for a transition into learning to argue. Thus, both orientations play a role in helping students write argumentative essays. We illustrate the arguing to learn orientation to help students gain deeper insight into a topic as a first step, one that involves them in dialogic interactions with peers before they move on to several steps concerning the argumentative writing itself and engagement in learning to argue.

Step 1: Warm-Up Exercises

Heavily influenced by *Zhongyong*, dialectical thinking, *Yin* and *Yang*, and intuitive thinking, some Chinese English learners may approach a controversial topic by taking the middle ground to achieve harmony rather than reasoning in one direction. Thus, it helps to ease them into a new way of thinking. This initial step in arguing to learn is aimed at sharpening students' understanding of a topic through an analytic process (Hirvela, 2017); the model follows an inductive approach that guides them gradually into taking a side in an argument to build sound arguments with skills. This process begins by asking students to watch a video clip entitled "The Bystander Effect" (https://www.youtube.com), which asserts that individuals are less likely to offer help to a victim when there are other people present; the greater the number of bystanders, the less likely it is for any one of them to intervene in an emergency situation.

The video clip contains three experiments, the results of which seem to disprove the classical bystander effect view, so that exploring numerous context clues in the three episodes can lead students into building a claim about whether the bystander effect holds water or could be wrong. After watching the video clip, students are asked to answer a few questions to monitor their understanding of it. Here are a few possible questions to promote Chinese L2 students' deeper thinking:

❐ What situational factors contribute to the bystander effect?

❐ How real is the bystander effect?

❐ Why would people help someone in need?

To measure and enhance students' understanding, three follow-up steps can be taken.

1. Examining the controversial topic. Since details in the video clip help illuminate how conventional bystander apathy may not tell a whole story, students work in pairs or small groups examining the topic closely and from different angles to develop a better understanding of it. This is a rigorous process of gathering, analyzing, and evaluating the information needed to understand and address the debate over the bystander effect issue. This activity is used to prepare students to take a position based on a claim supported by evidence.

2. Understanding cause-and-effect situations Identifying cause-and-effect relationships helps create analytical and logical thinkers and minds that can work through complex problems. Lian (2010), Qin (2009), Yun (2005), and Zhang (2009) argue that many Chinese tend to understand things by using feelings as a result of the impact of *Wuxing* or intuition, so students may not exhibit linear thinking skills as defined in Western terms. At this stage, activities are devised for students to identify in the experiments an event that is responsible for the cause that led to an effect. As the analytical style of thinking is stepwise in progression, this activity in turn helps Chinese learners of English understand that good writing should follow a coherent thread through argumentation, flowing linearly from idea to idea.

3. Contributing diverse experiences as a lead-in activity to jumpstart debate

    Students are now instructed to share what actual events or situations happened in reality. Sharing diverse experiences can be used as an enhanced evidence-based practice to prepare students to jump start a debate about whether the commonly held bystander effect is a fact or myth. This activity is particularly helpful to those who may subconsciously struggle with embracing various perspectives. Therefore, the purpose of the debate is to help students understand that an argument is not meant to avoid leaning to either side or balance two sides; rather, it is supporting, negotiating, or defending their argument's position accordingly by persuading the audience to accept a particular point of view backed by strong evidence. Through the debate, Chinese L2 students also become aware that they should use solid evidence to convince the listeners rather than the use of metaphors, proverbs, or well-known people's words in the Chinese style.

Collectively, these three activities engage students in arguing to learn as they explore the assigned topic from different directions. By arguing to learn (about the bystander effect, in this case) to deepen their topic understanding, they are now prepared to move on to argumentative writing and learning to argue.

Step 2: Discussing Elements of Argumentation

Now the class begins shifting to the learning to argue mode, which enables students to gain a conceptual understanding of how elements of an argument work. Many Chinese learners of English may have limited argumentative knowledge and strategies for argumentative writing, or even have certain misconceptions about argumentation in the EFL context due to "potential L1-L2 differences related to argumentation" (Hirvela, 2017). Thus, it is beneficial for them to open up new frontiers and make "conceptual change" (Jonassen & Kim, 2010, p. 440). In this instance, by drawing on the Toulmin model of argument (1958), which clarifies the relationships between information for the audience, we have designed interactive classroom activities for a group discussion in which students share their understanding and explore the use of the basic parts of an argument, such as:

❐ claim

❐ data

❐ Warrant (The warrant interprets the data and shows how it supports a given claim. In other words, it points to how the evidence is relevant to the claim.)

❐ counterclaim

Essential elements are explicitly introduced as tools, and examples are discussed. More specifically, the differences between the three core elements presented in the *Chinese argumentative writing* section and those in the Toulmin model of argument are compared so that students come to realize that the same terms are used, but they may have significantly different connotations. In so doing, students comprehend what the core elements are in L2 writing, how they are logically related, and how they can be effectively used—all of which scaffold Chinese L2 students to apply Western reasoning patterns. After that, to deepen their conceptual understanding, students are asked to work in small groups deciphering and discussing how each essential element is skillfully applied in the bystander effect video to persuade its intended audience. The interpretation and exploration of the elements provide a rich source for preparing Chinese L2 students to learn to argue. Reading activities can then be utilized to deepen understanding of the elements.

Step 3: Preparing Students to Construct an Argument through Reading Activities

As a hybrid approach to argumentative writing, this reading assignment is used as a steppingstone to blend the learning to argue/arguing to learn model to ultimately lead students into argumentative writing. Published in the *Los Angeles Times* in 1991, the article "In Groups, We Shrink From Loner's Heroics" by Carol Tavris introduces the topic of bystander apathy in the U.S. by discussing the murder of Kitty Genovese and the late Rodney King's savage beating by police officers. Tavris argues that individuals in groups think and act differently than they would on their own. To prove her point, the author uses experiments to demonstrate powerfully that people in a group behave differently from individuals. The author concludes the article by stating that people commit an immoral act if they only stand and watch.

In the article, Tavris structured an argument by using two experiments through which she persuaded the audience to believe that she was factual in her argument. The author presents a linear pattern of claim-justification-conclusion, which is in stark contrast with the Chinese dialectical approach, so a critical analysis of the text organization is constructive to Chinese L2 students in terms of adapting to Western-style critical argumentation. At this step, students are asked to engage in critical-thinking activities to promote comprehension of the text. Once they achieve a baseline understanding of it and to enrich their knowledge of argument strategies, they are guided to analyze the text's argument by discussing how the author arrived at that argument, how she developed it without digressing from the topic, how she built logical connections between sentences and paragraphs, if she addressed opposing points of view, and if she successfully convinced the audience to accept her conclusion.

In brief, the objective of the reading stage is for students to discover how to make a point and then prove it. Meanwhile, the analysis of the article also works toward reinforcing Chinese students' linear thinking that in turn helps strengthen Chinese students' argumentative writing in L2. Thus, reading leads to learning to argue.

Step 4: Crafting a Summary after Reading

To reinforce what was learned through the reading activities and to give students some practice in their use of language, after a review of the main elements a strong summary addresses, students are now asked to identify in their own words the author's main argument and major supporting points. The purpose of having students write a summary at this point is for them to sharpen their analytic skills as well as to demonstrate a basic understanding of how an argumentative text is structured so that they will be able to perform the task effectively.

Step 5: Addressing Counterarguments and Making Presentations

At this particular point, students will add a rebuttal paragraph to Tavris's article where they will challenge the author's argument. In the EFL teaching context in China, influenced by *Zhongyong* thinking, counterarguments may not be required. For many students, they do not even take a stance, much less address counterarguments. In contrast, addressing the opposing viewpoint in argumentative writing makes the argument more persuasive in the Western context because it allows students to anticipate doubts a skeptical reader might have. To raise the awareness of how to strengthen an argument, we ask students to gather and analyze the evidence from the bystander effect video to rebut an opposing argument. To complete this task, students need to share their writing with a partner and critique each other's rebuttal paragraph. After paired interaction, students take turns to present the writing to the entire class.

Through this persuasive writing activity, students earn that favorably agreeing with both sides to achieve the goal of the Confucian ideal of harmony may clash to some extent when meeting with Western norms of critical debate in the U.S. English classroom. This is an important component of learning to argue.

Step 6: Argumentative Writing Assignment

By this point, students have already spent much time watching the video and reading and discussing the article. Now it is time for them to choose one side of the topic—either support it or argue against it. The focus of the essay should be on students' thorough understanding of their claim, with persuasion as the heart of the argument. Thus, at this stage, students have engaged in both arguing to learn and learning to argue activities that pave the way to composing an argumentative essay.

Directions for Writing This Argumentative Essay (essay length: 1200–1500 words)

This assignment is complex enough to confuse many Chinese students from their L1-based *Yin and Yang* and intuition backgrounds. However, when they are guided to follow a clearly articulated series of steps (such as prewriting, drafting, revising, and editing), they learn how to write a strong argumentative essay. While drafting it, students have to include their position (claim), reasons(s), evidence, counterargument, conclusion, and use standard citation format in the essay. This writing assignment is used to help students understand that even the strongest stance will not be persuasive if it is not organized appropriately and supported with valid reasons and solid evidence. Before they begin writing, students will engage in two important preliminary steps:

Research

To better understand their position, students will first conduct research to investigate both sides of the controversial topic. They read three to four relevant scholarly articles about it and collect and evaluate evidence. Finally, they will write a proposal (of about a page in length) describing their research findings and ideas about their claim. All these activities aim to enhance students' analytical thinking abilities before they take a fully informed position.

Follow-Up Group Discussion

This pre-writing activity is designed to ensure that students find the right articles and understand the reading materials. They will work together in a small group and take turns reading, discussing, and critiquing each other's proposals, based on which students then start their writing task.

Following completion of a full draft of their essay, students will engage in a rigorous process of revision of their first draft and preparation of a new one.

Revising the First Draft

After completing the first draft, students will follow a self-assessment worksheet that includes such actions as looking to see if the writing stays on topic and if it has the correct cause-and-effect rhetorical pattern to avoid putting a lot of responsibility on the reader to figure out the logical connections between ideas. The objective of this phase is for students to improve the draft by rearranging, adding, or deleting content to make it appropriate for the intended audience.

Peer Review

The students then work in pairs to peer edit each other's essay using a peer review worksheet to ensure that the writing follows a linear pattern of introduction-claim-proof-refutation-conclusion to resonate with English readers. The purpose of the peer review activities is for each peer reviewer to critique the partner's work.

Further Revision and Peer Review

Students peer edit each other's final draft with another editing worksheet. At this final stage of revision, they will underline the argument/claim and examine the paragraphs where the partner defends and proves their argument with convincing evidence that will be appreciated by English readers. The goal is to ensure that their writing meets the expectations of readers in the SLW domain.

A Portfolio Preparation for Final Submission

Students have been developing an argumentative writing portfolio throughout the writing process, including a final version of the essay, an author letter, any essay outlines, three drafts, and all editing worksheets. They will write an author letter, a two-page document summarizing and discussing their strengths and weaknesses both as a reader and as a writer. The purpose of collecting a portfolio should be to provide a rich assessment of Chinese students' growth over time.

Step 7: Final Assessment

Finally, together with the final version of the argumentative writing, the portfolio is now turned in; it is worth 50 percent of the final grade. Brooklyn College's (2020) *Rubric 2: Holistic Grading* is used to evaluate student writing. We assign each essay to a scoring category according to its domains. To help students understand how much they learn from the assignment, we provide them with explicit written feedback rather than giving only one holistic score. In this respect, students are given the rubric at the beginning of the semester because it is helpful for them to keep each domain's separate qualities in mind.

A Brief Review of the Pedagogical Approach

At the heart of our hybrid model of learning to argue through arguing to learn is a focus on helping move Chinese learners of English from their L1-based orientation to argument through *Zhongyong*, dialectical thinking, and intuitive thinking into the kind of Toulmin-based argumentation that is more likely to be successful in their English writing classes and those across the curriculum that require the use of argumentative writing. This involves, at a broader level, an overlapping three-stage model that starts with students arguing to learn through initial exposure to a topic via an argumentatively oriented video, which they explore from various perspectives. Next, the model is coordinated with a reading assignment, along with a follow-up summary writing activity. The reading and summary writing, constituting the second stage, combine arguing to learn and learning to argue because students are focused on both general understanding of the topic as well as its argumentative features. In this way, they build knowledge of argumentation that can be transferred to their own argumentative writing. In the final stage, students engage in an involved process of essay writing and revision where they participate fully in learning to argue.

Embedded in the step-by-step process outlined in this chapter is the use of scaffolding to help Chinese learners of English enhance critical thinking to write an argumentative essay through key socio-cognitive stages of researching, reading, thinking, understanding, discussing, analyzing, applying, revising, and reflecting. Our hybrid model that blends arguing to learn to learning to argue is arranged so that arguing to learn and early learning to argue activities scaffold, or support, the fully developed learning to argue process that students experience as they compose their essays.

While our model demonstration is built on the use of a video and related article to lead students into an assigned topic, students may select their own topic. In our experience, it is important, when feasible, to ask them to choose a manageable topic via research that actually enables them to read and analyze relevant articles, thus reinforcing arguing to learn knowledge about the topic, which in turn can help them subsequently build their claims supported by ample evidence as they learn to argue.

Closing Thoughts

As with a large number of other L2 learners, Chinese students may face challenges in writing in English with regard to argumentative thinking. We believe that there is value in connecting arguing to learn and learning to argue in the hybrid model we have proposed. What is essential, in our view, is finding ways to combine arguing to learn and learning to argue instead of treating them as separate approaches. We view them as closely related partners in helping Chinese L2 students develop understanding and command of the reasoning processes at the heart of Western argumentation. Learning to argue through arguing to learn will, we believe, enhance their argumentative experience in English. In our approach to learning to argue through arguing to learn, the two modes receive approximately equal treatment as students move through the six steps prior to assessment. Future applications of this hybrid model might experiment with different proportions for these two essential components of the model.

We hope our model can assist Chinese learners of English and their instructors in broadening their repertoire to include not only Chinese-oriented *Zhongyong*, dialectical thinking and intuitive thinking, but also the culturally preferred processes of critical thinking and logical reasoning embedded in the argumentative writing common in U.S. colleges and universities.

REFERENCES

Abrams, E. (2000). *Essay structure.* Hard College Writing Center of Harvard University. Retrieved from https://writingcenter.fas.harvard.edu/pages/essay-structure.

Brett, J., Behfar, K., & Sanchez-Burks, J. (2013). How to argue across cultures. *Harvard Business Review.* Retrieved from https://hbr.org/2013/12/how-to-argue-across-cultures

Brooklyn College. (2020). Rubric 2: Holistic grading. Retrieved from http://www.brooklyn.cuny.edu

Chen, B. (2007). *The spirit of the Doctrine of the Mean* (中庸的思想). Beijing: SDY Joint Publishing Company.

Chen, L. (2005). Persuasion in Chinese culture: A glimpse of the ancient practice in contrast to the West. *Intercultural Communication Studies, 14*(1), 28–40.

Chen, G. H., & Chung, J. (1994). The impact of Confucianism on organizational communication. *Communication Quarterly, 42*(2), 93–105.

Guang, X. (2013). Buddhist impact on Chinese culture. *Asian Philosophy,* *23*(4), 305–322.

Hinds, J. (1987). Reader versus writer responsibility: A new typology. In U. Connor & R. B. Kaplan (Eds.), *Writing across languages: Analysis of L2 text* (pp. 141–152). Reading, MA: Addison Wesley.

Hirvela, A. (2017). Argumentation & second language writing: Are we missing the boat? *Journal of Second Language Writing, 36,* 69–74.

Jonassen, D. H., & Kim, B. (2010). Arguing to learn and learning to argue: Design justifications and guidelines. *Education Technology Research Development, 58,* 439–457.

Kirkpatrick, A., & Xu, Z. (2012). *Chinese rhetoric and writing: An introduction for language teachers.* Anderson, SC: Parlor Press.

Li, D., & Zhang, H. (2002). Reflections on the faults in English writing Chinese students with thinking differences (从思维差异看中国学生英语写作中的失误). *Shangdong Foreign Language Education, 89*(4), 43–46.

Lian, S. (2006). Chinese and Western thought patterns: Wuxing and rationality (中西思维方式:悟性与理性). *Foreign Languages and Their Teaching, 208*(7), 35–39.

Lian, S. (2010). *Contrastive studies of English and Chinese.* Beijing: Higher Education Press.

Liu, X., & Fan, J. (2014). The study of the Chinese People's inductive inclination in communication. *Journal of Language Teaching and Research, 5*(4), 786–790.

Liu, Y. (2007). An introduction to the college English test (band 4) in writing (英语四级考试写 作终极归纳之基础篇). Retrieved from http://www.sina.com.cn

Liu, Y.-Q. (2007). Cultural factors and rhetorical patterns in classical Chinese argumentation. *Intercultural Communication Studies, 16*(1), 197–204.

Liu, Y.-Q. (2009). The impact of cultural factors on Chinese and American college students' rhetorical choices in argumentative discourse: A contrastive study. *Intercultural Communication Studies,* XVIII: 1.

Lu, X. (1998). *Rhetoric in ancient China, fifth to third century B.C.E.: A comparison with classical Greek rhetoric.* Columbia: University of South Carolina Press.

Peng, K., Spencer-Rodgers, J., & Nian, Z. (2006). Native dialecticism and the Tao of Chinese thought. In U. Kim, K.S. Yang., & K. K. Hwang (Eds.). *Indigenous and cultural psychology: Understanding people in context* (pp. 247–262). New York: Springer.

Qin, P. (2009). *Fifty thinking differences between Easterners and Westerners* (东方人与西方人的50个思维差异). Harbin, Heilongjiang: Harbin Press.

Ren, Z. (2013). Influence of Chinese cultural patterns of thinking on discourse organization in English dissertation writing. In T. Coverdale-Jones (Ed.), *Transitional higher education in the Asian context* (pp. 149–160). London: Palgrave Macmillan.

Ren, J., & Wang, N. (2015). A survey on college English writing in China: A cultural perspective. *English Language Teaching, 8*(1), 21–30.

Sun, L. (2017). A corpus-based study on the influence of Chinese circular thought pattern and collectivism on English writing. International Conference on Frontiers and Management Sciences (FETMS 2017).

Tavris, C. (1991). In Groups We Shrink From Loner's Heroics. *The Los Angeles Times*. Retrieved from https://www.latimes.com/archives/la-xpm-1991 -03-22-me-433-story.html

Toulmin, S. (1958). *The uses of argument.* Cambridge, England: Cambridge University Press.

Wang, M., & Li, J. (1993). The survey of the English discourse thinking pattern of the Chinese students. *Foreign Language Teaching and Research, 4,* 59–64.

Yun, M. (2005). *The Chinese Wuxing* (中国人的悟性). Retrieved from http://gb.cri.cn/3601/2005/01/14/882@423245.htm

Yuan, Y., & Yang, Y. (2010). The cultural basis and feasibility of the post-quake "bare-foot psychotherapist". *Schweizer Archiv Fur Neurologie und psychiatrie* [Swiss Archives of Neurology and Psychiatry], *161*(8), 316–318.

Zhang, D. (2009). *Culture and philosophy* (文化与哲学). Beijing: Remnin University Press.

6

Expertise and the Teaching of Argumentative Writing

ALAN HIRVELA

Abstract

Since emerging as a field in its own right in the 1980s, the second language (L2) writing field has focused primarily on students and their writing. Despite their importance in helping students learn how to write, teachers have remained on the margins of L2 writing scholarship. Hence, we know relatively little about what they teach and how they teach it. This includes their approaches to perhaps the most dominant type of writing students are expected to produce: argumentative essays. As a result, we lack understanding of what constitutes expertise in teaching argumentative writing. This chapter suggests a model of expertise that could be used in framing understanding of expertise in argumentative writing instruction, as well as some of the pedagogical content knowledge that would help teachers achieve such expertise.

The history of the second language (L2) writing field has been dominated by an interest in *learning*. We have wanted to know how students learn to write in a language other than their native language: how they compose, what influences their composing processes, what challenges they encounter, what actually transfers from instruction to their written products, and how they respond to feedback. This deep interest in learning is understandable, and we have come a long way in demystifying the learning process and its various dimensions. However, this has also meant that the *teaching* of writing has taken a back seat to learning, as have those who do the teaching. This does not mean that we have ignored teaching and teachers. However, over the four decades in which L2 writing has been a field in its own right, relatively little has been learned about L2 writing instruction and L2 writing teachers (Hirvela, 2019). What teachers actually do in their writing classrooms is still something of a mystery. Another mystery is what actually constitutes expertise in L2 writing instruction. There are resources that provide declarative and procedural knowledge about how to teach L2 writing (e.g., Ferris & Hedgcock, 2014; Hyland, 2016; 2019), and rubrics tells us, indirectly, what kinds of knowledge and skills teachers should consider in their instruction. But the actual features of L2 writing teacher expertise remain a subject that is vague at best. What Ilona Leki (1995) said about identifying good student writing—"I know it when I see it"—seemingly applies to L2 writing teacher expertise as well: we know it when we see it, or at least we think we do. This is not a desirable situation, especially with respect to argumentative writing, perhaps the most dominant and complex kind of writing to teach and to learn (Hirvela, 2017).

This chapter makes connections between expertise scholarship, on the one hand, and argumentation on the other. First, relevant expertise literature is reviewed. Then, the topic turns to argumentation and aspects of argumentation of special importance to L2 writing teachers are discussed. In closing, a model of expertise that draws from the earlier discussions is presented.

The Quest to Understand Expertise

Models of Expertise

Scholars have been studying expertise in various fields since the 1960s, but it was not until the 1980s that a focus on expertise in teaching emerged. That work has moved in two primary directions: (1) **who** should be studied and (2) **what** constitutes the primary characteristics of expertise in teaching? Seminal work by Berliner in 1986 set the initial framing for the investigation of teacher expertise. In his view, it was necessary to study and compare novice and expert teachers, especially because "the performance of experts, though not necessarily perfect, provides a place to start from when we instruct novices" (p. 6). His work, along with that of Dreyfus and Dreyfus (1986), led to the first major model of expertise in teaching. Often called the "stages" model, their work places teachers along a five-stage continuum: **novice, advanced beginner, competent, proficient,** and **expert.**

Two points stand out in this work. First is the emphasis on the novice-expert distinction, which has had major ramifications for teacher expertise research. The second is the use of the amount of teaching experience as a key variable in classifying teachers relative to expertise. However, even as Berliner (1986, p. 9) promoted the importance of teaching experience, he acknowledged complications in "confounding experience and expertise," and those complications were partly why some scholars began to look for different ways of studying and measuring expertise.

An important and influential alternative model was introduced in the work of Bereiter and Scardamalia (1993), who argued for the study of **experts** and **experienced nonexperts**. In their view, much more was to be gained by examining the instruction of those who already have some teaching experience and understanding why some teachers become experts and others do not, as opposed to novices and experts. As they explained:

> The career of the expert is one of progressively advancing on the problems consituting a field of work, whereas the career of the nonexpert is one of gradually constricting the field of work so that it more closely conforms to the routines the nonexpert is prepared to execute. (1993, p. 11)

Also important in their work is their distinction between what they call **crystallized** and **fluid** expertise. Crystallized expertise involves "intact procedures, well-learned through previous experience, that can be brought forth and applied to familiar kinds of tasks" (p. 36), while fluid expertise constitutes "abilities that are brought into play in novel or challenging tasks or tasks that the expert has elected to treat in a challenging way" (p. 36). While the experienced nonexpert locks into crystallized expertise, among expert teachers, "crystallized and fluid expertise interact" (p. 36) in creative and productive ways relative to the situated context in which instruction occurs.

A third major model emerged from the work of Hatano and Inagaki (1986), who suggested that "there are two courses of expertise, adaptive and routine" (p. 268), leading to distinctions between the **routine expert** and the **adaptive expert**. This has become known as the **adaptive expertise model**. Routine experts "learn merely to perform a skill faster and more accurately, without constructing or enriching their conceptual knowledge," so that they "lack flexibility and adaptability to new problems" (1986, p. 266), thus limiting their professional growth and expertise. Adaptive experts, on the other hand, continue to build conceptual knowledge and use it to make adjustments in their work as circumstances demand. Thus, they avoid reliance on the automatized practices characteristic of routine experts. Unlike the routine expert, the adaptive expert is open to change and embraces opportunities to adapt instruction as is deemed necessary. As Hayden, Rundell, and Smyntek-Gworek (2013, p. 396) explain, adaptive experts are willing and able to "identify instructional roadblocks, then generate and enact success-ful responses." These teachers recognize what they call "critical incidents," and their "identification of critical incidents, followed by rich reflection and adaptation, is therefore a marker of adaptive expertise" (p. 399). The routine expert fails to respond in such ways.

Key Characteristics of Expertise

Another important topic of interest that developed as education scholars began studying expertise concerns the kinds of knowledge teachers need to possess. Here the work of Shulman has been considered groundbreaking. In Shulman (1986) and then in later work, he identified and defined what he saw as three core domains of knowledge that teachers must possess. First there is what he called **content knowledge**, which refers to knowledge of the subject matter being taught. Then there is **pedagogical knowledge**, which refers to knowledge related to teaching itself: teaching strategies, knowl-edge of classroom management, and so forth. Third is **pedagogical content knowledge**, which comprises knowledge of instructional approaches and techniques that allows the teacher to present content knowledge effectively. This feature of Shulman's taxonomy, commonly referenced as **PCK**, has been especially useful in expertise scholarship. While other scholars have offered variations on Shulman's model, it remains the foundation of work on teacher knowledge.

L2 Writing Teacher Scholarship and Expertise

As noted earlier, L2 writing scholarship has been dominated by a focus on students and the writing they produce. Directly and indirectly, the aim of this work has been to define expertise in writing itself—that is, what the expert student writer does or needs to do. There has been far less attention devoted to teachers of L2 writing, and almost none concerning argumentative writ-ing instruction (Hirvela, 2017). Just as rare are direct references to the term *expertise*. In addition to the primary interest in students and their writing, this situation may be due in part to the nature of expertise itself. As Geisler (1994, p. xi) has observed, "The concept of expertise is a difficult one," and that may cause L2 writing scholars to avoid it. Regarding L2 teachers, says Tsui (2003, p. 1), "what exactly constitutes their expertise is something that is not yet fully understood." In the final analysis, scholarship about writing teachers has occupied the fringe of the L2 writing field, leading Hirvela and

Belcher (2007) to call for an increase in such scholarship. It was also this enigmatic nature of expertise and the failure of L2 writing specialists to pin it down that inspired a focus on expertise as the theme of the 2016 *Symposium on Second Language Writing.*

Expertise and Argumentative Writing Instruction

If L2 writing teachers are to teach argumentation effectively and researchers are going to study them, working from a model of expertise can be a helpful step forward. Adoption of such a model establishes a foundation on which to build, a place to start when classifying teachers and their instruction and when making useful comparisons of them. The intent is not to pass judgment on writing teachers, but rather to better understand them, a point we will return to later. However, there is also the question of what, specifically, to teach, and how to teach it—that is, the realm of pedagogical content knowledge (PCK) previously mentioned. This is also part of the expertise equation and is where the L2 writing field appears to operate in something of a vacuum, especially regarding argumentation. I have written elsewehere (Hirvela, 2017) of how the mainstream or L1 writing field has what I have called an "argument industry." By that I mean a large number of textbooks and teacher resource books devoted solely to argumentation. Such resources are nonexistent in the L2 field, and argumentation in L2 writing textbooks, if present at all, occupies only some space and can hardly be considered comprehensive in coverage.

In a recent content analysis of 29 well-known L2 writing textbooks, I concluded that textbook representations of argumentation are uneven in depth and scope (Hirvela, 2020). Three outcomes may commonly accrue from this situation. The first is that L2 writing teachers may turn to the perhaps better known and more abundant L1 resources, which do not account for the nuances of L2 writing and writers, making it difficult for teachers to transfer that input to their instruction effectively because the transfer process can be a complicated one. Second, L2 writing teachers, lacking exposure to useful resources, may latch on to an existing and well-known approach, such as the ubiquitous "Toulmin Model," and try to fit it into the L2 writing course, rather than searching for other approaches that may be more beneficial for their students. Here it may well be the case that the Toulmin model has become the default pedagogical choice for many L2 writing teachers. Third, these teachers may rely on L2 textbook treatments of argumentation that, again, vary considerably in their coverage. The net result is that many

L2 writing teachers, however well-intentioned, may work with insufficient or underdeveloped PCK, leading to instruction that lacks depth and efficacy as well as underdeveloped expertise.

Outside of textbook treatment of argumentative writing, there have been a handful of attempts to describe different ways of teaching L2 argumentative writing. Bacha (2010) and Mitchell and Pessoa (2017), for example, have explored the use of instructional scaffolding in taking students into argumentation. Eckstein, Chariton, and McCollum (2011) have shown how a multidraft composing pedagogy can strengthen argumentative writing, while Liu and Stapleton (2014), focusing on counterargument, draw attention to the value of explicit instruction aimed at an important and especially difficult component of argumentation. Poole (2016) has presented and demonstrated the benefits of a corpus approach in helping students acquire language related to argumentation. Salter-Dvorak (2016) discusses how a pedagogy that starts with speaking for argumentative purposes (e.g., debate) and then moves to writing prepares students to produce argumentative essays. Wingate (2012) has focused on the value of first carefully examining definitions of argumentation in a three-part definition process that prepares students to engage in argumentative writing. Hirvela (2014) has reviewed a range of pedagogical options available to teachers.

However, such resources, while useful, represent only a miniscule amount of L2-oriented PCK-type information that L2 writing teachers of argumentation can utilize. Compared to the L1 domain, L2 writing instructors confront a relative chasm in the resources category, and with what could be unfortunate consequences. This in itself could be part of an expertise-oriented study of L2 argumentative writing instruction: the resources teachers utilize and what they do when they lack such resources.

With respect to the kinds of information that can strengthen argumentatively oriented PCK, one option is to draw attention to some larger frameworks through which to view argumentation. Mendelson (2002, p. xvi), for example, explains that, on the whole, approaches to argumentation fall within two camps: one that foregrounds it in **logic** and the other that foregrounds it as a process of **dialogic reasoning** where the goal is to shed deeper light on an issue through different kinds of interaction. These two orientations lead to very different kinds of argumentative writing instruction and in themselves can contribute to the development of expertise by offering teachers a meaningful launching point for instructional decision making and design. Another is the **learning to argue** and **arguing to learn** distinction, where instruction focuses on argument as a structurally oriented

product or endpoint generated through correct uses of patterns of organization (learning to argue) or as a **process** through which deeper insight into a topic is achieved by using elements of argumentation (arguing to learn)—or, in other words, argument as a means, not an end. L2 writing teachers can benefit from being aware of these choices and deciding which is most suitable relative to their students' needs.

Also worth noting is the **argument-persuasion** distinction that is often made in literature on argumentation. As Lunsford, Ruskiewicz, and Walters (2019, p. 7) explain:

> . . . the point of argument is to discover some version of the truth, using evidence and reasons. Argument of this sort leads readers toward conviction, an agreement that a claim is true or reasonable or that a course of action is desirable. The aim of persuasion is to change a point of view or to move others from conviction to action. In other words, writers or speakers argue to find some truth; they persuade when they think they already know it.

Here, too, this distinction has significant implications for classroom handling of argumentation, and it is important for teachers to understand this dichotomy, especially since it may matter in other instructional contexts where students write essays. My analysis of L2 writing textbooks revealed that few authors address this distinction and that argument and persuasion are used interchangeably.

Because so few studies have looked at how L2 writing teachers teach argumentation, we do not know the extent to which these teachers are aware of these more general options, let alone make thoughtful decisions as to which to adopt. This is another area in which expertise in L2 argumentative writing instruction can be built within the context of building appropriate PCK.

Just as these distinctions might come as a surprise to some, perhaps many, L2 writing teachers, an even bigger surprise may exist with respect to the existence of many ways of viewing argument. To put it another way, the Toulmin model, however useful or appealing, is just one option. Here is a brief look at several that might attract the interest of L2 writing teachers.

❐ **Nonadversarial argumentation** (Belcher, 1997). Drawing from feminist theories, this approach steers away from what has been called the adversarial "argument as war" pedagogy in which there must be a winner and a loser. Instead, writers engage in what Belcher calls a "cooperative discourse" with their readers.

☐ **Single argument** (van Eemeren & Grootendorst, 2004). This approach features only one primary reason to argue for or against a standpoint or claim, with significant development of that reason.

☐ **Solo argument/arguing with one's self** (Baumtrog, 2018). Here the writer uses argument to achieve personal clarity or understanding about an issue as opposed to writing for a wider audience. Argument is used to create a kind of inner dialogue.

☐ **Arguing to display identity** (Hample & Irions, 2015). Argument is used to help the writer develop commitment to a cause or idea, resulting in an identity arising from that commitment.

☐ **Reflective argument** (Hoffman, 2016). Argument is used to reflect on the writer's reasoning concerning an important issue or decision, thus helping to ensure wise decision-making through careful evaluation.

☐ **Practical reasoning argument** (Macagno & Walton, 2018). Here, similar to reflective reasoning, argument is used to justify a decision that the writer has made.

☐ **Case-to-case argument** (Stevens, 2018). In this approach, the writer cites and develops precedents or past decisions to argue for a current position or action, rather than other forms of evidence.

☐ **Argument as critical discussion**, also known as the **pragma-dialectical approach** (van Eemeren & Grootendorst, 2004). The objective here is to use evaluative procedures to analyze evidence and reasoning toward the ultimate purpose of resolving differences in viewpoint.

☐ **Coalescent argument** (Gilbert, 1997). Like the pragma-dialectical approach, the goal of an argumentative process or engagement is to produce agreement, with the exploration of opposing points of view coalescing into a mutually agreed upon perspective.

☐ **Argument as inquiry** (Kuhn, 2005). Working from the arguing to learn direction, this approach engages students in peer reasoning activities through which they use elments of argumentation to construct arguments that allow them to enrich understanding of an issue by viewing it from multiple perspectives.

☐ **Argument as problem-solving** (Hillocks, 2011). In this approach, students are assigned a problem to solve and to use argumentative elements for that purpose.

☐ **Collaborative reasoning** (Reznitskaya, Anderson, McNurlen, Nguyen-Jahiel, Archkodidou, & Kim, 2001). Students work in small groups discussing an assigned literary text and collaboratively, through dialogic interaction, construct an argumentative essay concerning an issue or dilemma posed in the text.

Then there is the "Toulmin Model" first developed by Stephen Toulmin in 1958 and deeply embedded in scholarship concerning argument pedagogy. While many writers characterize the approach as including several components, Toulmin himself (1958, p. 175) boils it down to three core elements: **claim or thesis (C), data or evidence (D),** and **warrants (W)** that connect data to the claim. That is, they explain why the evidence is appropriate. For example, if a student claims that high school students should be required to wear school uniforms and indicates, as evidence, that wearing uniforms would save money, the warrant could be a statement along the lines of "and it is commonly agreed that saving money is a good thing." Because the quality of an argument depends heavily on the accuracy of the warrants employed, Toulmin also discusses the importance of backing (B), the statements that verify the strength of the warrants. These four elements represent the essence of his model, and it is these elements that teachers bring to students' attention from a learning to argue orientation.

Also of importance in Toulmin's work is a crucial point many authors fail to present when describing his approach, and that is how he portrays the relationship between claim and data. He sketches it out this way: D→C. That is, data leads to a claim, rather than an approach many teachers and students may adopt in which they begin with a claim and then seek out data which supports it.

The value of a menu of options like this one is that it shows teachers that argumentation can serve multiple purposes and that considering such options will better serve their students' interests and needs than locking onto the kind of approach that leads to the long-standing and deeply entrenched thesis-support framework at the heart of the five-paragraph essay model that has seemingly dominated L2 writing instruction for decades (Caplan & Johns, 2019). Developing expertise in argumentative writing instruction can derive in part from awareness of such options and the ability to make wise choices among them. Equipping teachers with knowledge of these and other options is another path toward developing suitable PCK and thus argumentative expertise.

Another important dimension in the development of L2 writing teachers' PCK that can lead to expertise in argumentation is awareness of some key features of argumentation that have emerged in recent years. These supplement such core and well-known elements as claim, data/evidence, warrants, backing, counterargument, and rebuttal. A few of them are reviewed next.

One of these is the notion of **argument schema** (Reznitskaya et al., 2001)—that is, understanding, or background knowledge, of core elements of argumentation that students can draw upon while writing arguments. This might include knowledge of argumentation from their L1 writing background that can be transferred to their L2 writing. The pedagogical goal here is to build a core set of such schema that will form the foundation L2 writers draw from while building arguments.

Closely related to argument schema is what are called **argument strategems** (Reznitskaya, Anderson, & Kuo, 2007). These are specific strategies to employ during the writing process, such as an expression like *one reason in support of this idea is.* . . . There are specific strategems for different components of argumentation, such as stating claims and linking evidence to claims. The popular book *They Say/I Say* (2018) provides numerous examples of these strategems. L2 writing teachers can build a solid repertoire for argumentative PCK, and thus expertise, by developing their knowledge of these schema and strategems.

Another pedagogical tool that can be especially helpful in developing argumentative PCK is awareness of a common phenomenon called **myside bias**. As Wolfe, Britt, and Butler (2009, p. 183) explain, this refers to "the tendency to ignore or exclude evidence against one's position." This can be a problem for many novice L2 writers, who may feel pressure to support their claim and thus limit the scope of the evidence they employ in their essays. Accounting meaningfully for such bias can enrich L2 writing teachers' PCK and their expertise concerning argumentation.

Also, Pessoa, Mitchell, and Miller (2017) have recently introduced an especially interesting and useful term they call **emergent arguments**. They explain that these are "texts that meet some of the expectations for argumentative writing, but not others" (p. 42). They use this term to stress the importance of understanding the developmental nature of L2 writers' engagement with argumentative writing. In both teaching and assessing argumentative writing, L2 writing instructors' expertise can be enhanced by understanding and embracing this developmental perspective, especially given the challenges associated with learning how to write quality argumentative essays.

A Recommended Approach to Expertise in Argumentative Writing Instruction

Connecting the information presented so far, we can present some possible ways forward in the study of expertise in L2 argumenative writing instruction. First in this process is the matter of expertise itself and a framework or fameworks from which to view it.

In his plenary address at the 2016 *Symposium on Second Language Writing*, Alister Cumming, noting the field's lack of emphasis on expertise in teaching, suggested, as a starting point, the use of a three-stage model comprising these options: **novice, competent**, and **expert**. The model involves identifying and comparing the characteristics of teachers at each of these stages of development and performance.

Tsui (2003, 2009; see also, Tsui & Ng, 2010) has built on the expert-experienced nonexpert work of Bereiter and Scardamalia in a number of case studies involving secondary school teachers with varying degrees of experience and expertise. Utilizing this framework, including analysis of their writing instruction, she concluded that, "I characterize expertise as constant engagement in exploration and experimentation, in problematizing the unproblematic, and responding to challenges" (pp. 277–278). She encourages "studies of teachers' work and teachers' lives [which] show that the knowledge and skills teachers develop are closely bound up with the specific contexts in which they work and in their own personal histories" (p. 2), thus accounting for expert and experienced nonexpert similarities and differences.

L2 writing as a field would benefit from exploration of the modified stages model suggested by Cumming. Given the long and successful history of stages-oriented research and its continued use in other fields, it is important to know what a stages approach would yield regarding L2 writing teachers' expertise, particularly in their treatment of argumentation, and how useful that information would be. In addition, Tsui's studies have already demonstrated the value of her approach in capturing the intricate dynamics of teachers' instructional lives, and it would be beneficial to know how applicable her definition of expertise is in the realm of L2 argumentative writing instruction.

In my own work (Hirvela, 2019), after reviewing expertise scholarship and research on L2 writing teachers conducted over the past 30 years, I have proposed the use of the adaptive expertise model, asserting that it "has the advantage of providing a degree of flexibility not available in the more common novice-expert distinction" (p. 25). Lee and Yuan (2021) have also drawn attention to its benefits in studying teachers of L2 writing. To elaborate, this model is not tied to amount of teaching experience or to specified stages of development as a teacher. Routine and adaptive experts can be found at any stage in the teaching career. In addition, while at first sight this model may seem to position the routine expert strictly as deficient and the adaptive expert as outstanding, a closer look at the model suggests that is not quite the case. The routine expert may also do good work—to a certain point—and the adaptive expert possesses routine expertise. However, the adaptive expert is also willing and able to deviate from routine expertise when such a move is desirable or required to ensure greater student learning. In other words, it is not always necessary to be adaptive, and the routine-adaptive expert distinction need not be treated as an either-or construct.

As such, research on teaching argumentative writing would benefit from exploring the characteristics of routine expertise in that domain and then look at adaptive expertise. We need to know what routine expertise in argumentative writing instruction entails, in part because many L2 writing teachers may belong to that category, and in part to better understand what constitutes adaptive expertise. This, in turn, makes it possible to better understand adaptive experts and the transitions they make from routine expertise. Descriptions and comparisons of the two types of expertise relative to argumentative writing instruction would give teachers at any point in their career a meaningful frame of reference to use in constructing, understanding, and adjusting their own pedagogical repertoire. While all three models discussed make this possible, it may be that routine-adaptive comparisons and contrasts will be especially useful.

To augment use of the adaptive expertise model, I have suggested elsewhere (Hirvela, 2019, p. 17) that a working definition of L2 writing teacher expertise takes into account "the instructional beliefs, knowledge, and skills that may be considered as essential at a certain level of proficiency in order for teachers to guide students towards the acquisition of beneficial L2 writing ability" (p. 17). Adopting the adaptive expertise model in conjunction with this portrait of pedagogical content knowledge in studies of L2 writing teachers teaching argumentative writing would shed valuable light on what actually takes place in the L2 writing classroom and allow us to begin charting the specific features of expertise in teaching argumentative writing, of both the routine and adaptive varieties. We would know what to look for, and what to adjust, while studying L2 argumentative writing instruction.

Given the complexity of argumentation and the challenges commonly acknowledged in teaching it, making comparisons between routine and adaptive experts may provide our richest opportunity to unravel what takes place as argumentative writing is taught, and perhaps what we believe should take place. Equipped with such knowledge, we will then be in a better position to discuss expertise as it applies to argumentative writing instruction. And then, to return to Leki (1995), we will be able to say, with some authority:

"Expertise in argumentative writing instruction—I understand it because it has been categorized and delineated in meaningful terms."

Concluding Thoughts

As with the L2 writing field itself, we have a long way to go in developing concrete and reliable awareness of what constitutes expertise in teaching argumentative writing. An important starting point in this process is making the quest to identify such expertise a topic of active discussion and investigation. In short, we need to foreground expertise. Establishing a specific model or models of expertise to work with and from would be an important step in this foregrounding. Here it may be especially beneficial to initally employ all three expertise models discussed and then compare what they reveal and what benefits they provide. However, we also need to arrive at a clear understanding of what represents high-quality L2 argumentative writing itself, which will in turn enable us to pin down the specific dimensions of pedagogical content knowledge we deem necessary for teachers to aquire. These dimensions, along with a concrete model or models of expertise, can be used in teacher preparation courses, professional development workshops, and materials about L2 writing instruction. In this way we can establish concrete pathways toward expertise and equip teachers to tackle the demands of argumentative writing.

This work is doable, provided we shift more attention to studying writing teachers, to making the study of expertise a priority, to having an appropriate model or models of expertise to work from, and to articulating the components of argumentative pedagogical content knowledge and the options available to teachers. Ultimately, we can then can do what we are unable to do now: talk meaningfully about teachers and what takes place in the L2 writing classroom when argumentation is taught.

REFERENCES

Bacha, N. N. (2010).Teaching the academic argument in a university EFL environment. *Journal of English for Academic Purposes, 9,* 229–241.

Baumtrog, M. D. (2018). Reasoning and arguing, dialectically and dialogically, among individual and multiple participants. *Argumentation, 32,* 77–98.

Belcher, D. D. (1997). An argument for non-adversarial argumentation: On the relevance of the feminist critique of academic discourse to L2 writing pedagogy. *Journal of Second Language Writing, 6,* 1–21.

Bereiter, C., & Scardamalia, M. (1993). *Surpassing ourselves: An inquiry into the nature and implications of expertise.* Chicago, IL: Open Court.

Berliner, D. C. (1986). In pursuit of the expert pedagogue. *Educational Researcher, 15(7),* 5–13.

Caplan, N. A., & Johns, A. M. (2019). *Changing practices for the L2 writing classroom: Moving beyond the five-paragraph essay.* Ann Arbor: University of Michigan Press.

Cumming, A. (2016). A jack(al) of all trades? Expertise in studies of SLW. Plenary address at the *Symposium on Second Language Writing,* Tempe, AZ.

Dreyfus, H. L., & Dreyfus, S. E. (1986). *Mind over machine.* New York: Free Press.

Eckstein, G., Chariton, J., & McCollum, R. M. (2011). Multi-draft composing: An iterative model for academic writing. *Journal of English for Academic Purposes, 10,* 162–172.

Ferris, D. R., & Hedcock, J. S. (2014). *Teaching L2 composition: Purpose, process, and Practice* (3rd ed.). New York: Routledge/Taylor & Francis.

Freeman, D. (1996). The "unstudied problem": Research on teacher learning in language teaching. In D. Freeman & J. C. Richards (Eds.), *Teacher learning in language teaching* (pp. 351–378). Cambridge, England Cambridge University Press.

Geisler, C. (1994). *Academic literacy and the nature of expertise: Reading, writing, and knowing in academic philosophy.* Hillsdale, NJ: Erlbaum.

Gilbert, M. A. (1997). *Coalescent argumentation.* Mahwah, NJ: Erlbaum.

Graff, G., Birkenstein, C., & Durst, R. (2018). *They say/I say: The moves that matter in academic writing with readings* (4th ed.). New York: W. W. Norton and Company.

Hample, D., & Irions, A. L. (2015). Arguing to display identity. *Argumentation, 29,* 389–416.

Hatano, G., & Inagaki, K. (1986). Two courses of expertise. In H. Stevenson, H. Azuma, & K. Hakuta (Eds.), *Child development in Japan* (pp. 262–272). New York: W. H. Freeman and Company.

Hayden, H. E., Rundel, T. D., & Smyntek-Gworek, S. (2013). Adaptive expertise: A view from the top and the ascent. *Teaching Education, 24,* 395–414.

Hillocks, G., Jr. (2011). *Teaching argument writing, grades 6–12.* Portsmouth, NH: Heinemann.

Hirvela, A. (2020). Argumentative writing and textbooks: Implications for teaching, learning, and development. In L. Grujicic-Alatriste & C. Crosby (Eds.), *Second language writing in transitional spaces: Teaching and learning across educational contexts* (pp. 237–262) . Ann Arbor: University of Michigan Press.

Hirvela, A. (2014). Preparing English language learners for argumentative writing. In L. C. de Oliveira & T. Silva (Eds.), *L2 writing in secondary classrooms: Student experiences, academic issues, and teacher education* (pp. 67–86). New York: Routledge/Taylor & Francis Group.

Hirvela, A. (2017). Argumentation & second language writing: Are we missing the boat? *Journal of Second Language Writing, 36*, 69–74.

Hirvela, A. (2019). Exploring second language writing teacher education: The role of adaptive expertise. In L. Seloni & S. Henderson Lee (Eds.), *Second language writing instruction in global contexts: English language teacher preparation and development* (pp. 13–30). Bristol, England: Multilingual Matters.

Hirvela, A. & Belcher, D. (2007). Writing teachers as teacher educators: Exploring writing teacher education. *Journal of Second Language Writing, 16*, 125–128.

Hoffman, M. H. G. (2016). Reflective argumentation: A cognitive function of arguing. *Argumentation, 30*, 365–397.

Hyland, K. (2016). *Teaching and researching writing* (3rd ed.). London: Routledge.

Hyland, K. (2019). *Second language writing* (2nd ed.). Cambridge, England: Cambridge University Press.

Kuhn, D. (2005). *Education for thinking.* Cambridge, MA: Harvard University Press.

Lee, I., & Yuan, R. (2021). Understanding writing teacher expertise. *Journal of Second Language Writing, 52.* https://doi.org/10.1016/j.jslw.2020.100755.

Leki, I. (1995). Good writing: I know it when I see it. In D. Belcher & G. Braine (Eds.), *Academic writing in a second language: Essays on research & pedagogy* (pp. 23–46). Norwood, NJ: Ablex.

Liu, F., & Stapleton, P. (2014). Counterargumentation and the cultivation of critical thinking in argumentative writing: Investigating the effects of washback from a high-stakes test. *System, 45*, 117–128.

Lunsford, A. A., Ruszkiewicz, J. J., & Walters, K. (2019). *Everything's an argument* (8th ed.). Boston: Bedford/St. Martin's Press.

Macagno, F. & Walton, D. (2018). Practical reasoning arguments: A modular approach. *Argumentation, 32*, 519–547.

Mendelson, M. (2002). *Many sides: A protagorean approach to the teaching, practice, and pedagogy of argument.* Dordrecht, The Netherlands: Kluwer Academic Publishers.

Mitchell, T. D., & Pessoa, S. (2017). Scaffolding the writing development of the Argument genre in history: The case of two novice writers. *Journal of English for Academic Purposes, 30*, 26–37.

Pessoa, S., Mitchell, T. D., & Miller, R. T. (2017. Emergent arguments: A functional approach in analyzing student challenges with the argument genre. *Journal of Second Language Writing, 38,* 42–55.

Poole, R. (2016). A corpus-aided approach for the teaching and learning of rhetoric in an undergraduate course for L2 writers. *Journal of English for Academic Purposes, 21,* 99–109.

Reznitskaya, A., Anderson, R. C., Kuo, L-J. (2007). Teaching and learning argumentation. *The Elementary School Journal, 5,* 449–472.

Reznitskaya, A., Anderson, R. C. McNurlen, B., Nguyen-Jahiel, K., Archodidou, A., & Kim, K-Y. (2001). Influence of oral discussion on written argument. *Discourse Processes, 32,* 155–175.

Salter-Dvorak, H. (2016). Learning to argue in EAP: Evaluating a curriculum innovation from the inside. *Journal of English for Academic Purposes, 22,* 19–31.

Shulman, L. S. (1986). Those who understand: Knowledge growth in teaching. *Educational Researcher, 15(2),* 4–14.

Stevens, K. (2018). Case-to-case arguments. *Argumentation, 32,* 431–455.

Toulmin, S. (1958). *The uses of argument.* Cambridge, England: Cambridge University Press.

Tsui, A. B. M. (2003). *Understanding expertise in teaching: Case studies of second language teachers.* Cambridge, England: Cambridge University Press.

Tsui, A. B. M. (2009). Distinctive qualities of expert teachers. *Teachers and Teaching: Theory and Practice, 15,* 421–439.

Tsui, A. B. M., & Ng, M. M. Y. (2010). Cultural contexts and situated possibilities in the teaching of second language writing. *Journal of Teacher Education, 61,* 364–375.

van Eemeren, F. H., & Grootendorst, R. (2004). *A systematic theory of argumentation: The pragma-dialectical approach.* Cambridge, England: Cambridge University Press.

Wingate, U. (2012). 'Argument' helping students understand what essay writing is about. *Journal of English for Academic Purposes, 11,* 145–154.

Wolfe, C. R., Britt, M. A., & Butler, J. A. (2009). Argument schema and myside bias in written argumentation. *Written Communication, 26,* 183–209.

7

A Multilingual Orientation to Preparing Teaching Assistants to Teach Argumentation in First-Year Writing

PARVA PANAHI

Abstract

Argumentation is a main learning outcome of the first-year writing (FYW) course. As the number of multilingual students continues to increase in FYW classes, the education of teachers who teach argumentation in FYW needs to include a solid grounding in multilingual writing and an enhanced understanding of difference. In this chapter, I propose a pedagogical model for promoting an understanding of *difference as resource* among early-career graduate teaching assistants who teach a large fraction of FYW courses. The model can also be useful in improving the teaching and learning of argumentative writing in L2 contexts.

Argumentation, generally referring to forms and practices of reasoning, stating claims, and offering support to justify beliefs to influence others (Inch & Warnick, 2010), is recognized as a key determinant of good writing ability in higher education settings in the United States and many other countries. It plays a central role in writing courses and also in the disciplines (Hirvela, 2017), and students at all degree levels are expected to be able to comprehend, evaluate, and construct arguments.

At U.S. institutions of higher education, the first-year writing (FYW) course represents one of the few places in the academic curriculum, in some institutions the only place, where students learn the basics of argument as a genre of writing. FYW, also often referred to as college composition, academic writing, first-year composition, introductory composition, or the like, is an integral part of U.S. higher education today. At most institutions, it is a required general education course or sequence of courses for undergraduate students from all backgrounds and disciplines. In this course, argumentation is often taught generically, and students learn to argue by writing generic, context-neutral academic essays in preparation for writing assignments in other courses as they move through the academic curriculum. The "Outcomes Statement for FYW," developed by The Council of Writing Program Administrators (CWPA, 2014) and supported by a large body of research, views argumentation as central to students learning to write in FYW classes. It identifies skills specific to argumentative writing that are taught and learned, such as composing appropriately qualified and developed claims and attending to relationships between assertion and evidence.

Students enrolled in FYW in the United States come from diverse linguistic and cultural backgrounds, including domestic majority and minority students as well as international visa and immigrant students from around the globe. While the teaching of FYW may be done by part-time faculty, full-time non-tenured or tenured faculty at universities with graduate programs in English, a significant amount of FYW teaching is done by graduate student teaching assistants (TAs) (sometimes also referred to as graduate student instructors, or GSIs). These early-career graduate students, who often have little to no teaching experience, learn on the job by participating in primarily faculty-led teacher preparation programs where they receive professional support and supervision during their initial year of teaching FYW. These TA training programs (aka the practicum) are led by writing program administrators and faculty and usually last one to two semesters.

As a result of the influx of international visa and immigrant students into U.S. universities, the enrollment of multilingual students in FYW classes has increased and continued to grow. The increasing presence of multilingual students in FYW has significant implications for the preparation of TAs who teach the course. Early-career graduate students with no background in teaching diverse groups of students need preparation, professional support, and resources to successfully work with students with linguistic, cultural, and educational backgrounds that often differ significantly from the majority of domestic students.

The education of TAs in FYW programs, because of the unique and ubiquitous role of these programs in supporting multilingual writers (MLWs) at U.S. institutions, is an essential step for writing program administrators (WPAs) who supervise graduate TAs and build TA training programs that fit their particular institutional needs and circumstances. The growing multilingual (and multicultural) nature of FYW environments makes it critical that prospective FYW teachers, especially those working with MLWs, receive adequate programmatic support that will help them acquire new knowledge, adapt and transform it to their multilingual classroom contexts, and develop effective pedagogies accordingly. Provision of such support involves rethinking current assumptions and practices within TA preparation programs about how to attend to linguistic and cultural difference in FYW. The curricular emphasis underlying the education of early-career TAs should be on broadening discussions of and enhancing understanding of *difference* in FYW. TA training, if based on an understanding of *difference as resource* or a desire to promote it, can create a prime space for providing TAs with the support and preparation they need to work with MLWs, including the teaching and learning of argumentation. However, for a variety of reasons, this may be lacking at many institutions.

This chapter argues for the need to create a multilingual space within TA preparation programs in order to prioritize and enhance an understanding of difference as a resource in FYW and thus enhance the learning experience for MLWs. An orientation to difference is also key to fostering the development of writing skills in L2 students across learning contexts and, therefore, should be a component of teacher expertise for L2 writing teachers. This could be especially helpful in facilitating MLWs' development of argumentative writing skills. The chapter first provides some background on typical frameworks of TA preparation in FYW in the U.S. and identifies a set of assumptions and practices that have historically posed barriers to attending to cultural and linguistic difference in this space. Then it proposes a small first step for laying the foundation for a multilingual orientation to prepare TAs to respond to difference in the context of teaching argumentation to MLWs in FYW. Finally, some pedagogical implications and affordances of the multilingual orientation are discussed.

Background on GTA Preparation and Response to Difference in FYW

The increasing multilingual character of FYW classes is a unique opportunity for WPAs to re-envision current practices and assumptions about difference in TA preparation, generally known as mentorship or practicum, in English programs. Decisions regarding the planning, execution, and evaluation of mentorship programs are made under the purview of WPAs, and, therefore, they are in a good position to support TAs' pedagogical journeys through linguistic and cultural diversity in FYW by providing opportunities early when training TAs to help them cultivate an appropriate mindset towards diversity, also addressing ways of recognizing and supporting MLWs' practices of integrating their unique linguistic and cultural resources into writing in FYW pedagogy, including how to teach argumentation. It can be challenging for early-career TAs to effectively address linguistic and cultural difference in their writing pedagogy or to teach inclusively to all MLWs they encounter in their FYW classes (Ferris, Jensen, & Wald, 2015), but creating awareness and purposefully navigating and addressing linguistic and cultural difference are essential places to start.

Most WPAs say they value linguistic and cultural diversity; however, in practice, the way in which the training of most TAs in FYW is traditionally designed and facilitated is still rooted in the assumption that students' other languages constitute problems that need to be solved (Hall, 2009; Schneider, 2018). Many writing programs are structured around "myths" that character- ize MLWs as a small minority that can be placed in separate sections of FYW (often referred to as L2-specific or sheltered sections, as opposed to main- stream sections that are designated for domestic L1 students), where there is more focus on grammatical issues than rhetorical ones (Miller-Cochran, 2010). Such common responses to the increasing diversity in FYW tend to make a clear line of demarcation between the languages students use, thus creating an L1/L2 binary that can lead to a (mis)understanding of *difference as problem*. The L1/L2 dichotomy can be clearly seen in the planning and execution of TA training where separate mentoring is focused independently for mainstream and L2-specific sections of FYW.

The Conference on College Composition and Communication (CCCC) Statement on Second Language Writing and Multilingual Writers (first published in 2001) emphasizes the need for MLWs to receive high-quality instruction, based on up-to-date developments in relevant disciplines, from experienced instructors. To address this need and create conditions for TAs to gain experience, new TAs are often first trained to teach domestic students in mainstream sections of FYW and then, after one or two semesters teaching these students, they transition to L2-specific sections of FYW and are offered mentoring for this audience. This TA training model seems to have been established under the assumption that once new teachers gain experience teaching L1 students, they will then be experienced enough to teach MLWs. L2-specific training was originally conceived as an add-on to TA preparation for mainstream FYW; here writing instruction is often approached from a remedial or basic skills perspective that sees MLWs as a homogeneous group in need of simpler instruction and assignments, disregarding MLWs' linguistic, cultural, and educational repertoire that puts them at an advantage (Siczek & Shapiro, 2014; Rose & Weiser, 2018). Such teacher preparation practices reinforce binaries (e.g., ESL vs. mainstream) in writing instruction, leading to TAs feeling caught between the desire to accommodate MLWs and the repercussions of identifying them as a discrete group of learners (Ferris, 2009; Ortmeier-Hooper, 2010). TAs supported by these programs might inadvertently plan their instruction in ways that impede their students' learning by ignoring their linguistic and cultural resources, as well as their past educational experiences.

The WPA assumptions and practices described illustrate an ideology of monolingualism as the norm. While the legitimacy of monolingualism is increasingly in question in the United States and globally, monolingual ideologies still remain dominant in college composition programs (Horner & Tetreault, 2017). A monolingual orientation prescribes curricular and pedagogical practices that attempt to erase differences to achieve what Matsuda (2006) calls "the myth of linguistic homogeneity." The prevalent monolingual ideology reveals a dilemma WPAs are grappling with and also a paradox in their curricular and pedagogical responses to difference in FYW. The paradox, according to Lyons (2010), is that most writing programs are in the business of assimilation, yet at the same time they say they value diversity (cited in Miller-Cochran, 2010, p. 212). Nevertheless, the existence of the paradox should not be seen as a barrier but rather as a step on the way toward developing a better approach to structuring writing programs and preparing writing teachers (Miller-Cochran, 2010). The paradox can provide the impetus for coming to terms with linguistic and cultural difference in FYW and fully escaping the monolingual assumptions surrounding TA training in FYW.

Rose and Weiser (2018) encourage WPAs to consider how the increasing presence of MLWs serves as a catalyst for change through entire writing programs, and particularly for altering conventional ways of training new teachers in order to make teacher preparation more responsive to a diverse student population. It is imperative that WPAs take their responsibility toward MLWs seriously because, in a diverse world, "all writing teachers should be prepared to address issues of language diversity in writing classrooms" (Miller-Cochran 2010, p. 216). While understanding language diversity and difference is obviously beneficial for working with MLWs, this type of preparation can help address the needs of other groups of students as well.

This discussion suggests that WPAs need to take a broader multilingual perspective on the work of TA preparation for FYW. A multilingual orientation requires that WPAs promote a more nuanced understanding of linguistic and cultural difference and equip FYW teachers with knowledge, skills, and attitudes that will enable them to successfully work with MLWs. Such a multilingual orientation, as noted by Shuck and Wilber (2018), "is wholly preferable to retrofitting a set of pedagogical and administrative practices that were meant for monolingual, monocultural students" (p. 169). It can help develop what might be called a "multilingual mindset" in TAs.

Mentoring programs can be an ideal way to develop this multilingual mindset in TAs from the outset of their career development, and understanding difference is the first step in developing a multilingual orientation to TA preparation for FYW. Most teachers are aware of the positive ways in which MLWs contribute to the classroom. However, they also feel a sense of frustration in having to develop and execute multilingual pedagogies without time, resources, or preparation. Therefore, the linguistic and cultural diversity of students should be an important consideration in TA preparation for FYW, and MLWs should be taught by instructors who are sensitized to their needs and trained to meet them (Ferris, 2009).

One question that needs to be addressed in this context is: If WPAs should see TA preparation through a multilingual lens, what would the first step look like? The answer to that is presented next.

A Multilingual Orientation to Teaching Argumentation

Cultivating the multilingual mindset as it relates to teaching argumentative writing is rooted in the desire to understand *difference as explanation* in the teaching and learning of argumentation. A multilingual orientation to GTA preparation can enable early-career graduate students to develop a multilingual mindset up front, widen their perspectives on argumentation and its cultural dimensions, and benefit from this enhanced, expansive view of argument in their instruction by providing better accommodation for MLWs learning to comprehend and construct arguments in the FYW class.

Typical mentorship programs for TAs who have little to no experience with MLWs mostly attend to practical aspects of teaching to equip them with pedagogical skills that get them through their first semesters of teaching FYW to MLWs. The conceptualization, teaching, and learning of argumentation in these programs are aligned with current L1 models of argumentation (e.g., the Classical, the Romantic, and the Toulmin models), which were originally conceived for monolingual and monocultural learners. The monolingual ideology underlying these models conceives the "learning-to-argue" process as the unidirectional acquisition of a set of argumentation norms and conventions in English, while devaluing the linguistic and cultural resources MLWs bring to their texts and contexts. These monolingual models, when used with MLWs, overemphasize the instructional use of English to the exclusion of students' L1, with the goal of enabling MLWs to think in the target language with minimal interference from their L1.

A multilingual conceptualization of argumentation and its teaching and learning, on the other hand, views MLWs as resourceful writers who are able to negotiate with not only academic genres and conventions they know, but also the instructional context. Consistent with Canagarajah's (2002) suggestion that the linguistic and cultural peculiarities that MLWs display should be viewed as resources to enrich the academic discourse community and be valued as representations of their unique voices and identities, the multilingual orientation aims to make MLWs, to use Valdes' (1992) language, a "profession-wide concern" in GTA preparation for FYW—with "concern" meaning to take as a subject of interest and inquiry, rather than a problem or deficit. The multilingual orientation recognizes that MLWs draw on their collective linguistic and cultural repertoires to make meaning as they try to meet genre expectations, and—following Schleppegrell's (2005) argument for the need to identify the linguistic resources of multilingual students–encourages writing teachers to identify the various resources that these students can focus on as they work on complex texts and tasks, such as arguments. The multilingual orientation also encourages FYW teachers to assist their multilingual students in strategically negotiating with academic conventions and expectations of advanced genres such as argument, as these students inevitably bring their values and discourses into their writing.

To make multilingualism a central theme in conceptualizing, teaching, and learning argumentative writing in FYW, an important first task for WPAs and writing faculty is to find ways to enrich teaching argumentative writing relative to existing models of argumentation by drawing on MLWs' linguistic and cultural backgrounds and resources. One such way will be to integrate research on MLWs into these mentoring programs and expand the foundation of argumentation research beyond the limits of monolingualism by drawing on research-based, cross-disciplinary concepts and practices that shed light on multilingualism and MLWs' practices of integrating their linguistic and cultural resources into argumentative writing. Faculty-mentors could include scholarly pieces on these concepts and practices in their syllabi and design activities to help TAs gain a foundational understanding of MLW pedagogy, while also engaging them in discussions and reflections on how to transfer these concepts and practices to FYW pedagogy. Some concepts and practices that, if integrated into TA training, can help TAs to not only enhance their declarative knowledge of multilingualism but also enrich their procedural knowledge about suitable pedagogies and content for teaching argumentative writing in FYW are discussed.

Expansive View of Argument

An expansive notion of argument views argument as both a form of reasoning (a product) and a form of inquiry (a process) and sees writing as an analytical tool that fosters the development of argumentative skills. The expansive view also recognizes that different cultures might hold what Ratcliffe (2005) calls differing cultural logics and highlights the impact of cultural perspectives on all communication, including approaches to developing and presenting arguments. According to this view, what constitutes an argument and how to effectively present an argument vary across cultures. Therefore, when discussing argument structures and strategies, individuals need to remember that not everyone argues in the same way, to keep cross-cultural differences in mind, and to respect those differences. The expansive view reinforces the shifting nature of logic, illustrating the impact of cultural norms on structuring arguments and defining what is normal or even logical in different contexts.

Biliteracy

Biliteracy, defined as "the conjunction of literacy and bilingualism" (Hornberger, 2003, p. 3), posits that individuals formulate, produce, and reproduce a general view of writing within a certain cultural context that can continue to influence literacy learning over a lifetime. A biliteracy perspective on the teaching of writing genres such as argument attempts to combine insights from research in literacy and bilingualism to shed light on how MLWs develop and use genre expertise in more than one language. This perspective has the potential to shed light on an important pedagogical question about argumentation: How can writing teachers help MLWs draw on the knowledge of the argument genre they have gained in one language when they write in another?

Interdependence

This theory proposed by Cummins (2000) suggests that there is considerable interdependence between one's ability in the L1 and L2, and transfer from the former to the latter is especially noticeable in academic language (of which argumentative writing is an example). Cummins' interdependence hypothesis postulates that concepts learned in one language can readily transfer into the other language and need not be reacquired in another. All that is needed are new labels in another language for those concepts already present in the L1.

Transfer

Transfer, also known as cross-linguistic influence, is traditionally defined as the influence resulting from similarities and differences between the target language and any other language that has been previously acquired (Odlin, 1989). Recent transfer research trends (e.g., Bardovi-Harlig & Sprous, 2017) favor positive transfer from the first language to the second and vice versa.

Heteroglossia

This notion proposed by Bakthin (1981) accounts for the heterogeneity of signs and forms in meaning-making, which describes the coexistence of distinct varieties within a single language. Heteroglossia challenges mono-lingual norms, providing theoretical grounding for multilingual practices that involve teaching and learning strategies allowing for and making use of practices that build on students' multiple resources to enhance metalinguistic awareness (Creese & Blackledge, 2010).

Dialogical Critical Thinking

This notion, introduced by Gieve in 1998, emphasizes the universal importance of critical thinking regardless of students' cultural backgrounds. According to Gieve, critical thinking, when defined in the dialogical view, is not merely a Western product, but belongs to all existing successful cultures in the world and has a significant value for students in any society and culture. Advising against overly simplistic stereotyping of nationalities and writing styles, the notion of dialogical critical thinking assumes that it is the responsibility of instructors to ascertain that students do benefit from dialogical critical thinking and use it to improve themselves.

Translanguaging

Translanguaging refers to the multiple discursive practices in which multi-linguals engage to make sense of their multilingual worlds (Garcia, 2009). Translanguaging operates under the notion that a multilingual mind is one linguistic repertoire within which different linguistic systems continually interact and engage with one another. Classrooms where translanguaging is encouraged provide safe spaces for multilinguals to draw on the multiple resources they already possess to be able to participate fully in all learning events (García, Johnson, & Seltzer, 2017). Translanguaging techniques, when intentionally used to raise students' consciousness about L2 writing strategies, makes students more aware of their discursive resources in writing processes and helps them strategically mediate their writing with a multitude of resources, find the true meaning of writing, and gradually develop themselves into better writers (Adamson & Coulson, 2014; Makalela, 2015).

A Pedagogical Model for GTA Training in Teaching Argumentation to MLWs

In this section, drawing on my own experience as a teacher of first year writing and information provided earlier in this chapter, I present a detailed description of how a FYW course that includes or is aimed at MLWs can approach the teaching of argumentative writing. This model could be shared with TAs as part of a training/mentoring program. Focused discussion of the model would be used to help TAs transition into teaching argumentation in ways that would be relevant to and meaningful for MLWs.

To develop a model for teaching the argument genre to MLWs, I relied on the existing models of argument that are commonly used in the teaching and learning of argument in the FYW course. Toulmin's model of argumentation, though not originally directed to rhetoric and composition, has been adopted in many composition coursebooks and is therefore widely used in FYW courses. Involving six main components that are used for constructing and analyzing persuasive arguments, Toulmin's model is clear and easy to follow, providing writers with basic guidelines for creating a map of an argument. Given the specific characteristics of MLWs and their unique linguistic and cultural resources, I modified Toulmin's model by expanding it to make it more effective for argument instruction based on *difference as explanation*.

The motivation for doing this stems from the fact that Toulmin's model focuses predominantly on linguistic and structural expectations of argument as a product and neglects the rhetorical, cognitive, and metacognitive dimensions of argumentation as a process, particularly in the process of learning to argue in the L2. Furthermore, as used in the FYW course, Toulmin's model only tells students that they must develop an argument in a certain way, when what most MLWs are looking for is something that will show them what is meant by argumentation, how it works, and what it looks like in text. Therefore, my model includes an additional consideration for teaching argumentation to MLWs that places emphasis on the cognitive and metacognitive aspects of argumentation as a process. This addition helps create opportunities for prioritizing discussion and understanding of *difference* and benefiting from it as *explanation* when teaching argumentative writing to MLWs. It allows writing instructors to make *difference as resource* part of a shared language between themselves and their students, helping students in FYW understand culturally related differences in argumentation and learn that writing is not only genre-bound but also culture-bound.

Discussions of difference can be facilitated among students with the main goal of elucidating ways in which acts of argumentation work in different cultures. To meet this goal, writing instructors can design activities that focus on different ways in which argument is conceptualized; the rhetorical strategies that can be deployed in the making of an argument; the linguistic and cultural dimensions that influence an argument's construction, form, force, and nuance; and how argument is carried over into writing (in the formal academic essay in the case of FYW). Through such guided, direct engagements with difference, students will be able to make sense of the different spheres of personal, linguistic, and cultural knowledge that they work within and can draw upon when they learn to argue in a new language.

Metacognitive Activities in Argumentation Instruction

My argument model adopts a metacognitive approach to instruction. Metacognitive practices have proven to be effective in helping students gain a level of awareness beyond the subject matter they are learning. They also increase students' abilities to think about the tasks and contexts of different learning situations and themselves as learners in these different contexts. Weimer (2012) encourages teachers to adopt a metacognitive approach to instruction and create opportunities, in explicit and concerted ways, for developing students' metacognitive awareness of themselves as learners and for improving their critical thinking skills. It is therefore necessary that teachers regularly engage their students in discussions on not only what they are learning but also how they are learning it. As such, metacognitive activities, if effectively embedded and fostered in argumentation instruction, could be an effective way of getting students to understand culturally related differences in argumentation and provide opportunities for deep learning of how to argue in the L2.

CCC Levels

While Toulmin's model of argumentation offered initial guidance in developing my argument model, I turned to my teaching experiences with MLWs in both L1 and L2 contexts to identify meaningful components that could create an expansive model for teaching the argument genre to MLWs in the FYW class. The three levels in the model are explained next.

The three levels to teaching argumentation to MLWs are: comprehension, construction, and communication. At each level, difference can be made explicit and used as a resource to foster student thinking and learning. At the level of **comprehension**, the emphasis is more toward the cognitive considerations of argumentation, while it is on the structural at the **construction** level and on the rhetorical and linguistic expectations at the **communication** level. As all these levels might pose challenges for MLWs, using metacognitive activities can help students to benefit from their collective linguistic and cultural resources to learn how to argue better.

1. Comprehension

In my model, grasping argument concepts takes precedence over argument production, as facilitating argument comprehension yields better results in terms of students' ability to produce effective arguments. At the comprehension level of argument instruction, MLWs' navigation of conceptualizations of argument in L1 and L2 is facilitated and cultural differences in this regard are made explicit. The assumption here is that argumentation, as it is defined and practiced in English, might be an unknown concept to many MLWs who come to the FYW class with different perceptions of and experiences with argument. Therefore, it is necessary that writing instructors make the differences between the L1 and the L2 explicit and visible through metacognitive practices. These practices help foster students' thought processes about argumentation, as critical-thinking skills are important to meet the expectations and challenges surrounding argumentation. Often, students find it difficult to think critically and need a great deal of structured guidance when completing tasks which require higher-order thinking skills, such as argumentative writing.

Writing instructors can design class discussions (in pairs or groups) and also reflective writing tasks with prompts intended to improve argumentation comprehension in MLWs. Discussion and writing prompts that ask students whether they argue in their L1 and L2 in the same way or how they think their language and culture shape their argumentation preferences (i.e., the way they conceptualize, develop and present arguments) can help to raise their awareness of linguistic and cultural influences on their argumentation style, key aspects of argumentation in their L1 and L2, and the use of L1 as a resource while learning to argue in the L2. Incorporating such questioning techniques provides scaffolding for MLWs' argumentation comprehension and critical-thinking ability. To benefit from the affordances of online resources, teachers can also incorporate online discussion forums so that students can share and respond to their thoughts, assumptions, and experiences regarding argumentation in a different interactive learning environment.

2. Construction

In the FYW course, the argumentative essay's minimum requirement is a clear claim in a thesis statement with reasons and evidence to support the claim. As claims, reasons, and evidence are parts of an argument in Toulmin's model, clear definitions and illustrations of this model, as well as other common models of argument, such as Stasis theory (a series of analytical questions that helps writers collect and use information about their research topics) and approaches to appeals, will be beneficial to MLWs. While these are addressed in the argument unit of the FYW course, they are often discussed without explicit references to the MLWs' linguistic and cultural background or having them think about the differences that might exist between methods of constructing arguments in their L1 and L2. Explicitly teaching the structural expectations of argument using the differences between the L1 and the L2 as explanations, with the goal of raising students' awareness of how claims, reasons, and evidence are made to make sense in L1 and L2, is a metacognitive practice that can help students focus their thinking, understand the elements, form and lay out an argument, and develop good critical-thinking habits.

The practical question at the construction level is: how can argument be taught so MLWs learn to identify parts of an argument as well as they write arguments? Writing instructors can design identification exercises using short examples of arguments and take time to define elements of an argument and have students identify each element in argument examples—for example, interesting editorials that stir up a debate. It is also recommended that teachers create opportunities for students to think about the structural expectations of argument in their own language by having them find and analyze short arguments in their L1 and compare them with arguments written in the L2. Students can be asked to pay careful attention to L1-L2 differences in terms of how claims are made, how reasons and evidence are provided to support claims, and how assumptions, or warrants, link the claim, reasons, and evidence.

Instructors can also engage students in short in-class argumentative writing by requiring them to compose arguments with a specific audience in mind. Students can be asked to construct a claim and provide reasons before finding evidence from credible sources of information to support their claims. By concentrating on claim and reason before adding strong evidence from various sources, students might gain a better understanding of the lines of an argument and its functional and structural elements. Instructors can also require students to do the same writing activity in their L1 outside class and then reflect upon how their argumentative writing practices would differ in the L1 and L2. The variety of metacognitive activities introduced here make the structural expectations of an argument and the differences between the L1 and the L2 in this regard so explicit that the claim-reasons-evidence relation can be more easily grasped by MLWs.

It is also recommended that writing instructors make MLWs' experiences with argument construction less stressful for them by using terms such as *argument, claim, reason, evidence,* and *assumption* in earlier units of the course. While it is important to prepare students for engaging with concepts and practices that might be different from their L1 experience, it is equally important that instructors stress the fact that the ability to reason and think critically is universal and argumentative writing—whether in the West, East, or places in between—is premised on claims supported by reasons and evidence. This is particularly important, as it prepares students to overcome the anxiety that is experienced when learning a new concept or starting work on a new writing project.

3. Communication

At this level, metacognitive practices are used to help MLWs to present their arguments effectively in the form of the academic essay. While students are in the process of writing their argumentative papers, teachers need to schedule feedback sessions—both individual and small group conferences—to give students specific guidance for the improvement of their arguments. The emphasis here is on providing explicit feedback on structural, linguistic, and rhetorical features of arguments. Feedback should be expressed using terminology understood by the students. TAs are encouraged to use questioning techniques during feedback sessions to help students metacognitively assess their own argumentation, articulate their strengths and weaknesses regarding the expression of argument in the academic essay genre, and discuss whether and if yes how their argument construction and presentation has been influenced by their L1 rhetorical preferences and argumentation style. Once the student has reflected on and articulated the nature of the difficulty, the teacher and the student can work through their responses to it together. Such retrospective thinking and assessments push students to monitor their own thinking and the influences of their multilingual repertoire when they form and present arguments in their papers.

These metacognitive exercises can also be conducted by planning revision workshops where students are provided with instructions as well as rubrics (or checklists) with clearly defined categories and criteria that can help them discuss and assess their own and their peers' arguments in groups. A post-workshop activity would be brief self-assessment writing in which students apply the criteria to articulate their strengths and weaknesses withing the argumentative paper or over the course of learning to argue in the argument unit.

Closing Thoughts

This chapter argued that a multilingual orientation is integral to preparing TAs to teach argumentative writing to MLWs in FYW classes. Current models of TA preparation housed in many writing programs are still influenced by the monolingual ideology which, once applied in argumentation instruction to MLWs, will lead to inadequate teaching and learning of argumentative writing. WPAs can consider a myriad of ways to orient TAs to a multilingual pedagogy, but an essential first step is to focus on broadening discussions on and understanding of *difference as explanation*. The pedagogical model presented here is a step toward this goal and helps TAs to benefit from understanding the potential differences between students' L1s and L2s regarding argumentation in teaching MLWs in the FYW course. The CCC levels of the model enable writing teachers to approach the cultural dimension of argumentation in ways that not only make difference a central theme in the comprehension, construction, and communication of arguments but also use it as a resource to better accommodate MLWs in their process of learning to argue in the L2. The proposed model is based on a definition of argument that is widely accepted and adopts a generic approach to teaching argumentation to be generally applicable across L1 and L2 writing contexts.

REFERENCES

Adamson, J., & Coulson, D. (2014). Pathways towards success for novice academic writers in a CLIL setting: A study in an Asian EFL context. In R. Al-Mahrooqi, A. Roscoe, & V. Thakur (Eds.), *Teaching writing in EFL/ESL: A fresh look.* (pp. 151–171). Hershey, PA: IGI Global.

Bakhtin, M. M., (1981). *The dialogic imagination: Four essays.* Austin: University of Texas Press.

Bardovi-Harlig, K. & Sprouse, R.A. (2017). Negative versus positive transfer. In J.I. Liontas and M. DelliCarpini (Eds.), *The TESOL encyclopedia of English language teaching.* https://doi.org/10.1002/9781118784235.eelt0084

Canagarajah, S. (2002). *Critical academic writing and multilingual students.* Ann Arbor: University of Michigan Press.

Creese, A., & Blackledge, A. (2010). Translanguaging in the bilingual classroom: A pedagogy for learning and teaching? *The Modern Language Journal, 94,* 103–15.

Cummins, J. (2000). *Language, power, and pedagogy: Bilingual children at the crossfire.* Clevedon, England: Multilingual Matters.

CWPA. (2014). WPA outcomes statement for first-year composition (3.0). Retrieved from http://wpacouncil.org/aws/CWPA/pt/sd/news_article/243055/_PARENT/layout_details/false

Ferris, D. (2009). *Teaching college writing to diverse student populations (Michigan series on teaching academic English in U.S. postsecondary programs).* Ann Arbor: University of Michigan Press.

Ferris, D., Jensen, L., & Wald, M. (2015). Writing instructors' perceptions of international student writers: What teachers want and need to know. *CATESOL Journal, 27*(2), 55–72.

García, O. (2009). *Bilingual education in the 21st century: A global perspective.* Malden, MA: Wiley-Blackwell.

García, O., Johnson, S., & Seltzer, K. (2017). *The translanguaging classroom: Leveraging student bilingualism for learning.* Philadelphia: Caslon.

Gieve, S. (1998). A reader reacts. *TESOL Quarterly, 32*(1), 123–128.

Hall, J. (2009). WAC/WID in the next America: Redefining professional identity in the age of the multilingual majority. *WAC Journal, 20,* 33–40.

Hirvela, A. (2017). Argumentation and second language writing: Are we missing the boat? *Journal of Second Language Writing, 36,* 69–74.

Hornberger, N.H. (Ed.). (2003). *Continua of biliteracy: An ecological framework for educational policy, research and practice in multilingual settings.* Clevedon, England: Multilingual Matters.

Horner, B. & Tetreault, L. (2017). *Crossing divides: Exploring translingual writing pedagogies and programs.* Boulder, Colorado: University Press of Colorado.

Inch, E. S., & Warnick, B. (2010). *Critical thinking and communication: The use of reason in argument.* Hong Kong: Allyn & Bacon.

Lyons, S. R. (2010). There's no translation for it: The rhetorical sovereignty of indigenous languages. In B. Horner, M. Lu, & P. K. Matsuda (Eds.), *Cross-language relations in composition* (pp. 127–141). Carbondale: Southern Illinois University Press.

Makalela, L. (2015). Moving out of linguistic boxes: The effects of translanguaging strategies for multilingual classrooms. *Language and Education, 29*(3), 200–217.

Matsuda, P. (2006). The myth of linguistic homogeneity in U.S. college composition. *College English, 68*(6), 637–65.

Miller-Cochran, S. (2010). Language diversity and the responsibility of the WPA. In B. Horner, M. Lu, & P. K. Matsuda (Eds.), *Cross-language relations in composition* (pp. 212–220). Carbondale: Southern Illinois University Press.

Odlin, T. (1989). *Language transfer: Cross-linguistic influence in language learning.* Cambridge, England: Cambridge University Press.

Ortmeier-Hooper, C. (2010). The shifting nature of identity: Social identity, L2 writers, and high school. In M. Cox, M., J. Jordan, C. Ortmeier-Hooper, & G. Schwartz (Eds.), *Reviewing identities in second language writing* (pp. 5–28). Urbana, IL: NCTE.

Ratcliffe, K. (2005). *Rhetorical listening: Identification, gender, whiteness.* Carbondale: Southern Illinois University Press.

Ringbom, H. 2007. *Cross-Linguistic similarity in foreign language learning.* Clevedon, England: Multilingual Matters.

Rose, S. K. & Weiser, I. (Eds.). (2018). *The internationalization of U.S. writing programs.* Logan: Utah State University Press.

Schleppegrell, M. J. (2005). *Helping content area teachers work with academic language: Promoting English language learners' literacy in history.* Santa Barbara: University of California Linguistic Minority Research Institute.

Schneider, J. (2018). Learning how to support multilingual writers: A framework for faculty education. *Pedagogy 18*(2), 345–374.

Shuck, G. & Wilber, D. (2018). Holding the language in my hand: A multi-lingual lens on curricular design. In S. K. Rose & I. Weiser (Eds.), *The internationalization of U.S. writing programs* (pp. 168–184). Logan: Utah State University Press.

Siczek, M., & Shapiro, S. (2014). Developing writing-intensive courses for a globalized curriculum through WAC-TESOL collaborations. In T. Myers Zawacki & M. Cox (Eds.), *WAC and second language writers: Research towards linguistically and culturally inclusive programs and practices* (pp. 329–346). Anderson, SC: Parlor Press.

Valdes, G. (1992). Bilingual minorities and language issues in writing: Toward profession-wide response to a new challenge. *Written Communication 9*, 85–136.

Weimer, M. (2012, November 19). Deep learning vs. surface learning: Getting students to understand the difference. *The Teaching Professor Blog.*

Part 2

Applications and Research in the Classroom

8

The New Bricolage: Assembling and Remixing Voice and Images in a Multimodal Argumentative Text

JOEL BLOCH

Abstract

This chapter examines *bricolage* in digital storytelling as a form of argumentation in an academic writing course. Three digital stories created by graduate students in an academic writing class are discussed to show the similarities and differences with voice and textual borrowing in argumentative discourse.

Argumentation has become more prominent in composition courses as new pedagogical approaches and forms of literacies have been introduced. Its role in multilingual writing classrooms has similarly evolved, although often at a slower pace. This evolution accelerated with the popularization of "paradigmatic shifts" in scientific discourse (Kuhn, 1962) that emphasized greater skepticism, which can require more emphasis on argumentation for producing agreement between the creator and the audience. Academic discourse has long been argumentative; however, the arguments often occurred outside the research paper, which relied primarily on clearly enunciating the research and its methodology for establishing a claim (Shapin, 1996) rather than, as Latour (1987) noted, by creating increasingly stronger arguments.

Older pedagogies for multilingual composition similarly exemplified this lack of argumentation in favor of organization and style, as exemplified in Bander's (1971) *American English Rhetoric.* However, a greater skepticism in establishing claims opened the way for more emphasis on argumentation. Swales (1990) further developed the role of argumentation in academic genres by examining problem-solution statements and the use of textual borrowing to open gaps and support claims, which was later incorporated in textbooks, such as Swales and Feak's (2012) *Academic Writing for Graduate Students.*

Incorporating argumentation further evolved with the introduction of multimodal literacies, often associated with new technologies. Technology has long impacted academic writing, as exemplified in the 17th century scientists such as Galileo, Boyle, and Newton, who used various technologies to conduct research (Shapin, 1996). Latour (1987) argues that researchers still use technologies in their labs to address possible "dissenters." Today, multimodal literacies, although still controversial, have allowed students to bring more of their own arguments into the classroom.

While not universally accepted (Casanave, 2017), Belcher (2017) has argued in favor of the importance of these multimodal literacies to take advantage of the affordances they offer. Multimodality was later appropriated into multilingual academic writing classrooms in various formats (Bloch, 2015, 2018, 2019; Hafner, 2015; Hessler & Lambert, 2017). This chapter discusses one such multimodal approach, called **digital storytelling** (Lambert, 2020), to exemplify possible roles for multimodal literacy for argumentative writing.

Digital Storytelling as a Form of Multimodal Argumentation

Using digital stories was motivated by the problems that students seemed to have in print assignments that asked them to express their voices and use texts to support their claims. Digital storytelling can create alternative social contexts for argumentation by providing affordances (Norman, 2007), such as recording podcasts of writers' narratives and mixing the narrative with internet images, that can be used in creating arguments. With these alternative affordances, the digital story can help create new relationships between the authors and their audiences, who Ede & Lunsford (1984) described as both "addressed" and "invoked." Instead of only addressing a teacher and perhaps a peer reviewer, the digital storyteller may address the entire class, as was attempted in our viewing parties, and, if the stories are posted online, an even larger audience.

Both the undergraduate and graduate courses in our program, which contained multiple sections taught by different instructors, combined a print assignment on arguing about plagiarism and a digital story that focused on an important moment in the students' lives. Both assignments required personal voices and textual borrowing, which were captured in the digital stories with podcasts of the students' narratives that were then mixed or assembled with visual texts, for exploring the meanings of their narratives. Differences in the social contexts resulted in part from the differences in the assignments. In the print assignment, the students were given a topic related to plagiarism and a set of papers to be summarized and evaluated. In the print assignment, the students first summarized and evaluated three texts assigned by the course instructor, wrote a synthesis paper arguing about the issues raised in the texts, and then wrote a more traditional argumentative paper on their attitudes toward plagiarism. Each week the students blogged about their opinions toward plagiarism. In the digital story, the students first wrote their text, recorded it in a podcast, and then chose images that could be assembled into a short movie (Bloch & Wilkinson, 2013). Unlike the assigned texts used in the print assignment, digital storytellers used whatever materials they could access, whether they be personal photographs or images downloaded from the internet, along with music if desired, rather than relying only on teacher-sanctioned texts.

In the digital story assignment, there was no requirement for argumentation, although, as discussed, many students created arguments on their own. Lambert (2020) discusses various approaches to digital storytelling, but our approach was constrained by our course goals, which primarily valued evaluation and textual borrowing. With digital storytelling, students began with their narrative and then, consistent with Canagarajah's (2018) framework, used "bricolage" to choose their images, and then "assembled" them with images into a short movie. Their choices could provide an alternative social context for argumentation but with similar goals. Each claim had to be evaluated using these images, as it would be with texts, although there would be differences because of the differences in the modes of expression.

Digital Storytelling in the Multilingual Writing Classroom

In the print arguments, the social contexts were largely created by the course instructors for discussing plagiarism (Newell, Bloome, & Hirvela, 2015); in the digital story, however, each student could create social contexts by choosing their topics and the texts to assemble for their story, so as to explore political and personal issues. A major difference between the assignments was in students' relationships with their audiences, although both approaches retain voice and textual exploring of personal experiences for addressing an "invisible audience" (Ong, 1975). However, instead of writing primarily for the teacher, the digital storyteller could "perform" in front of the class and with permission, post it online, making their potential audiences both larger and more interactive.

By providing more flexibility in choosing topics and images, there was greater autonomy in the digital story assignment for development of the writer's voice and the use of textual borrowing, even without making argumentation a requirement of the assignment. Allowing the students to foreground their own voices could better facilitate expressing authorial identity (Ivanic, 1998), which was found to be more difficult in the print texts, where student evaluative voices were often lacking and had to be supplemented by "cut and pasting" from other, more personal literacy forms, such as their blogs. By starting with a narrative and then choosing whatever images they wanted, digital storytelling provided an opportunity to better integrate their voices with the images. The blogs could then still be used more for reflecting on the relationship between the assignments.

By combining assignments with print and digital literacies, our pedagogical goals were expanded to provide alternative ways of assembling their movies, which fostered alternative ways of creating arguments (Bloch, 2018, 2019). Our students could choose a topic and then search online to find related images, becoming what Canagarajah (2018) has called a "*bricoleur*" for using whatever images they could find and then "assembling" or mixing them with their narratives. Canagarajah borrowed the term *bricolage* from Lévi-Strauss (1966) to challenge assumptions about valuing textuality and *assemblage* in the writing classroom.

The students used assemblage in both print and digital contexts for argumentation by mixing their voice and their chosen texts. While assembling was found in both approaches, *bricolage* was emphasized to a greater degree in the digital story. The main resulting difference was in the types of texts or images being borrowed. A *bricoleur* can borrow any found objects, here often accessed from the internet or from their own photos. By becoming bricoleurs (Lévi-Strauss, 1966), the creators can use whichever multimodal texts they can find, thus challenging the domination of print texts usually found in the academic writing course.

In digital storytelling, the *bricoleur* must work with whatever artifacts are at hand to create "brilliant, unforeseen results" (Lévi-Strauss, 1966, p. 17), but in more chaotic teaching and learning contexts. Framing image choice as *bricolage* increased the rhetorical value and introduced new ethical considerations regarding intellectual property law for borrowing and transforming these images in an educational context—both of which further supported our classroom goals (Bloch, 2012). These borrowed texts may not be used as often as the more commonl print texts, but they allowed the class to meet the same rhetorical goals for transforming texts and provided students with greater autonomy to do so.

Thus, both assignments could incorporate argument, although sometimes with different consequences. Both assignments relied on student voice, although digital storytelling provided an expanded personal narrative voice that differed from a more evaluative voice common in written academic argumentation. Again, with different forms of expression, these voices were consistent with Medawar's (1984) discussion of storytelling in scientific writing, as well as with Latour's (1987) theory of the author becoming an actor using a network of texts for establishing claims.

However, textual borrowing was used to align with some rhetorical purposes that did not always meet the course goals of the print text for finding supporting allies or creating author *etho* (Latour, 1987). Student use of intellectual property for textual borrowing became part of the course discussion, although with different manifestations. Although their print texts contained citations within the paper, both forms of texts required reference lists at the end.

Creating narratives in digital storytelling had other consequences for using classroom language. The students had the autonomy to create and record their narratives without teacher interference using their own lexicogrammatical forms of English, which provided varying degrees of support for interpersonal relationships with their audiences (Newell et al. 2011).

Becoming Bricoleurs in Developing Argumentative Texts

Although the teachers lost some control over the course content, this approach allowed students to become *bricoleurs* for choosing various types of images—movie stills, cartoons, photos—for exploring the meanings of their narratives without regard for their valuation in institutional contexts.

The impact of this *bricolage* in digital storytelling could readily be seen in the argumentative stories. In one story that will be discussed (see Table 8.1), a Libyan student argued how she hoped to change Westerners' views of Islam using various images, some of which directly expressed her argument and others provided more space for audience interpretation.

Canagarajah (2018) used these terms, *bricolage* and *assemblage*, to illustrate "shifts" in "translingual" perspectives for using language and rhetoric, which could be seen in both the foregrounding of a personal voice and the choice of images. The results of these shifts could be seen regardless of the rhetorical purposes for the digital stories. In one example, a Taiwanese student mixed personal photos, images from movies, and cartoons for arguing her perspective on leaving her boyfriend. She borrows different images to reach her invisible audience in different ways, reflecting Newell et al.'s (2011) finding that arguments are combined with their social contexts, types of users, and forms of literacy employed. As a *bricoleur*, for example, she chose movie stills from the popular movie *Twilight*, possibly reflecting her assumptions about audience prior knowledge. The use of these images, in some cases, creates a large space for audience interpretation. In another story, a Korean, using his own photos, attempts to persuade his audience that he would be a better father than his father was. In one image, there is a man in front of a ship, implying his father did not spend much time with the family but never explicitly even identifying the man.

These shifts often resulted in creating different learning contexts through repurposing of the digital tools, such as the blogs and storyboards, for facilitating greater reflection on the relationships between the assignments. The storyboards were used initially in the digital story to organize texts and images but later, along with the blogs, were repurposed to reflect on the rhetorical connections by asking the students to "name what they know," which can facilitate transfer between the assignments by having students identify both their rhetorical strategies and purposes (Adler-Kassner & Wardle, 2015) for each image and text to support transferring these understandings from one assignment to the other.

However, there were still institutional constraints on digital storytelling. Because the print texts were more frequently used in university writing assignments, it was necessary to ensure that they were used in this assignment. Parallel assignments could help students use the different affordances to make different decisions regarding how to achieve similar rhetorical purposes. As Newell et al. (2015) found, argumentation can involve multiple forms of speech, writing, and related semiotic resources, all addressed for persuading a real or imagined audiences. These pedagogies for teaching multilingual students often contain such multiple literacies (Matsuda, 2006), allowing greater flexibility in understanding the choice of rhetorical forms for meeting the course goals.

Argumentation in Student Digital Stories

Three digital stories, each using a different approach to argumentation, are examined to explore the consequences of these issues. As Latour (1987) found, all academic writing is argumentative, but here the stories expressed specific arguments for persuading their audiences. Table 8.1 introduces the first story, "Being a Muslim"

By focusing on important moments in their lives, the students' social contexts often reflected their perceptions of crossing boundaries—in this case from Libya to the United States—to enter a U.S. university and culture. This student created her context for arguing about her experiences as a Muslim in a non-Muslim country in response to her perceptions of her audience. The student responds to the dilemma of being a Muslim in a country she perceives to be overtly hostile toward Muslims both by addressing her

Table 8.1
Storyboard for Being a Muslim

Frame #	Image Description	Text	Image Purpose	Rhetorical Goal
1	Dove	Islam is a religion of peace.	Goal for argument	Positive image of Islam
2	Muslim girls	And teach us to deal with people and respect people morally	Support claim	Positive image of Islam
3	Koran	And how Islamic law	Support argument	Basis of Islam
4	Muslim protestors against terrorism	Is against hurting innocents	Support argument	Differences among Muslims
5	Islam	So, Muslims life in non-Islamic countries has become not as easy as before.	Support argument	Expression of opinion

perceptions of her audience after the 9/11 attack on the World Trade Towers and by borrowing images that expressing her perceptions of Islam to mix with her narrative.

In Table 8.1, Columns 2 and 3 illustrate her goals for choosing images and mixing them with her text to address possible concerns about Islam. Columns 4 and 5 illustrate how this assemblage was used to express her perception of the beliefs of an extensive audience by arguing that Islam was different from what her audience might think, in Perelman's (1982) terms, the distinction between "persuading" and "convincing" audiences, to convince her audience of her perceptions of Islam by refuting the audience's possible misperceptions.

As a *bricoleur*, she uses the warrants, which connect a claim to its underlying assumptions, with each image to address her perceptions of her audiences. In Frame 3, she presents an image of the Koran providing background for the audience about the background of Islam, another assumption about what the audience may not know about Islam. In Frame 4, she addresses other possible audience concerns that Islam supports terrorism by presenting an alternative argument—that Islam "is against hurting innocents"—using an image of Muslim protestors against terrorism for presenting a counterargument to her audience's prejudices to support her own claim about the peaceful intents of Islam. Finding images allows her a personal dimension in creating her argument. In Frame 5, she uses her narrative to evaluate life in non-Islamic countries, again using an image illustrating possible audience perceptions. In these examples, *bricolage* can be seen in the way that her images create a dialectical relationship with her audience, which also allows more space for creating meaning.

Assemblage of the images with her text is one strategy for creating arguments. In Frames 1 and 2, the student argues that "Islam is a religion of peace" that teaches "to deal with people and respect people" using two images representing her views: the first is a dove, often recognized as symbolizing peace, and the second is an image of Muslim girls playing a sport popular in the U.S., basketball. Both images seem to address her audience's understanding of Islam. As a symbol of peace, the dove supports her argument that Islam is a religion of peace, by which she hopes to persuade her audience, but the basketball image adds a more abstract meaning to the perceptions of her audience, particularly for those familiar with the sport, for extending her argument that Muslims are "normal" people. In the latter example, her warrants appear not to be about basketball but about the similarity of Islam to U.S. values.

The interactions of *bricolage* and *assemblage* transform their roles in creating meanings beyond those expressed in each mode, providing a rhetorical strategy reflecting Newell et al.'s (2011) argument about the importance of students considering diverse views to "convince" her audience. Thus, by becoming a *bricoleur*, she, in Latour's (1987) terms, builds her argument using her experiences and beliefs to strengthen her argument and disarm her dissenters.

Table 8.2 introduces the second story.

This story also discusses crossing boundaries, first between Hong Kong and China and then from China to the United States, for creating a personal argument about choosing a major. In discussing these crossings, the student also becomes a *bricoleur* by finding images describing her motivations to convince her audience about her later decisions. Choosing an issue connecting her background and career choice illustrated her goals for "convincing" her audience about her motivations for her career decisions. Her movie begins with three images of an audience applauding an unspecified performance that may have been hers (Frames 1, 2, and 3).

Bricolage is used to create a visual argument about her childhood. Her choices of images reflect her concerns with her emotional problems. The images are mixed with a text describing a man (possibly her father) being abusive to a woman (possibly her mother), mixed with abstract images of a fist coming out of a man's mouth hitting a woman in the head, which leads to another sequence of young boys, obviously not her, responding to an unknown terror. The transformative nature of this assemblage makes the images more personal while providing a space for the audience to create their own meanings. By showing the enthusiastic response of the audience to these decisions, her audience can know the responses to her play, but also, at a metaphorical level, how she coped with her emotional problems.

Had she addressed this content in a traditional academic paper, she might have chosen texts about the effects of abuse. Her choice of images, however, had a similar rhetorical intent but offered the audience greater space for connecting the images and the narration to explore how the images expand on her story. The images do not simply restate the narrative or even fuse the narrative and the image but transform her more clinical description of spousal abuse to demonstrate the consequences of the abuse, as visualized by the pained face of the woman (Frame 8). This image does not merely support the text by restating the argument but connects the verbal and physical abuse to demonstrate its consequences.

Her use of images reflects the findings of Newell et al. (2015), where students recognize their text structures by providing appropriate evidence

Table 8.2

Storyboard for Toi Kwan's Digital Story

Frame #	Image Description	Text	Image Purpose	Rhetorical Goal
1, 2, 3	Audiences applauding	The audience first gave thunderous applause, which died down to lingering [inaudible] as the play *Runaway Girl* drew to an end.	Audience reaction	Support claim
4	Self-image holding camera	Directed by and starring myself	Insert self into the story	Show the author of play and movie
5	Chinese child	This drama recounted a Hong Kong girl, who with the infliction and violence of the family.	Background	Growing up
6	Tiananmen Square in Beijing	Escaped to Beijing. And finally found a solution and. solutions there	Background	Show searching for solution
7	Reality Sign	Actually, I was the girl not only in that story but in real life. Born in Hong Kong, I had undergone a miserable childhood.	Background	Reason for problem
8	Man, with fist coming out of mouth hitting a woman	My father was a disabled man who engaged in domestic violence which stemmed from the tragedies and biases of workplace.	Causality	Reason for problem
9	Man, with fist coming out of mouth hitting a woman	My mother came from Mainland China and did not get respectful treatment from her husband and expressed a strong preference towards sons.	Causality	Reason for problem
10	Young boy	I was often confronted with	Causality	Result of problem
11	Young boy with hands over ears	The argument of my parents and the violence of my father	Causality	Result of problem

that shows, in this case, the relationship between her childhood and career choice, and then offering reasons and rebuttals for possible disagreements with her argument. She seems to recognize how the structures of the images may differ from what might be presented in print texts, although their rhetorical purposes may be similar. Her transformation of text and image into an argument about the consequences of childhood abuse illustrates how mixing narrative and image transforms both elements by assembling both personal and social contexts. Her approach exemplifies the traditional form of argumentation that uses a series of causalities, what Perelman (1982) refers to as "liaisons of succession" (p. 81), where the audience can evaluate her arguments by their consequences—how her childhood experiences led to her current concern for mental health and a graduate program in social work.

The third story is introduced in Table 8.3 (https://vimeo.com/34129517).

In this story, the student discusses a more personal argument concerning her learning English that her immediate audience, all of whom were English language learners, had experience with. She expresses her attitudes about learning English, problems with learning English, and her dislike of her courses. Her English language voice could have resulted from the personal social context for her experience. The student immerses herself in the emotional process of argumentation, which may be more expansive than in our print text assignment.

With the greater abundance of texts available on the internet for borrowing, the *bricoleur* is no longer constrained in constructing her argument by the limited number of available materials that Lévi-Strauss (1966) described about the traditional *bricoleur*. As Lévi-Strauss argued, the materials the *bricoleur* can use are not tied to a unique topic but can be remixed in ways that make them appear appropriate, in this case for criticizing both her English language speaking and writing skills and the learning approaches she endured. The print assignment, however, had only those texts prescribed by the instructor, although that number was slightly expanded by using student blogs.

These factors provided greater autonomy in creating their arguments. For example, Images 1, 2, and 3 describe her emotions as an individual student by providing her premise for her argument about learning English (#1) and then its consequences: a student receiving an F on a test (2) and a group of frustrated students (3). The images may not be of her class but mixing them with her narrative makes the images appear as if they were her and her classmates.

Her argument about teaching and learning can be seen throughout her choice of images. Her image of a class (7) not only argues against the

Table 8.3

Storyboard for "Why I Hate English"

Frame #	Image Description	Text	Image Purpose	Rhetorical Goal
1	Cat Holding Pen saying, "I hate English."	She knew very well that I hate English language	Attitude towards learning English	Support claim
2	Test paper with F	And everything connected with this subject. And why? Because I failed	Frustration with English	Support claim
3	Frustrated Student with lots of books	In the high school. Then my English teacher taught me that I didn't have English aptitude.	Problem with existing school	Background of problem
4	Wordle of words connected with English language	And I will never speak English in my life throughout three years in this school	Consequences of problems	Consequence of problem
5	Cartoon of adult in child's class for grammar and punctuation	Because there are so many words, the grammar is more complex, the way of thinking	Perception of English class	Support claim
6	Painting of man with book struggling to read	Is totally different from Chinese and the pronunciation, which is very hard to imitate perfectly	Difficulty in learning English	Support claim
7	Picture of large class	The English course in my school was boring. We need to do all the things we need to do	Criticism of Chinese English classes	Critical
8	Professional-looking writing	To pass them. The last thing I wanted to do was writing	Difficulty in writing	Critical
9	Chinese characters superimposed on English text	Every time I write an English essay I want to kill myself.	Causes of difficult	problem
10	English with line striking	I don't even know what to write in Chinese then how can I write in English. I was really never looking forward about English.	Difficulty with English	problem
11	Expression about negative level of English	So, my English remain at a poor level for a long time.	Negative perception of English	Support claim about problem

pedagogy of large classes but also her frustration with learning English, thus demonstrating her evaluative voice that was often found difficult to find in the print assignments. Her argument about her writing problems similarly resulted from assembling her narrative with images for expressing her emotional response to her learning. None of her images directly related to her experiences but were transformed into an expression of her frustration. In Images 8, 9, and 10, she mixes claims about her writing problems, again demonstrating its emotional consequences; thus, her transformative assemblage builds her argument concerning the negative impact of language pedagogy.

Her arguments illustrated the process of connecting texts and narrative, again using *bricolage* to choose images—cartoons, photographs, digitally enhanced images—and *assemblage* to expand the meanings of her narrative. This approach to creating argument can affect conceptions of genre-based discourse, which in a digital context of innovations in genre, as described by Tardy (2016), may require more complex understandings of intellectual property, fair use, and transformative nature of remixing for using internet content (Aufderheide & Jaszi, 2012). This borrowing of multimodal texts incorporates our course goals for discussing textual borrowing in terms of how intellectual property laws apply to writing. *Bricolage* provides an alternative for creating "allies," in Latour's (1987) terms, as well as new approaches for textual borrowing in multimodal literacy spaces.

Discussion and Closing Thoughts

This chapter examines how *bricolage* and *assemblage* in a digital storytelling assignment create a space for argumentation in a multilingual academic writing course. Excerpts from three stories were presented to discuss previously identified pedagogical problems with argumentative assignments, particularly with voice and what Bazerman (2013) identified as the danger of being "written" by borrowed texts. In comparison with the print text assignment, digital storytelling provided an alternative approach to argumentation where authors became *bricoleurs* for strategically assembling new and transformative texts to create their arguments. Both assignments involve rhetorical decisions, such as borrowing images or creating narrative arguments, similar to what is found in classical forms of argumentation, where appropriate texts are cited at the appropriate time (Sheridan, Michael, & Ridolfo, 2009), often referred to as *kairos*.

There are important differences between the print and digital arguments both in terms of their institutional positions and pedagogies. The print assignment has a longstanding status in the university while the multimodal assignment is relatively recent. In the print assignment, the author often provides the name of the author and can use reporting verbs or modals to express stances toward the cited texts (Hyland, 1999). Providing these references is one way that can help establish *ethos* by demonstrating familiarity with the existing research (Latour, 1987); however, in the digital story assignment, images were mixed without their creators' names or with using reporting verbs so they did not have the same impact on the argument, although authorship could be recognized by creating "reference" lists at the end of the movie. The use of voice in the digital stories also differed, focusing more on expressing personal stories than on evaluating competing claims of other researchers. However, the narratives remained important in presenting the claims for developing the argument.

As Canagarajah (2018) argues, such new pedagogies require new teaching and learning spaces where these rhetorical processes can be more valued and provide writers with more autonomy. Digital storytelling, therefore, was an alternative approach for creating arguments. These stories present alternatives to personal voice and textual borrowing in the print assignments as well as for rethinking the relationship between the authors and their audiences. This approach also places more responsibility on the students for choosing texts for expressing their arguments. *Bricolage* and *assemblage* involve more than just reconstructing language; it involves using intellectual property in transformative ways for addressing an audience (Ong, 1975; Park, 1982) and "repurposing" of openly available texts (Wiley, 2019) through *assemblage*, so its transformative nature addresses the criteria for the fair use of intellectual property (Aufderheide & Jaszi, 2012).

Assembling images with a narrative creates new, transformative approaches that incorporate similar rhetorical purposes for citation, intellectual property use, structures of academic writing, and open access (Wiley, 2019) from different perspectives and sometimes with different rhetorical goals. However, both assignments required creating social contexts for creating arguments by using personal voices and textual borrowing, whether their stories were political, personal, or a mixture, along with strategies for reaching their audiences.

Comparing the components of every argument—its claims and use of supporting evidence and warrants—can also be different or similar across modes. The domination of print texts outside the writing classroom has made multimodality more problematic. Since multimodality is not yet a major form in academic writing, questions concerning the transferability (Perkins & Salomon, 1988) between the print and digital texts remain important for teaching argumentation.

Using these two forms illustrates how their different affordances can impact our pedagogy. For example, the social context of the print assignment was often derived from genre research or questions peer reviewers often ask about the significance of the research or its adaptability to diverse audiences. In the digital story, the students created their own social contexts and strategies for responding to their audiences. There were, however, important differences in textual borrowing, such as in establishing authorial creditability (Latour, 1987), being able to share resources, or even supporting the truths of the claims.

Both assignments were implemented simultaneously to provide alternative perspectives, as well as different tools and affordances, for academic writing, although more class time and a greater percentage of the grade was allocated to the print assignment. Their simultaneous implementation necessitated discussing their connections and possible areas of transfer. Despite the "dissonance" (Horner, 2020) between these modes, the transfer of academic forms (Anson & Moore, 2017) may increase the value of digital storytelling either as an alternate literacy and/or a bridge to the print forms.

This potential for transfer impacted our uses of tools in both assignments. For example, using Perkins & Salomon's (1988) framework on reflection and transfer, storyboards and blogs were repurposed for exploring the connections between the two forms, which allowed students to identify the rhetorical potential of *bricolage* and *assemblage*. However, there was no evidence of transfer. Nevertheless, these digital and print forms of argumentation are evolving as are print genres (Tardy, 2016), thus especially increasing the value of multimodality for providing alternate perspectives on argumentative literacies.

REFERENCES

Adler-Kassner, L. & Wardle, E. (2015). *Naming what we know: Threshold concepts of writing studies.* Ogden: Utah University Press.

Anson, C.M. & Moore, J.L. (2017). *Critical transitions: Writing and the question of transfer.* Boulder: University of Colorado Press. Retrieved from https://wac.colostate.edu/docs/books/ansonmoore/transfer.pdf

Aufderheide, P. & Jaszi, P. (2012). *Reclaiming fair use: How to put balance back in copyright.* Chicago: University of Chicago Press.

Bander, R. (1971). *American English rhetoric: Writing from models for bilingual students.* New York: Holt, Rinehart and Winston.

Bazerman, C. (2013). *A theory of literate action: Literate action. Volume 2.* Fort Collins, CO: WAC Clearinghouse. Retrieved from https://wac.colostate.edu/books/perspectives/literateaction-v2/

Belcher, D. (2017), On becoming facilitators of multimodal composing and digital design, *Journal of Second Language Writing, 38,* 80–85.

Bloch, J. (2012). *Plagiarism, intellectual property and the L2 writing classroom.* Bristol, England: Multilingual Matters.

Bloch, J. (2015). The use of digital storytelling in an academic writing course: The story of an immigrant. In M. Roberge, K. M. Losey, and M. Wald (Eds.), *Teaching U.S.-educated multilingual writers: Practices from and for the classroom* (pp. 178–204) Ann Arbor: University of Michigan Press.

Bloch, J. (2018). Digital storytelling in the L2 academic writing classroom: Expanding the possibilities. *Dialogues,* 2. https://dialogues.ojs.chass .ncsu.edu/index.php/dialogues/article/view/30

Bloch, J. (2019). Digital storytelling in the L2 graduate classroom: Expanding the possibilities of personal expression and textual borrowing. In S. Khaddka & J.C. Lee (Eds.), *Bridging the multimodal gap* (pp. 182–200). Ogden: Utah University Press.

Bloch. J., & Wilkinson, M.J. (2013) *Teaching digital literacies.* Alexandria, VA: TESOL Press.

Canagarajah, A. S. (2018). Translingual practice as spatial repertoires: Expanding the paradigm beyond structuralist orientations. *Applied Linguistics, 39,* 31–54.

Casanave, C.P. (2017). *Controversies in second language writing* (2nd ed.). Ann Arbor: University of Michigan Press.

Ede, L. & Lunsford, A. (1984). Audience addressed/audience invoked: The role of audience in composition theory and pedagogy. *College Composition and Communication, 35,* 155–171.

Hafner, C.A. (2015). Remix culture and English language teaching: The expression of learner voice in digital multimodal compositions. *TESOL Quarterly, 49,* 486–509.

Hessler, B., & Lambert, J. (2017). Threshold concepts in digital storytelling: Naming what we know about storywork. In G. Jamisson, P. Hardy, Y Nordkvelle, & H. Pleasants (Eds.), *Digital storytelling in higher education* (pp. 19–35). Basel, Switzerland: Springer Nature.

Horner, B. (2020). Afterword. Postmonolingual projections: Translating translinguality. In A. Frost, J. Kierna, & S.B. Malley (Eds.), T*ranslingual dispositions: Globalized approaches to the teaching of writing* (pp. 295–303). Ft. Collins, CO: The WAC Clearinghouse. Retrieved from https://wac .colostate.edu/docs/books/translingual/afterword.pdf

Hyland, K. (1999). Disciplinary discourses: Writer stance in research articles. In C. Candlin & K. Hyland (Eds.), *Writing: Texts, processes, and practices* (pp. 99–121). London: Longman.

Ivanič, R. (1998). *Writing and identity: The discoursal construction of identity in academic writing.* Amsterdam: John Benjamins.

Kuhn, T. (1962). *The structure of scientific revolutions.* Chicago: University of Chicago Press.

Lambert, J. (2020). *Digital storytelling: Capturing lives, creating community* (5th ed.). Berkeley, CA: Digital Diner Text.

Latour, B. (1987). *Science in action.* Cambridge, MA: Harvard University Press.

Lévi-Strauss, C. (1966). *The savage mind.* Chicago: The University of Chicago Press.

Matsuda, P. (2006). The myth of linguistic homogeneity in U.S. college composition. *College English, 68,* 637–651.

Newell, A., Beach, R., Smith, J. & VanDerHeide, J. (2011). Teaching and learning argumentative reading and writing: A review of research. *Reading Research Quarterly, 46,* 273–304.

Newell, G.E., Bloome, D. & Hirvela, A. (2015). *Teaching and learning argumentative writing in high school English language arts classrooms.* New York: Routledge.

Norman, D. (2007). *Emotional design: Why we love (or hate) everyday things.* New York: Basic Books.

Ong, W.J. (1975). The writer's audience is always a fiction. *PMLA, 90,* 9–21.

Park, D.B. (1982). The meaning of "audience." *College English, 44,* 247–257.

Perelman, C. (1982). *The realm of rhetoric.* South Bend, IN: University of Notre Dame Press.

Perkins, D.N., & Salomon, G. (1988). Teaching for transfer. *Educational Leadership, 46,* 22–32.

Shapin, S. (1996). *The scientific revolution.* Chicago: University of Illinois Press.

Sheridan, D., Michel, T., & Ridolfo, J. (2009). Kairos and new media: Toward a theory and practice of visual activism. *Enculturation,* 6. http://enculturation.net/6.2/sheridan-michel-ridolfo

Swales, J. (1990). *Genre analysis: English in academic and research settings.* Cambridge, England: Cambridge University Press.

Swales, J.M., & Feak, C.B. (2012). *Academic writing for graduate students: Essential skills and tasks* (3rd ed.) Ann Arbor: University of Michigan Press.

Tardy, C.M. (2016). *Beyond convention: Genre innovation in academic writing.* Ann Arbor: University of Michigan Press.

Wiley, D. (2019 Aug. 15). Everything old is new again: Textbooks, the printing press, the internet, and OER. https://opencontent.org/blog/archives/6104.

9

Remediating L2 Students' Argumentation in an ESL Composition Class: From Print to Digital Argumentation

NUGRAHENNY T. ZACHARIAS

Abstract

This chapter explores how a Vietnamese second language (L2) writer reme-diated her print essay into a digital argument. It focuses on the way visual images afforded a student's digital argumentation design. The findings show that utilizing of visual modes to express digital arguments has both strengths and weaknesses. Visual modes gave her additional rich and new ways to support her claim, even though the linguistic element in the digital argu-mentation version was somewhat limited. Pedagogical implications about using DMC in the L2 writing classroom are also discussed.

In higher education, it is perhaps safe to say that students' ability to argue is an important factor for students' educational success. For L2 writers, in particular, the ability to put forward a convincing and well-organized argu-ment is "an important marker of second language writing ability" (Hirvela, 2017, p. 69). In addition to being adopted in some form in many high-stakes tests to measure students' L2 competence, argumentative writing is also the most common type of writing students will encounter in academic settings (Nesi & Gardner, 2012). However, at present, most knowledge concerning students' argumentation skills continues to be drawn from studies of print argumentation where arguments are perceived to have "linear sequences of claims, counter-claims, and evidence" (Handa, 2004, p. 305). In this chapter, 'print' refers to traditional essay or written essay. Since digital technologies have enabled new possibilities to construct and circulate arguments digitally (or digital argument, for short), it is important to understand whether digital media composing (or DMC) would strengthen L2 writers' overall ability to argue.

One semiotic tool afforded by DMC is "representational images" (Hill, 2004), or visual images, which is the focus of this chapter. Representational images are designed to represent "a recognizable person, object, or situation" (Hill, 2004, p. 25) and can take the form of still images such as a photo, cartoon, and illustration, or moving/animated images such as videos or GIFs (Graphical Interchange Format) that display a continuous looping succession of frames. A few studies have shown that allowing students to complement written argument with images may contribute to L2 students' overall argumentative skills.

Among these studies, Navera, Garinto, and Valdez (2019) studied how memes affect argumentation by assigning students the task of challenging fallacious arguments embedded in existing online memes. They found that student-created memes depicted arguments that were more dialogical and rich and that demonstrated a strong awareness of socio-political issues. Also, Shin and Cimasko (2008) explored the experience of 14 undergraduates in a first-year ESL composition class who were tasked with composing argumentative digital web pages. Although not focusing on the use of visual images per se, they found that students used concrete photographs to provide vivid contexts for their arguments. For example, in arguing against China's examination-based educational system, rather than using statistics depicting a nationwide testing average, a student named Lin inserted a photograph showing the exhaustion students experience after taking a major examination. Another student used graphs and pie charts to argue for the advantages of South Korea's English curriculum over a state-based ESL curriculum from the U.S.

What is interesting in these cases is how the students used visual modes to address issues in their country of origin while writing to an audience outside those countries. In other words, the visual images were a rhetorical strategy the students utilized to appeal to more international audiences. In another study, Tardy (2005) explored how four L2 graduate students used visual images in scientific presentation slides to develop their arguments. She found that the visual elements of DMC performed rhetorical functions that aligned these students with their disciplinary community's conventions and viewers' expectations, as well as exerting their individual identity. Tardy's findings illustrate the significant role of visual resources in making scientific arguments.

Despite this emerging evidence of the value of visual resources to develop argumentation, it is likely that some, perhaps many, L2 writing teachers are still somewhat skeptical of the value of including visual modes when teaching argumentation. One of their concerns may be that students will spend an unnecessary amount of time on selecting images and play with a variety of digital platforms, rather than on developing rhetorical strategies for argumentation. In short, visual modes are often perceived as interfering with "the difficult . . . business of print literacy practices" (Leander, 2009, p. 147). These concerns are understandable considering how few studies have examined how the teaching and use of visual images can contribute to the way students develop an argument in L2 writing. However, in the digitally oriented 21st century, there is a need to take a more extensive look at whether visual images can actually strengthen students' argumentation. This chapter aims to address this gap by exploring the design process employed by one L2 writer from Vietnam (Stephanie, a pseudonym) when remediating her original argument into a digital platform of a website. It also will address this research question: What affordances do visual images of DMC offer a student's digital argumentation design?

Theoretical Framework: Writing as a Design Approach (WDA)

The current research looks at the visual images in Stephanie's digital argumentation based on the concept of "writing as a design approach" (WDA) (Cimasko & Shin, 2017, p. 390). Approaching texts from a design perspective is different from approaching them from a traditional literacy perspective that privileges linguistic text (Belcher, 2017). A *text* is no longer defined as something that includes linguistic elements; non-linguistic elements, such as images, sounds, and spacing, are now part of the *text* (Yi, Shin, & Cimasko, 2020). Visual images are perceived as a *mode* that has "meaning-making resources" (Yi, Shin, & Cimasko, 2020, p. 2). For example, an essay has resources such as sentences, paragraphs, and topic sentences, while verbal images have resources such as colors, pictures, spatial positions, and angle shots.

One potential reason that the call to integrate multimodality into the L2 writing classroom has recently increased is because of the way that WDA views the author, or designer. In a traditional L2 writing classroom, students are *learners* who are often perceived as error producers, so, therefore, their writing needs to be "corrected." Within a design perspective, learners are *designers* who are "strategically and creatively negotiating" (Kress, 2000, p. 103) to create and convey their intended meaning. Producing a multimodal text also allows designers to bring their everyday media experiences into the classroom. In DePalma's study (2015), for example, one participant drew on her experience as a professional photographer when composing her digital story for the course. Another participant was able to create dramatic tension in her digital story due to her knowledge and skill in creating musical compositions.

However, while WDA focuses on the designer's agency, Jewitt, Bezemer, and O'Halloran (2016) warn that it should not be taken to mean that "anything goes." Nelson (2006) asserts that "authorship implies intentionality"; therefore, a focus on multimodality also needs to address the way that designers are able to verbalize the modal choices and how the intermodal relationship in a digital text accommodates "their interests, characteristics of audiences" (Cimasko & Shin, 2017, p. 390), and rhetorical situation.

When approaching a text from a design perspective, researchers focus on "the intentional deployment of resources in specific configurations to implement the purposes of the designers" (Kress, 2000, p 339). In other words, researchers are looking at the intermodal relationship in a text to accommodate the designer's rhetorical intention(s). In this respect, Jones and Hafner (2012) offer a way to understand the way that the linguistic and visual elements might relate to one another in multimodal texts. These elements can relate in three possible ways: concurrence, complementarity, or divergence. When textual and visual modes convey the same information, they are in **concurrence.** Textual and visual modes are **complementary** when they both project "slightly different information, which 'colors in' the details of the message in other mode" (p. 61). Unsworth (2008, p. 390, in Jones & Hafner, 2012) has discussed how images can complement texts in three ways: (1) enhancing: when the image explain "the 'how' or 'why' of an even tin the main text" (Jones & Hafner, 2012, p. 61); (2) extending: when the image provides additional information to the text; and (3) elaborating: "by restating or specifying what is in the main text" (Jones & Hafner, 2012, p. 61). Finally, visual and linguistic elements **diverge** when they carry pieces of information that are "incompatible with one another" (Jones & Hafner, 2012, p. 61). This happens when the "tone" of an image—"the attitudes and emotions that it conveys" (Jones & Hafner, 2012, p. 61)—differ from the textual mode. Jones and Hafner (2012) assert that visual modes sometimes diverge from the textual modes to create irony or humor. The current study will follow Jones and Hafner's intermodal relationship when exploring Stephanie's utilization of visual modes in her digital argumentation version expressed through a website.

Methodology

Context

The present study was conducted in one first-year ESL composition class at a U.S. university, where I implemented a project in which students were assigned to remediate their initial print argumentative essay into a digital argument. I use the word 'remediate' following Alexander, DePalma and Ringer (2016), to refer to a model of transfer where writers adapt existing writing knowledge and skills across different media as when moving from a print genre to a digital genre. The course, ENGL 109, operates with a baseline syllabus consisting of five units, where each unit represents a writing genre commonly encountered in academic settings. The argumentative essay and remediation task units were the ones where the majority of class instruction time was spent—that is, students produced a written argumentative essay in the third unit and then transformed it into a digital product in the fourth unit. According to Jonassen and Kim (2010), argumentation can be taught from two perspectives: *learning to argue*, which focuses on using elements of argumentation (e.g., evidence, warrants or claims, counterargument, etc.) to argue for a position, and *arguing to learn*, where students practice applying argumentative elements to learn about a particular topic. The teaching of argumentation in this study utilized both perspectives in conjunction with Toulmin's (1958) model of argumentation. The specific task assigned in this case was to learn about international students' (re)naming practices in a study abroad environment (in this case, the U.S.) Stephanie first wrote an essay in which she argued for international students' adoption of English names, a claim she later developed visually.

Once students completed writing their argument essay, it became the source material for the remediation task. The purpose behind engaging students with the remediating process that started with the written product was to offer a way to strengthen students' overall ability to argue to suit the rhetorical demands in a 21st-century context. In other words, they would be prepared to compose both in writing and digitally as their circumstances dictated. Students were given a range of digital genres to choose from, such as comics, websites, posters, and videos. In this way, they could choose a genre that they were familiar with and/or had previously created and thus could connect these out-of-class literacies with those of the classroom. Although students could only transform their print arguments into one of these digital genres, they still had the option to use it as a visual image. For example, when choosing a poster as a genre, students could insert a comic as a visual image to illustrate a particular element of their argument.

The remediation project lasted for 4 weeks. It began by analyzing two or three student samples of digital texts produced in each genre. Each of four class sessions was dedicated to working with a particular type of digital genre. The discussion questions/topics used for examination of each digital genre were: (1) What is the claim made by the student? (2) Who is the intended audience? (3) Identify two dominant rhetorical strategies the designer uses to express his/her argument. (4) Can you think of another rhetorical strategy to make the argument more appealing? The aim of these prompts was to help students think ahead about the affordances each digital genre can provide in relation to the argument the student intended to make. Students then spent another week participating in a series of mini-workshops where they experimented with different genres and then decided on one to use for their remediation task.

The final two weeks of the unit were spent on brainstorming features of their essay that would be remediated into the digital text. During these sessions, students were grouped according to the digital medium they had chosen and worked collaboratively to review mode choices, manage practical problems, and learn from one another about the most effective way to express their arguments. Students then published their remediation projects on a closed Facebook group that was only accessible to students in the class. The digital presentation in Facebook was followed up with peer feedback sessions, which lasted for the whole week. During this time, students also voted, through a Google forum, for the best use of a digital genre to achieve the argument. For each class meeting, students were expected to provide feedback to approximately four students. The feedback was posted on the comment thread beneath the digital texts. The feedback focused on: (1) two things they liked, with relevant supporting reasons; (2) one thing the student needed to improve; and (3) one question to ask the student who designed the digital product. The peer feedback students received helped them to write the reflection essay at the end of the remediation unit.

Participant

The participant for the current study was recruited from the cohort of students in the ENGL 109 composition class. To avoid conflicts of interest, students were contacted after they had completed the course and their grades had been released. The focal participant selected for this study was Stephanie (a pseudonym), an international student from Vietnam, who had only been in the U.S. for four months at the time she took the course. Among the four digital genres available, she chose a website. Her website includes four webpages which were the evidence for her argument. Also, a website allowed her to include visual elements to give further evidence on each webpage. For example, she intended to *transduct* ("changing semiotic materials from one mode to another" [Cimasko & Shin, 2017]) her personal experience into a comic and added still images to make her website more visual.

Stephanie was selected as the focal participant for the study because her website was chosen by her peers as displaying the Best Argument. Also, because she did not have any prior experience creating websites, I was curious to learn more about her composing process and design decisions, as a novice, when remediating her written essay.

Research Design, Data Collection, and Analysis

Stephanie's remediation of her argumentative essay into a website is presented using a qualitative case study approach (Denzin and Lincoln, 2003) because this approach would offer a more detailed view of how remediation functioned and the kinds of decision-making the student experienced when transducting (Cimasko & Shin, 2017) her print product into a digital argument presented through a website. I was particularly interested in seeing the specific visual modes she chose and how she used them in conveying a digital argument.

The data collection included multiple types of data: Stephanie's argumentative writing, reflective essays about her essay and the remediation project, website-related artifacts, and an interview. The primary data source to explore her remediation process was the website-related artifacts and her essay. My field notes and teaching journal entries (written reflections on my teaching), as well as the interview with Stephanie, served as supplementary data to provide contextual information about the design process not conveyed in the reflection essays. The interview lasted 40 minutes and was conducted four months after the class ended. Due to the considerable amount of time lapse between the interview and the remediation project, I utilized a stimulated recall approach where I drew attention to examples from the websites and reflection essays to remind Stephanie about her design process and the decision-making she engaged in during the entire remediation process.

Findings

The findings presented highlight the way Stephanie used visual images to remediate her print argument essay into a digital argument.

**How Visual Images Facilitate Author's Written Claim
for the Need to Use an English Name**

Stephanie addressed the question of whether international students should adopt an English name. When remediating her essay into websites, she wanted to find a way to make her claim more visual. She began by visualizing and highlighting her claim of the need for international students to use English names near the top of her created homepage, which acts as the "front door" of the website The homepage was designed to be read from top to bottom—following the reading path of a traditional essay—which is different from an "F-shaped" reading path commonly used when reading a webpage (Jones & Hafner, 2012).

   When entering her homepage, online viewers were greeted with a black and white photograph of a metropolitan skyline that seems intended to remind online viewers of the setting—the study abroad context—for her claim. The photograph shot from a high angle seems to project the idea of a vibrant and majestic world beyond one's home country that reflects international students when they are studying abroad (see Figure 9.1 for the text that appeared on Stephanie's homepage).

Figure 9.1

Text from Stephanie's Homepage

ENGLISH NAMES—A NECESSITY
FOR INTERNATIONAL STUDENTS

HOME · ABOUT · AUTHOR
ENGLISH NAME—AVOIDMISPRONUNCIATION
ENGLISH NAME—BOOST CONNECTIONS WITH AMERICANS
ENGLISH NAME—NO MORE BIAS
ENGLISH NAME--NEVER DISRESPECT PARENTS' HOPE IN REAL NAMES

INTERNATIONAL STUDENTS HAD
BETTER HAVE ENGLISH NAMES

The second visual element is an image of clouds foregrounding the call for action, "International students had better have English names," written in a multicolored arch. The first two images work together to contextualize her claim of the need to use an English name as a promise and/or key to achieve a positive study abroad experience.

Apart from the images that romanticize the world of international education, Stephanie deployed linguistic elements to quickly reorient online readers to her claim and the audience she wished to speak to. She did this by repeating the keywords "English names" and "international students" in different parts of this homepage: the site headline, navigation menu, and call for action. Stephanie also made several notable modal changes to fit her writing into the genre of a webpage. She transformed her essay's title "International Students Had Better Have English Names" into the call for action and recreated a concise headline for the homepage: "English Names— A Necessity." She was aware that a homepage headline needed to be "short and meaningful." This intention was also the reason why she chose to use a dash (–) in the navigation menu to succinctly relate the evidence to her claim: "Avoid Mispronunciation," Boost Connections with Americans," "No More Bias," and "Never Disrespect Parents' Hope in Real Names." When she was asked about a potential issue with her use of the dash, Stephanie admitted that that was a possibility, but prior to publishing her website she had shown the navigation menu to two of friends—both of whom are international students—and they both commented that her webpage was good and easy to understand.

Stephanie's remediation of the essay's introduction into the homepage made her claim more noticeable for online readers. She achieved this by employing images to enhance the reality of study abroad contexts by providing a relevant context for her claim. The images and textual elements on the homepage work together to project an idea such as "Use English names and you can have a happy study abroad experience." By doing so, Stephanie appears to make her claim more relevant or appealing to online viewers, positioning it as a promise that international students can achieve when accepting her claim.

Augmenting Affective Evidence of Name Mispronunciation through Visual Images

One significant remediation change that Stephanie made to strengthen the evidence of her claim for the need to use English names is by highlighting affective nuances of name mispronunciation through a combination of visual images. For example, on the webpage "English Name—Avoid Mispronunciation," transformed from the first supporting paragraph of the essay, Stephanie employed a combination of a comic and two GIFs. In this paragraph, she wrote this personal experience statement—a required element of the essay:

> *Through my experience of having such a unique name in my country Vietnam, I find out that the situation of being called with wrong names deeply hurt students' feeling. [. . .] In primary school, many Vietnamese teachers have always mistaken my middle name Uyên for my first name Phuong. When my teacher called my name wrong, I felt confused and depressed inside because I felt like my teachers did not care about me, so they did not even remember my name.*

Stephanie transformed this writing into a comic. In the paragraph, she did not write an explicit warrant of how having her name mispronounced by a Vietnamese teacher was relevant to her claim for the use of English names in the U.S. It is possible that her intention is to emphasize the pain of having one's name mispronounced by a teacher and thus did not think the different contexts mattered.

Regardless, when creating the comic, she seems to be aware of the lack of warranting in her evidence and then added a relevant warrant. She then created a setting that is most relatable to international students—the first day of class when a teacher does a roll call, a situation where many international students with a different (non-Western) given name could encounter embarrassment. To portray the scene, she created an eight-frame comic. After showing her arrival at school and then her classroom in the first few frames, the teacher is pictured sitting at her desk and calling out "Ho Phuong Uren?" The next frame shows Stephanie sitting at her desk and not responding. The teacher then says, "Who is Ho Phuong Uren?????" When there is still no reply, the teacher declares, with an angry look on her face, "ABSENT!!!" This is followed by the final frame, where Stephanie is sitting at her desk crying and saying "Why again??? My name Is Uyen Phuong, not Phuong Uyen."

A visual change she made to assert the pain of having a teacher mispronounce one's name is altering the sympathetic teacher character in the written text to a mean and unsympathetic teacher character in the comic. As a visual genre, the comic presented a way to create a storyline and narrative details that would show a more straightforward connection between the cause and (emotional) effect of teacher's misnaming behavior. In this way, Stephanie believed she could better show how what she wrote in her reflection to her online audience.

Following the comic, she added two direct quotations from published sources taken verbatim from the personal experience paragraph. These sources highlight the pain and discomfort of having one's name mispronounced. At the top, in the first text, readers see the words: "I felt very uncomfortable in class just like what Uyen Thi Tran Myhre state that 'it is difficult to build any kind of meaningful working relationship' with people calling me wrong." Then, in the first GIF, readers see two people having a conversation in a room. A girl in focus is shaking her head, and we see the words, "I couldn't be more unhappy." This is followed by more text from Stephanie's paragraph, which includes a secondary source:

> Besides, I was not the one who experienced this mispronunciation, but also almost every international student using their cultural name in foreign countries. In the article "How We Pronounce Student Names, and Why it Matters," Samira Fejzić also experienced sadness and ache when they mispronounced her name at graduation, even when she considered the mispronunciation of her name as ritual
>
> (Gonzalez, 1).

Beneath this text, the second GIF contains two images of an angry looking man saying "WRONG" in the first image and "WROOOONG!!!!!" in the image next to it.

Interestingly, the two GIFs interact differently with the written explanation framing them. The first GIF appears to visually complement the written text "very uncomfortable feelings [of teacher mispronunciation]," while the second seems to totally diverge from the accompanying text that describes the "sadness and ache" when Fejzić (the author of the secondary source she quoted) experienced her name being mispronounced during a graduation event.

The divergence between the animated GIF and the textual information might highlight the benefit of allowing the use of visual modes in an L2 writing classroom. Nelson (2006) explains that teachers can put L2 writers in a "modally impoverished semiotic environment" (p. 71) when they insist on only using linguistic elements of the L2 in student essays. She further argues that digital mediated communication can offer "a potential leveling effect" (p. 71) by providing an alternative tool to express an authorial intent not supported by the linguistic element of the L2. Stephanie pointed out that the second GIF aims to highlight the frustration international students feel when *multiple* teachers *repeatedly* mispronounce their given names—an affective dimension that is not expressed in her written reflection. However, the reason for not addressing the frustration expressed in the written version is unclear: did she intend to write it in her essay but could not find suitable words? Or was it that in the process of finding a suitable GIF for additional textual information, she came across an additional emotional effect of what happened when she heard her own name mispronounced? Either way, working with digital material allowed her to insert a verbal image that she believed could provide additional evidence that could not be inferred from a written explanation.

Although the use of digital images allowed Stephanie to present information she was unable to express in writing, adopting GIFs might also reflect an important issue commonly associated with visual images. Different from comics, which can be read in a linear and sequential way, images, including GIFs, tend to be, as Jones and Hafner (2012) note, more "polysemous" because of their capability "of sending numerous messages at the same time" (p. 52). When asked if online viewers might not understand how the GIFs relate to the webpage headline "English Name—Avoid Mispronunciation," Stephanie felt she did not need to explicitly connect the two GIFs with the page headline because the GIFs served as visual hooks. Stephanie's response might therefore indicate that instructors need to explicitly teach warranting where visual elements are used to connect evidence to the claim and how it is expressed digitally. This is something that I did not explicitly teach during this particular unit in ENG 109.

Using Visual Modes to Create Audience Experience

Smith (2018) explains that when composing in multiple modes, students sometimes design their digital text for "audience experience" as a way to make their design appeal to a wider audience; they do this by including "entertaining and interesting [elements] . . . even if these elements did not contribute to the substantive meaning of their works" (p. 204). Stephanie's desire to make her webpages attractive might explain why she inserted some "cute" images that did not have any substantive meaning related to her claim. One example is an image of Bob the Minion (from the movie "Minions") looking up to the text "English Names –Never Disrespect Parental Wishes," which she placed at the bottom of the page. Another example is a one-minute video on the page "English Name—Boost Connection with Americans" entitled "Cute Friendship Comfort Cartoon" describing a relationship between two different species.

Stephanie's employment of "cute" images highlights two issues related to the use of visual elements in the digital environment. First, following

Nelson (2006), Stephanie's use of divergent cute images can be an instance of "overaccommodation of audience" (p. 72) where her employment of funny visuals is simply meant to please the audience without any clear rhetorical intention that significantly contributes to her argument. Another possible reason is that students as designers can become attached to certain images and seem to be unable to resist the temptation to use them. This may well be what happened to Stephanie.

In addition to decorating her website with "cute" images, Stephanie sought to relate to online audiences with what she referred to as "funny" images. One example is two images she inserted, one on top of the other, on the webpage "English Name—Boost Connection with Americans." Stephanie hoped that the images would mean that online audiences would not take her claim too seriously, which may seem like an odd move to make in an argumentative text, but she was still supporting her claim. Next to the image the word "Pronunciation" is shown in large red letters. Stephanie explained that the first image—a boy with his tongue-tied (literally)—was supposed to provide a visual comedic exaggeration of why U.S. professors and peers could not pronounce the given names of international students. The second image shows a man holding his right hand over his face in obvious frustration, which is supposed to represent the sense of hopelessness and frustration of international students when their professors mispronounce their given names.

Stephanie's utilization of these types of images might make her evidence richer in the way it appeals to potential audiences, even though, as previously noted, she did not want readers to take her claim too seriously. The written explanation provides a logical reason for Stephanie's belief that international students should use English names. Additionally, the image of a man face-palming reminds international students of one possible emotional reaction when professors repeatedly mispronounce their given names. Perhaps more importantly, through the use of these types of images, she can address this issue more respectfully by not offending professors and/or criticizing them in a direct way.

Closing Thoughts and Pedagogical Implications

This chapter set out to explore how visual images could facilitate or compromise the digital argument created by Stephanie, a L2 writer from Vietnam, which she remediated from a written essay. The findings show that utilizing visual modes to remediate Stephanie's written argument had both strengths and weaknesses. One obvious strength is that the use of visual modes gave her rich new ways to support her claim, thus expanding her possibilities as a "designer" of argumentative texts. Through visual modes she seemed to overcome limitations associated with argumentative writing. For this to have happened to someone who was a novice creating web pages is significant and highlights the affordances that can be provided by digital argumentation.

Unlike previous remediation studies of remediation (Cimisko & Shin, 2017; Shin & Cimasko, 2008) where linguistic modes are often used as a gate-keeper of visual modes, Stephanie utilized visual modes in a more purposeful way to express what she could not in writing. In her essay, she supported her claim for the use of English names by highlighting the benefits of having an English name. In the digital argument, which she presented on a webpage she created, each benefit was transformed into a webpage headline. Even though the two versions were basically the same structurally, the design choices she made and the intermodal relationships she built between the visual modes in her digital version aimed to project deeper and richer affective evidence to support her claim.

Similar to research by DePalma (2015), Stephanie's reflection on the remediation project demonstrates her awareness of "rhetorical reshaping" (p. 267)—the process in which designers "remix, repurpose, recontextualize, or coordinate" (p. 267) across digital mediums—and thus, digital genres allowed her to develop richer ways to engage with an online audience. Stephanie recognized that the "serious and academic" tone of the language used in her written essay might deter her online audience, so she felt the need to strategi-cally coordinate interactions among diverse visual modes in ways that would allow her to engage with them in a more interesting way. To sustain online viewers' interest, she repurposed visual images to focus on creating humor and appeals to emotion to capture the distress and long-lasting emotional impact of name mispronunciation. In the process, it may have enabled her to experience argumentation itself more meaningfully.

While Stephanie was able to use a variety of visual modes to provide evidence for her claim, her remediation of the written explanation in the digital argumentation version was somewhat limited. That is, many sentences on her website were taken directly from the essay instead of being adjusted to better fit her visual content. There also is a lack of connection between the webpage headline and the visual content on the webpage. Echoing what Qu (2017) has advocated, this finding lends further empirical support for the need to continue focusing on the linguistic aspect of digitally mediated communication because in many digital genres, such as the website in the current study, "the words . . . anchor the interpretation" (p. 92). While in the digital era the teaching of writing needs to be broadened to include visual aspects, Qu argues that the linguistic mode still needs to be addressed as well, particularly when teaching L2 writers who need to be prepared for "courses and activities . . . overwhelmingly conducted in the target language" (p. 93) outside the L2 writing classroom.

One possible reason why Stephanie largely took the written explanation on the webpages directly from her written argument might be the A grade she received for her essay. For Stephanie, transforming the written words when used on a website might have looked like a risk that would put her satisfactory grade on the line. Thus, the transfer process from one modality to another may have been compromised. Despite her willingness to experiment with the visual modes in the digital argument, Stephanie apparently continued to assume a one-size-fits all view of the linguistic modes across writing contexts. This points to the need for teachers to focus specifically on the different ways prior learned linguistic skills acquired during the composing of a print argument can be repurposed to fit the platform of digital arguments.

Another potential pedagogical implication of the current study is to limit the digital genres into which students can remediate their writing. My initial intention in allowing students to select from a variety was to accommodate students' out-of-school digital practices, which I assumed were extensive, but it may have been the case that some students—like Stephanie—had only experienced the digital world as a consumer. Here, it should be remembered that Stephanie was a novice not only in website design but also in digital argumentation. Thus, the journey from the print essay to the digital remediation may have held challenges I did not anticipate as the teacher of the course. Then, too, providing a wide range of digital genre options, as I did, might not have been the best pedagogical choice. It might be better to limit inexperienced students' options and thus generate a more explicit scaffolding discussion on how the semiotic resources provided by a particular digital genre can work together to better accommodate a student's argumentation.

REFERENCES

Alexander, K. P., DePalma, M., & Ringer, J. M. (2016). Adaptive remediation and the facilitation of transfer in multiliteracy center contexts. *Computers and Composition, 41*, 32–45.

Belcher, D. (2017). On becoming facilitators of multimodal composing and digital design. *Journal of Second Language Writing, 38*, 80–85. http://doi .org/10.1016/j.jslw.2017.10.004

Cimasko, T. and Shin, D. (2017). Multimodal resemiotization and authorial agency in an L2 writing classroom. *Written Communication, 34*(4), 387–413.

Denzin, N., & Lincoln, Y. (2003). *The landscape of qualitative research.* Thousand Oaks, CA: Sage.

DePalma, M. (2015). Tracing transfer across media: Investigating writers' perceptions of cross-contextual and rhetorical reshaping in process of remediation. *College Composition and Communication, 66*(4), 617–642.

Handa, C. (2004). *Visual rhetoric in a digital world: A critical sourcebook.* Boston: Bedford/St. Martins.

Hill, C. A. (2004). The psychology of rhetorical images. In M. Helmers and C. A. Hill (Eds), *Defining visual rhetorics* (pp. 25–40). Mahwah, NJ: Lawrence Erlbaum.

Hirvela, A. (2017) Argumentation & second language writing: Are we missing the boat? *Journal of Second Language Writing, 36,* 69–74. http://dx.doi .org/10.1016/j.jslw.2017.05.002

Jewitt, C., Bezemer, J., & O'Halloran, K. (2016). *Introducing multimodality.* New York: Routledge.

Jonassen, D. H., & Kim, B. (2010). Arguing to learn and learning to argue: design justifications and guidelines. *Educational Technology Research and Development, 58*(4), 439–457.

Jones, R. H., & Hafner, C. A. (2012). *Understanding digital literacies: A practical introduction.* New York: Routledge.

Kress, G. (2000). Multimodality: Challenges to thinking about language. *TESOL Quarterly, 34*(3), 337–340.

Leander, K. (2009). Composing with old and new media: Toward parallel pedagogy. In. V. Carrington and M. Robinson (Eds.), *Digital literacies: Social learning and classroom practices* (pp. 147–164). London: Sage Publications Ltd.

Navera, J. A. S., Garinto, L. A. B., & Valdez, P. N. M (2019). Teaching against the meme: Politics, argumentation and engagement in an ESL classroom in the Philippines. *The Journal of Asia TEFL, 16*(1), 393–400.

Nelson, M. E. (2006). Mode, meaning, and synaesthesia in multimedia L2 writing. *Language Learning & Technology, 10*(2), 56–76.

Nesi, H., & Gardner, S. (2012). *Genres across the disciplines: Student writing in higher education.* New York: Cambridge University Press.

Qu, W. (2017). Disciplinary Dialogues: For L2 writers, it is always the problem of the language. *Journal of Second Language Writing, 38,* 92–93.

Shin, D., & Cimasko, T. (2008). Multimodal composition in a college ESL class: New tools, traditional norms. *Computers and Composition, 25,* 376–395.

Smith, B. E. (2018). Composing for affect, audience, and identity: Toward a multidimensional understanding of adolescents' multimodal composing goals and designs. *Written Communication, 35*(2), 182–214.

Tardy, C. (2005). Expressions of disciplinarity and individuality in a multimodal genre. *Computers and Composition, 22,* 319–336.

Toulmin. S. (1958). *The uses of argument.* Cambridge, England: Cambridge University Press.

Unsworth, L. (2008). Multiliteracies and metalanguage: describing image/text relations as a resource for negotiating multimodal texts. In J. Coiro, M. Knobel, C. Lankshear, & D. J. Leu (Eds.), *Handbook of research on new literacies* (pp. 377–405). Mahweh, NJ: Lawrence Erlbaum.

Yi, Y., Shin D., & Cimasko, T. (2020). Editorial for the special issue: Multimodal composing in multilingual learning and teaching contexts. *Journal of Second Language Writing, 47,* 1–7.

10

Blending Learning to Argue and Arguing to Learn in EFL Writing Instruction: A Classroom Inquiry

MIN ZOU, XIAOHUI LI, AND ICY LEE

Abstract

While argument is highly valued, EFL learners are generally unprepared to participate in argumentation and produce quality argumentative essays. Drawing on argument-based inquiry, this study implemented nine argument-focused activities to help students learn to argue and argue to learn in one EFL classroom in China. The findings revealed a significant growth in argumentative writing and skills. By helping students to internalize the argument schema and experience the joy of inquiry, the argument-based inquiry could also prompt them to transfer argumentative learning to other contexts.

Argument is seen as the essence of critical thinking and a key feature of successful writing across disciplines (Hirvela, 2017). Nevertheless, many students experience difficulties in constructing sound arguments (Bacha, 2010; Kuhn, Hemberger, & Khait, 2016a), primarily due to students' lack of prior knowledge, insufficient attention to argument in curriculum, and teachers' lack of pedagogical tools (e.g., Abdollahzadeh, Farsani, & Beik-mohammadi, 2017; Jonassen & Kim, 2010). In EFL contexts, while students are expected to develop arguments in internationally recognized tests (e.g., the TOEFL®), they are frequently found to be ill-prepared for English argumentative writing (e.g.,Qin & Karabacak, 2010). It is thus important to strengthen the teaching of argument in writing classrooms. However, little classroom-based research has focused on the teaching and learning of argument in EFL contexts (Hirvela, 2017). Drawing on argument theories and argument-based inquiry, this study centered on argument as a pathway to writing and thinking and aimed to investigate the effects of argument-based inquiry on students' argumentative learning in one EFL classroom in China.

Learning to Argue and Arguing to Learn

Despite the consensus about the importance of argument in education (e.g., Kuhn et al., 2016a), the term *argument* is used to refer to different practices, ranging from reasoning to inquiry (Hirvela, 2017). Derived from logic and rhetorical argument, argument-as-reasoning concentrates on the use of logic to construct a convincing argument and sees the well-structured argument as the ultimate product (Jonassen & Kim, 2010). A case in point is the Toulmin model (Toulmin, 1958): To produce a persuasive argument, writers need to reasonably justify their *claim* (assertion in response to a problem) by relating *data* (evidence to support a claim) to it through *warrants* (assumption bridging data and claim) and by using *qualifiers* (placing limits on the strength of the claim), *backing* (support of the warrant), and *rebuttals* (response to opposing views) appropriately. Argument-as-inquiry, however, sees argument as the social, collaborative practice of argumentation (Kuhn, 2018). It emphasizes using argumentative elements as a heuristic to rationally resolve questions, enhance thinking, and advance knowledge (Kuhn et al., 2016a). In this sense, argument becomes a tool toward a more important end.

In accord with the conceptual reasoning-inquiry dichotomy, a distinction is made between learning to argue and arguing to learn. Closely related to argument-as-reasoning, **learning to argue** involves providing students with argumentative elements and teaching them the reasoning processes helpful in constructing argumentative essays (Hirvela, 2017). For instance, Bacha (2010) provided explicit instruction in Toulmin's (1958) thesis-support argumentative element to help L1 Arabic students produce effective written arguments. Aligned with argument-as-inquiry, **arguing to learn** supposes that there exist some general argumentative skills in the coordination of claims and evidence and that acquiring them is "beneficial in supporting success and efficiency in acquiring new knowledge through the process of argumentation" (Hemberger, Kuhn, Matos, & Shi, 2017, p. 576). Teachers thus embed argumentation in the learning environment to develop argumentative skills and augment knowledge acquisition (Jonassen & Kim, 2010). Studies by Kuhn and her colleagues showed that students' argumentation with peers helped students to improve argumentative skills and transfer them to other topics (e.g., Kuhn et al., 2016a, 2016b). Similarly, Bloome et al. (2020) found that students' engagement in arguing to learn by reading literary texts and communicating with others contributed to better intertextual connections and deeper understanding.

Worthy of note is that learning to argue and arguing to learn should never be seen as an either-or choice. Indeed, both are part of a curricular continuum. Teachers are encouraged to integrate them in argumentative writing instruction, with students first taught learning to argue and then guided to draw on such knowledge and skills to deepen thinking through argumentation (Newell, Bloome, & Hirvela, 2015). Nevertheless, such a view is likely missing in most EFL writing pedagogy, which has primarily focused on the mastery of structural features of argument—that is, learning to argue (Bacha, 2010; Hirvela, 2017). To address the gap, this study attempts to integrate learning to argue and arguing to learn in EFL writing instruction through argument-based inquiry.

Argument-Based Inquiry

Argument-based inquiry is an umbrella term covering pedagogical approaches that engage students in argument in the context of doing inquiry, among which the Science Writing Heuristic Approach (SWHA) and argument-driven inquiry have gained much popularity.

Seeing argument as integral to science classrooms, SWHA integrates argumentation and writing into scientific inquiries through three phases (Hand, Norton-Meier, & Jang, 2017): (1) development of underpinning epistemic framework phase, in which teachers help students elicit prior knowledge and acquire the structure and practice of argument; (2) the argument phase, in which students negotiate their claims and evidence in groups and compare their ideas against source texts to learn scientific concepts; and (3) the summary writing phase, where students write on and/or present their current understanding and reflect on the inquiry process. Similarly, argument-driven inquiry emphasizes the role of argumentation in constructing and validating scientific knowledge through seven steps (Sampson, Grooms, & Walker, 2010): (1) teachers' identification of the task that captures students' interest; (2) generation of data, in which students work in groups to collect and analyse data; (3) production of a tentative argument comprising explanation of claims and evidence; (4) argumentation sessions, where groups share arguments and refine their explanations; (5) creation of a written investigation report by individual students; (6) peer review; and (7) revision and submission of the report. While their procedures slightly differ, both of these approaches emphasize well-structured tasks; teacher scaffolding; group discussion; opportunities for constructing, sharing, and revising argument; and a respectful learning atmosphere.

It is also suggested that sustained implementation of such an integrated model, which teaches students what counts as argument (i.e., learning to argue) and engages them in argumentation to develop a better understanding of content (i.e., arguing to learn), could empower students to engage in scientific argumentation, craft quality written arguments, and transfer their learning to new tasks (e.g., Jang & Hand, 2017; Sampson et al., 2010). Researchers (e.g., Walker & Sampson, 2013) thus contend that understanding the development of argumentative skills in coordinating claims and evidence as well as students' argumentative writing performance over time is crucial for implementing argument-based inquiry and designing curriculum materials. Yet, argument-based inquiry has been mainly applied to science classrooms. Little is known about how argument-based inquiry can be implemented in EFL classrooms and how students' argumentative writing and argumentative skills develop and transfer while participating in argument-based inquiry. Addressing these questions could provide valuable insights into the pedagogical exploration of argument in EFL contexts.

This Study

Research Questions

This study aimed to explore in what ways students developed their argumentative writing and argumentative skills through participation in argument-based inquiry in a writing-intensive course—Critical Thinking, Reading, and Writing at a university in Mainland China. It was guided by three questions:

1. How did the quality of students' written argument change when they engaged in argument-based inquiry?
2. How did students' argumentative skills change when they engaged in argument-based inquiry?
3. How might students transfer their argumentative learning from this course to other contexts?

Context and Participants

This study took place in one research-oriented university in southwest China, where great emphasis was placed on critical thinking (e.g., identifying and evaluating arguments) and writing in the college English curriculum. According to the curriculum, non-English majors needed to attend EFL courses in the first two years of their college study, and they were expected to write 500-word essays at the end of the first-year and 1,200-word essays at the end of the second year.

In this study, participants were 28 sophomores who enrolled in the elective course, Critical Thinking, Reading, and Writing taught by one author of this study (Li). The class met for two 45-minute classes per week during the 16-week semester. Students were from diverse disciplinary backgrounds, such as engineering, mathematics and law. Their English language proficiency was generally at the intermediate and upper-intermediate levels. Informed by the writing requirement stipulated in the college English curriculum in the university, students were required to write a 500-word argumentative essay on one controversial issue and gradually extend it to 1,200 words in this course.

Procedure

This inquiry featured nine argument-focused activities derived from the research on argumentative writing and argument-based inquiry, with more attention paid to learning to argue in the first ten weeks and arguing to learn in the following six weeks (Figure 10.1).

The first step was to help students understand argumentative elements through teacher explanation and text analysis. The teacher explained to students the components and principles of argument (Toulmin, 1958). Then students were guided to identify the structural and linguistic features (e.g., signposting words for refutation) of argumentative essays taken from Barnet and Bedau's (2014) book (the recommended textbook for the course) and the *New York Times*, use text maps to visualize their structures and content, and then write an analysis of argument. This step was designed to familiarize students with argumentative elements across texts and engage them in metacognitive discussions about how writers utilized relevant elements to make their argument persuasive (Newell et al., 2015).

The second step concerned teachers' identification of the task. Since confronting students with intriguing, important problems engaged them in active inquiries (Bean, 2011), the teacher selected three controversial issues

Figure 10.1

Argument-based inquiry

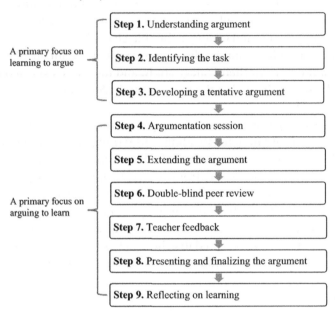

A primary focus on learning to argue

- **Step 1.** Understanding argument
- **Step 2.** Identifying the task
- **Step 3.** Developing a tentative argument

A primary focus on arguing to learn

- **Step 4.** Argumentation session
- **Step 5.** Extending the argument
- **Step 6.** Double-blind peer review
- **Step 7.** Teacher feedback
- **Step 8.** Presenting and finalizing the argument
- **Step 9.** Reflecting on learning

closely related to students' lives (see Part 1 in Appendix 10A). Then, students chose the topic that intrigued them most and constructed a 500-word written argument outside class within one week. The third step of developing a tentative argument was designed to orient students to different ideas on the selected topic and enable them to apply the argumentative elements to craft an argument.

During the fourth step, students were grouped with those who wrote on the same topic and engaged in dialogic argumentation. In the group, students read one another's 500-word essays and shared their claims with both same-side and opposing-side partners. This provided an actual audience (Kuhn, 2018) and made students' claims, evidence, and reasoning visible to others, which in turn enabled them to evaluate alternatives and their own conclusions and evidence (Walker & Sampson, 2013). Since text is a prop to foster dialogue and in-depth explorations, the teacher also guided students to search and synthesize topic-related texts and engaged them in "dialogic literary argumentation" (Bloome et al., 2020). Students read texts to juxtapose the multiple perspectives on the issue and shared with group members their reading and thoughts. The fifth step involved individual students extending their 500-word draft to a 1,200-word version by incorporating the multiple perspectives and rationalities they gained in argumentation sessions (see Part 2 in Appendix 10A), which was completed outside class in two weeks. The purpose was to challenge students to think critically about the claims and reasons in their initial argument in light of new information.

The sixth step was double-blind peer review of the 1,200-word argument essay. Once students finished their essay, they submitted a copy to the teacher, who then randomly distributed it to another student with a peer review sheet. The review sheet included specific criteria to assess argumentative elements, structure, and language as well as space to provide feedback. This was to help students develop and use rigorous criteria for quality argument, think about the problems and suggestions of developing arguments as both readers and writers, and form a community of learners who hold each other accountable (Sampson et al., 2010). Students revised their draft based on peer feedback and submitted it to the teacher during the seventh step. The teacher read each argument, decided whether it could be accepted as it is, and/or provided feedback about how to improve it. After the teacher's approval, students presented their argument in class and finalized it based on comments from the teacher and peers. During the final step, students reflected on their learning with the help of a reflection sheet, which was designed to help students take a metacognitive stance towards their engagement in argument, and reflect on the evolution of ideas (Bean, 2011).

Data Collection

Students' argumentative essays, reflection sheets, and interviews were collected to examine the influence of argument-based inquiry on their argumentative writing and argumentative skills. As written arguments require students to incorporate argumentative elements and argumentation to justify a claim and embody the "transfer of [argumentative] skill from the social to individual plane" (Kuhn & Crowell, 2011, p.545), students' initial 500-word argumentative draft and final 1,200-word essay were collected to document the changes in writing and thinking. The reflection sheets students completed in the end were also gathered to understand their inquiry process. To gain additional insight into their inquiry and transfer of argumentative learning, we invited six students, who provided detailed accounts about argumentative learning in their reflection, to participate in a 40-minute interview. The interviews were conducted in Chinese to make them feel ease at articulating ideas.

Data Analysis

The argumentative essays were firstly evaluated according to the Analytical Scoring Rubric for Argumentative Writing (ASRAW) developed by Stapleton & Wu (2015). Based on Toulmin's (1958) model, ASRAW contains descriptors of argumentative structural elements and reasoning quality as well as the weighting for each element, and thus can present a comprehensive picture of students' argumentative writing (Abdollahzadeh et al., 2017). One author of this study (Zou) and a tertiary EFL writing teacher with four years of teaching experience independently rated the 56 essays, and the average score was taken as the final score of each essay. The overall inter-rater reliability was 0.93 for the 500-word version and 0.90 for the 1,200-word version. Paired samples *t*-tests were then run on the scores to detect changes in students' argumentative writing.

As the use of evidence-based functional units of ideas are essential indicators of argumentative skills (Hemberger et al., 2017), the argumentative essays were divided into evidence-based idea units, which were operationalized as "a claim together with any reason and/or evidence supporting it" (Kuhn et al., 2016b, p.100). We then followed the coding system reported by Kuhn et al. (2016b) to identify the argumentative function each idea unit served: (1) *support my own* (M+)—a statement serving to support one's own position; (2) *weaken other* (O-)—a statement serving to critique and thereby weaken the opponent's position; (3) *support other* (O+)—a statement serving to acknowledge strengths of the opponent's position; and (4) *weaken my own* (M-)—a statement serving to acknowledge weaknesses of one's own position. Units that serve no identifiable argumentative function were categorized as *no argument*. A unit that was not substantively different from an earlier one was categorized as a *repeated argument*. Zou and the tertiary EFL writing teacher independently coded a randomly chosen 20 percent of the essays and achieved an interrater agreement of 97.79 percent for segmenting essays into idea units and 94.87 percent for assigning segments to argumentative functions. Differences were resolved via discussion, and the remaining essays were coded by Zou.

Additionally, student interviews were transcribed and translated. The interview data and reflections were read several times to identify emergent patterns and themes (e.g., the joy of inquiry) concerning how and why students' argumentative writing and argumentative skills changed and transferred, with salient points extracted to shed light on the results.

Findings and Discussion

Impact on Students' Argumentative Writing

The comparison of students' performance (Table 10.1) revealed a significant overall gain from 49.11 total points for the 500-word draft to 80.54 points for the 1,200-word essay. Regarding specific elements of argumentation, gains were seen in all but claim, for which the full credit (i.e., 5 points) was given if students stated points of view. Especially notable were gains in the use of counterargument data (from 5.71 to 15.44) and rebuttal data (from 6.25 to 17.59), and improvement in the use of data to support the claim (from 17.14 to 22.77). These gains suggest that continued focus on argumentation in the course strengthened students' mastery of argumentative elements and evidentiary reasoning ability, which was an important course goal, as shown in Table 10.1.

Table 10.1

Students' Performance on 500-Word and 1200-Word Argumentative Writing

Argumentative Elements and Weightings	N	500-Word Essay		1,200-Word Essay		t-Values	p-Values
		M	SD	M	SD		
Claim (5%)	28	5.00	0.00	5.00	0.00		
Data (25%)	28	17.14	2.23	22.77	2.29	−10.73	0.00
Counterargument claim (10%)	28	9.11	2.38	10.00	0.00	−1.99	0.06
Counterargument data (25%)	28	5.71	6.08	15.54	4.27	−8.29	0.00
Rebuttal claim (10%)	28	5.89	4.73	9.64	1.89	−4.28	0.00
Rebuttal data (25%)	28	6.25	6.86	17.59	4.98	−9.12	0.00
Total points (100%)	28	49.11	15.81	80.54	8.34	−13.63	0.00

Students' reflection and interview data uncovered two factors facilitative of argumentative writing. For one thing, the focus on argument throughout the course helped students understand the argumentative elements and translate them into practice, as these representative student comments indicate:

☐ *Teacher explanation and text analysis gave me the standard structures of organizing argumentative writing . . . and I consciously applied them to writing later.* (Reflection)

☐ *After repetitively using these structural elements to assess others' writing and revise my own, I had a better understanding of argument.* (Interview)

Thus, the emphasis on argument in teaching, learning, and assessment activities enhanced students' understanding of the structural elements of argument and heightened their awareness of applying them to argumentative writing practice (Bacha, 2010), especially in the use of data for various purposes.

In addition, the recursive writing process provided ample opportunities for feedback and revision. Along these lines, two student comments captured this point:

☐ *I noticed my problems in the clarity, relevance, and logic of ideas and possible counterarguments . . . through peer review, teacher feedback, and reading.* (Interview)

☐ *When reading, I learnt what ideas, evidence, words, and organizational strategies others use, thought over the quality of ideas in my own writing . . . and incorporated reading to make a better argument.* (Interview)

In this sense, the interactions with the teacher, peers, and texts in the argument-based inquiry empowered students to examine argumentative elements of their writing and integrate new information and organizational strategies to improve writing. In particular, reading topic-related source texts allowed students to appropriate words, structures, and ideas (Olsen, VanDerHeide, Goff, Dunn, 2018), which greatly facilitated their efforts to learn to argue.

Impact on Students' Argumentative Skills

One-way repeated-measures analyses showed that the total number of idea units changed significantly from the initial to final essays—an average of 18.75 idea units in the 500-word drafts and 42.29 in the 1,200-word versions, $F(1$,

27) = 189.06, $p = 0.00$, $\eta_p^2 = 0.88$. This increase was not surprising, since "we had to include more ideas, evidence, and counterarguments from reading texts and peers to extend the 500-word essay to a convincing essay of more than 1,200 words" (Reflection). Namely, extending texts was likely to push students to inquire into the problem, make intertextual connections, and incorporate new ideas to enrich their argument (Bean, 2011). However, while the increased length of their essay created the opportunity for this "push," students still had to execute it, and the results presented in Table 10.1 show that they embraced that opportunity. Meanwhile, text analysis revealed little change in the "no-argument" category in 500-word drafts (M=0.54) and 1,200-word essays (M=0.36), $F(1, 27) = 0.45$, $p = 0.49$, $\eta_p^2 = 0.02$, suggesting that the essays were mainly devoted to argumentative elements. To provide a direct comparison of students' argumentative skills, Table 10.2 compares the mean of idea units that served each argumentative function and the percentage of students who included each type of evidence-based functional unit at least once in argumentative essays.

As shown in Table 10.2, "support-own" statements (M+) were the most prevalent, which suggests that students focused on presenting positive attributes of their favored position—that is, supporting their claim (e.g., Iordanou et al., 2019). All the students included "support-own" statements, and there was a significant increase in its average number—10.46 in the initial 500-word draft to 24.96 in the final 1,200-word essay, $F(1, 27) = 125.65$, $p = 0.00$, $\eta_p^2 = 0.82$. The prevalence of support-own statements partly corroborated Christensen-Branum, Strong, and Jones's (2018) claim that

Table 10.2

The Use of Evidence-Based Functional Units in 500-Word and 1200-Word Essays

	N	M+		O-		O+		M-	
		M	P	M	P	M	P	M	P
500-word argument	28	10.46	100%	5.93	92.86%	1.68	71.43%	0.14	10.71%
1200-word argument	28	24.96	100%	11.93	100%	3.18	96.43%	1.86	71.43%

Note. M= the mean number of evidence-based idea units per essay, and P=the percentage of students who included the type of functional evidence-based claim in their writing.

people tend to choose evidence that validates their existing opinions. The second most frequent were "weaken-other" (O-) statements, accounting for 8.95 percent and 28.21 percent of the initial and final essays. The average number of weaken-other statements also significantly increased, $F(1, 27) = 33.94$, $p = 0.00$, $\eta_p^2 = 0.56$. While 92.86 percent of students included both support-own and weaken-other statements in the 500-word argument, all of them incorporated both in the 1,200-word argument. This was significant, as earlier studies have revealed rare attention to opposing positions in students' argumentation (e.g., Kuhn & Crowell, 2011). The juxtaposition of support-own and weaken-other statements revealed students' growing dual-perspective thinking in 1,200-word essays, which "requires assuming a stance contrary to one's own and reasoning about its implications" (Kuhn & Crowell, 2011, p. 546). In other words, the students improved in seeing both sides of an argument.

Compared with support-own and weaken-other statements, the use of "support-other" (O+) and "weaken-own" (M-) statements demonstrated less gain, echoing the developmental progression of argumentative skills (e.g., Kuhn et al., 2016b). In the 500-word argumentative essays, 71.43 percent of students made support-other statements, but their use was very low—a mean of 1.68. After participating in argument-focused activities, the mean increased significantly to 3.18 in the 1,200-word essays, $F(1, 27) = 7.91$, $p = 0.01$, $\eta_p^2 = 0.23$. Similarly, weaken-own statements were negligible in the 500-word essays and mentioned only by 10.71 percent of the students. In the final essays, however, 71.43 percent of students included weaken-own statements, and the average number of such statements ascended significantly from 0.14 to 1.86, $F(1, 27) = 17.67$, $p = 0.00$, $\eta_p^2 = 0.40$. While the increase in the average number of support-other and weaken-other statements was much less than support-own and weaken-other statements, their increases reflected students' growing ability to address evidence incongruent with their favoured position (Iordanou et al., 2019) and the slow emergence of an integrative perspective in thinking, which "gives voice to a set of arguments that lead in opposing directions" (Kuhn & Crowell, 2011, p. 546).

On the whole, the changes in students' argumentative skills were largely attributed to the instruction in argumentative elements and their engagement in argumentation in argument-based inquiry. As one student explained, the explicit teaching of argumentative elements inspired him "to purposively search for counterargument and evidence" (Interview), and thus contributed to dual-perspective thinking. At the same time, the opportunities for argumentation enabled him to "continuingly dig into the problem" (Interview), reflect on his initial argument, and integrate newly received knowledge from peers, source texts, and the teacher into the pre-existing knowledge system to transform thinking (Iordanou et al., 2019). As he said, "We should extract valuable evidence and ideas from both sides to develop our own argument" (Reflection), indicating a shift to more integrative reasoning.

The Possible Transfer of Argumentative Learning

An important element in teaching learning to argue and arguing to learn is promoting students' transfer of that learning to other writing situations. In our study, we did not measure transfer of argumentative learning, but we were interested in whether that possibility emerged. All of the six students interviewed mentioned the transfer of argumentative learning to other tasks and contexts, as exemplified by this comment:

❏ *When writing the term paper of the management course, I first searched evidence for and against my viewpoint, and considered how others may refute my points and how to respond to them. Then, I used the argumentative structure to logically organize the thoughts.* (Interview)

Echoing the previous research on argumentative learning (e.g., Kuhn & Crowell, 2011), most of these students reported a possible transfer of argumentative learning (e.g., addressing the opposing position and logically organizing ideas) to other contexts. The interview data revealed two potential cognitive and affective factors for the transfer: argument schema and the joy of inquiry. First, most of the interviewees internalized the structural and normative aspects of arguments—argument schema (Christensen-Branum, Strong, & Jones, 2018)—at the end of the study. Possession of such schema created a foundation from which transfer of their argumentative learning could occur, and that is an important goal of argumentative instruction: to instantiate the argument schema. The next interview excerpt suggests that this potential for transfer had been generated:

❏ *The reflective task allowed me to systemize the thinking process and strategies I had undertaken unconsciously in the writing process. . . . These successful strategies actually become a thinking mode which I can use in the future.* (Interview)

Thus, the engagement in argument-focused activities and reflective tasks allowed students to construct their own understanding of argument and develop "successful strategies" or "proactive executive control strategies" (Nussbaum & Asterhan, 2016) for dealing with argument-relevant information in similar circumstances (e.g., writing assignments in other courses).

Second, the joy of inquiry the interviewees experienced in the course motivated many of them to engage in argumentative practices in ways that could also lead to transfer of argumentative learning, as reflected here:

☐ *The teacher encouraged us to explore and construct our argument on interesting topics. I really enjoyed this process of inquiry and independent thinking . . . and I want to do more things like this.* (Interview)

The enjoyable experience of inquiring into the topic of interest fostered these students' positive beliefs about argumentation, which in turn prompted them to consider the possibility of engaging in the effortful argumentative reasoning in the future.

Implications and Closing Thoughts

In contrast to research emphasizing students' learning to argue (e.g., Bacha, 2010) and advocating for arguing to learn (e.g., Iordanou et al., 2019), this study took an integrative approach to help students learn to argue and argue to learn simultaneously in the EFL writing classroom. Through an explicit focus on argument in the process-oriented writing classroom, students familiarized themselves with argumentative elements and applied them to construct arguments in their efforts to learn to argue. In the process, they appeared to acquire argument schema available for future use. Consistent with research on arguing to learn (e.g., Kuhn & Crowell, 2011), the argument-focused activities, especially dialogical argumenta-tion, allowed students to engage deeply with the content surrounding their topic and use argumentative elements to enter into sophisticated analyses of and dialogues with the topic, wherein they sharpened argumentative skills (e.g., addressing evidence weakening one's position). By helping students to internalize the argument schema and experience the joy of inquiry, the argument-based inquiry in this study may also enable students to transfer argumentative learning to other contexts. Worthy of note is that such transfer might not have taken place for all the students, since only six students who included detailed accounts about argumentative learning in the reflection were interviewed and the transfer writing tasks the students mentioned were not examined in the study. Still, the data suggested the possibility of transfer of learning.

Although it is not the intention of this chapter to make generalizations based on the findings of a small sample, several tentative implications can be generated for argumentative writing instruction in EFL classrooms from the study we conducted. First, EFL teachers aiming at blending learning to argue and arguing to learn can intentionally embed argument in the teaching, learning, and assessment activities in the recursive writing process. Before writing, teachers might focus more on learning to argue by taking inductive and deductive steps (e.g., exemplars) to introduce argumentative elements (i.e., Step 1 of the argument-based inquiry). Students would then apply them to construct their argument on intriguing problems. This inquiry process not only provides opportunities to write and to deepen students' understanding of argument (learning to argue) but also expands their understanding of a topic and sharpens argumentative skills (arguing to learn), hence helping them learn to argue and argue to learn. After writing, students can reflect on their argumentative learning to enhance their metacognitive understanding of argument and promote transfer (Nussbaum & Asterhan, 2016)—an essential aspect of arguing to learn (Hemberger et al., 2017).

Second, this study shows that students' engagement with source texts, peers, and teachers helped them to borrow lexis, organizational structures, and ideas to improve their argumentative essays (learning to ague) and to shift from my-side reasoning to more integrative reasoning (arguing to learn). Teachers thus might pay more attention to such interactions in EFL writing classrooms and engage students in dialogical argumentation—for example, Steps 4 and 7 in the argument-based inquiry (Bloome et al., 2020; Kuhn & Crowell, 2011).

Third, the result revealed less gain in statements that address the opponents' merits and one's weaknesses than support-own and weaken-other statements, since reconciling evidence incongruent with writers' position is cognitively demanding (Kuhn et al., 2016b). Thus, more attention can be paid to scaffolding students' ability to address the evidence against their favored position. For instance, teachers can emphasize counterarguments and rebuttals in argumentative practices (Abdollahzadeh et al., 2017) or include a prompt to remind students of the incongruent evidence (Iordanou et al., 2019).

Last, teachers may attend to both cognitive and motivational aspects of argument to enhance the possibility of students' transfer of argumentative learning to other contexts (Kuhn & Crowell, 2011). Teachers can create an active, reflective learning environment (e.g., Step 9 of the argument-based inquiry) to help students experience the joy of inquiry and form their argument schema.

The study is not without limitations. First, since no control group was set up, it is difficult to detect the exact relationship among the change in students' idea units, text length (i.e., 500-word essay and 1,200-word essay), and the argument-based inquiry adopted in this study. Also, the present study merely relied on students' self-reported data to investigate the transfer of argumentative learning and did not track and analyze students' work in other contexts after the pedagogical intervention. Future research can conduct pedagogical experiments to explore the effects of argument-based inquiry on students' argumentative learning and its transfer over a longer period.

REFERENCES

Abdollahzadeh, E., Farsani, M. A., & Beikmohammadi, M. (2017). Argumentative writing behavior of graduate EFL learners. *Argumentation, 31*(4), 641–661.

Bacha, N. (2010). Teaching the academic argument in a university EFL environment. *Journal of English for Academic Purposes, 9*(3), 229–241.

Barnet, S., & Bedau, H. A. (2014). *Critical thinking, reading, and writing: A brief guide to argument* (8th ed.). Boston: Bedford/St. Martin's.

Bean, J. C. (2011). *Engaging ideas: The professor's guide to integrating writing, critical thinking, and active learning in the classroom* (2nd ed.). San Francisco: John Wiley & Sons.

Bloome, D., Newell, G., Hirvela, A. &., & Lin, T. J. (2020). *Dialogic literary argumentation in high school language arts classrooms: A social perspective for teaching, learning, and reading literature.* New York: Routledge.

Christensen-Branum, L., Strong, A., & Jones, C. D. O. (2018). Mitigating myside bias in argumentation. *Journal of Adolescent & Adult Literacy, 62*(4), 435–445.

Hand, B., Norton-Meier, L., & Jang, J. (2017). Examining the impact of an argument-based inquiry on the development of students' learning in international contexts. In B. Hand, L. Norton-Meier & J. Jang (Eds.), *More voices from the classroom: International teachers' experience with argument-based inquiry* (pp. 1–9). Rotterdam, the Netherlands: Sense Publishers.

Hemberger, L., Kuhn, D., Matos, F., & Shi, Y. (2017). A dialogic path to evidence-based argumentative writing. *The Journal of the Learning Sciences, 26*(4), 575–607.

Hirvela, A. (2017). Argumentation & second language writing: Are we missing the boat? *Journal of Second Language Writing, 36*, 69–74.

Iordanou, K., Kuhn, D., Matos, F., Shi, Y., & Hemberger, L. (2019). Learning by arguing. *Learning and Instruction, 63*, 101–107.

Jang, J., & Hand, B. (2017). Examining the value of a scaffolded critique framework to promote argumentative and explanatory writings within an argument-based inquiry approach. *Research in Science Education*, *47*(6), 1213–1231.

Jonassen, D. H., & Kim, B. (2010). Arguing to learn and learning to argue: Design justifications and guidelines. *Educational Technology Research and Development*, *58*(4), 439–457.

Kuhn, D. (2018). A role for reasoning in a dialogic approach to critical thinking. *Topoi*, *37*(1), 121–128.

Kuhn, D., & Crowell, A. (2011). Dialogic argumentation as a vehicle for developing young adolescents' thinking. *Psychological Science*, *22*(4), 545–552.

Kuhn, D., Hemberger, L., & Khait, V. (2016a). *Argue with me: Argument as a path to developing students' thinking and writing*. New York: Routledge.

Kuhn, D., Hemberger, L., & Khait, V. (2016b). Tracing the development of argumentative writing in a discourse-rich context. *Written Communication*, *33*(1), 92–121.

Newell, G. E., Bloome, D., & Hirvela, A. (2015). *Teaching and learning argumentative writing in high school English language arts classrooms*. New York: Routledge.

Nussbaum, E. M., & Asterhan, C. S. (2016). The psychology of far transfer from classroom argumentation. In F. Paglieri (Ed.), *The psychology of argument: Cognitive approaches to argumentation and persuasion* (pp. 407–423). London: College Publications.

Olsen, A. W., VanDerHeide, J., Goff, B., & Dunn, M. B. (2018). Examining intertextual connections in written arguments: A study of student writing as social participation and response. *Written Communication*, *35*(1), 58–88.

Qin, J., & Karabacak, E. (2010). The analysis of Toulmin elements in Chinese EFL university argumentative writing. *System*, *38*(3), 444–456.

Sampson, V., Grooms, J., & Walker, J. P. (2010). Argument-Driven Inquiry as a way to help students learn how to participate in scientific argumentation and craft written arguments: An exploratory study. *Science Education*, *95*(2), 217–257.

Stapleton, P., & Wu, Y. A. (2015). Assessing the quality of arguments in students' persuasive writing: A case study analyzing the relationship between surface structure and substance. *Journal of English for Academic Purposes*, *17*, 12–23.

Toulmin, S. E. (1958). *The uses of argument*. New York: Cambridge University Press.

Walker, J. P., & Sampson, V. (2013). Learning to argue and arguing to learn: Argument-driven inquiry as a way to help undergraduate chemistry students learn how to construct arguments and engage in argumentation during a laboratory course. *Journal of Research in Science Teaching,* *50*(5), 561–596.

APPENDIX 10A

Part 1: The Prompt for the 500-Word Essay

Please choose one of the following questions to write an essay of about 500 words.

1. Should those children who can learn quickly be taught separately or together with other students?
2. Students in university should specialize in one subject rather than to develop a wider range of subjects. To what extent do you agree or disagree?
3. In the past, the role of teacher was to provide information. Today, students have access to wide sources of information. There is, therefore, no role of teacher in modern education. Do you agree or disagree?

Part 2: The Prompt for the 1,200-Word Essay

Based on your reading of topic-related articles and discussions with group members, please further develop your 500-word essay to 1,200 words by considering the following elements:

1. new arguments and ideas related to the issue
2. possible counterarguments that challenge your arguments
3. examples, statistics, and other evidences which support your arguments and/or counterarguments

11

An Action Research Study Aimed at Improving Chinese High School Students' Argumentation in EFL Writing

QILING WU AND ZEHANG CHEN

Abstract

The issue of ability to persuade readers of the validity of writers' arguments has received considerable attention from L2 writing researchers. The current study explores practical ways to support high school EFL students' development of argumentative writing skills in China through an eleven-week action research project. The results suggest that students' overall argumentation ability has increased and the study indicates the importance of integration of structural aspects of arguments with an emphasis on reasoning processes in order to develop students' thinking capacity.

In today's world, the ability to write effective argumentative essays is beneficial in various ways. However, research has consistently shown that many students struggle with such writing, including the language necessary to convey arguments successfully (e.g., Perin et al., 2017). At the same time, argumentation plays an important role in prominent assessments of writing ability (Hirvela, 2017) and is increasingly emphasized in recent curriculum reforms across many countries, such as the Common Core State Standards Initiative (2010) in the United States.

Studies of L2 writing have led to a deep exploration of the structure of argumentative writing. One possible argument framework or schema might include arguments, counterarguments, and refutation (Piolat, Roussey, &

Gombert, 1999); another is Toulmin's (2003) frequently cited model featuring six elements of argumentation, namely claim, data, warrant, backing, qualifier, and rebuttal. **Claim** is the assertion one wishes to prove; **data** refers to rationale or evidence for the claim; **warrant** is the underlying connection between the claim and data; **backing** tells the readers why the warrant is a rational one; **qualifier** places limits on the strength of the claim; and **rebuttal** addresses potential objections to the claim. A simplified version featuring claim, data, and warrant, called the Claim-Evidence-Explanation (CEE) model in current research, has also been applied in argumentative studies (e.g., Erduran, Simon, & Osborne, 2004).

These models are useful in guiding students to understand core elements of argumentation. However, an overemphasis on teaching the structure of an argument may lead to the neglect of logic—that is, insufficient awareness of the importance of reasoning in argumentation. Thus, some researchers have stressed the importance of accounting for both the reasoning nature of an argument and its surface structure (e.g., Stapleton & Wu, 2015; Wen & Liu, 2006). In China, where this study reported took place, argumentation is also emphasized with respect to critical-thinking ability among the key competencies for high school English learners to acquire contained in the National English Curriculum Standards (2017) produced by the Chinese Ministry of Education (MOE). Thus, building on the need to include both the structure and content of arguments and a growing interest in the infusion of critical-thinking ability in language learning and writing instruction in China, this chapter examines the impact of an action research project featuring an instructional intervention intended to improve the quality of Chinese students' argumentative reasoning and writing.

Argumentation: Structure Application and Reasoning Ability

Argument can be seen as "a reasoned, logical way of demonstrating that the writer's position, belief, or conclusion is valid" (CCSS, 2010, Appendix, pp. 23). Argument is also often characterized as "using reasons to support a point of view, so that known or unknown audiences may be persuaded to agree" (Cottrell, 2017, p. 52). We agree that reasoning and argumentation are closely related, but we also agree with the idea that argument is "predictive of counterarguments" (Newell, VanDerHeide, & Wynhoff Olsen, 2014). In other words, an argumentative essay is not only meant to present a viewpoint in a reasoned way but also to approach arguments from a communicative perspective to convince those readers potentially holding alternative or opposite views of the claim. This orientation underscores the importance of teaching constructs of argument, counterargument, and rebuttal.

In research on argumentative writing, it is well established that understanding argument structure contributes to students' expressing their views in a more logical way (e.g., O'Hallaron, 2014). However, to account for the quality of content in argumentative writing, some researchers in the field of L2 writing have added the concept of informal reasoning to their approach. Informal reasoning is a "goal-dependent process that involves generating or evaluating evidence (or both) pertaining to a claim or conclusion" (Means & Voss, 1996, pp. 141). Some scholars assert that informal reasoning is inextricably linked to argumentation. For example, Mercier and Sperber (2011, p. 57) state that the "main function of reasoning is argumentative," as "people are skilled arguers, using reasoning both to evaluate and to produce arguments in argumentative contexts." Put simply, when people make arguments in their daily conversations or in written forms, they consciously or unconsciously activate the reasoning mechanism by arguing for their claims and assessing these arguments. Thus, adopting Sandoval and Millwood's (2005) definition, we treat argumentation as the ability to make effective judgments about the structure of arguments and to engage in successful informal reasoning. The intervention examined in this chapter was built on this view of argumentation.

With recognition of the significance of knowledge of structure and reasoning ability contributing to the quality of arguments, there is an emerging consensus that assessment of informal reasoning through writing is also important. For example, some researchers have put forward the term *acceptability*, which refers to the degree to which a reason can be reasonably accepted and "whether the reason supports the conclusion, sometimes termed relevance" (Means and Voss, 1996, p. 141). Related research has examined the overall number of reasons used in support of a claim and the reasons supporting counterarguments (Schwarz, Neuman, Gil, & Ilya, 2003), and the adequacy of premises to support the conclusion or claim (Hughes & Lavery, 2015). Thus, to assess students' argumentative writing ability, some current research advocates a combined focus on elements of argumentative writing and on the acceptability, relevance, and sufficiency of reasoning to reflect students' argumentation ability in general. Our intervention was inspired by this approach.

Instruction Aimed at Improving Argumentative Writing

Among pedagogical attempts to improve students' argumentative writing, O'Hallaron's (2014) study is frequently cited. In that classroom-based study, the teacher gave students explicit instruction regarding structural elements and stages of the argumentative writing process involving instructional scaffolding of learning. Moving in a different direction, Resnick et al. (1993) stressed the importance of counterargument and found that participants "appear to build complex arguments and attack structure. People appear to be capable of recognizing these structures and of effectively attacking their individual components as well as the argument as a whole" (pp. 362–363), thus expanding their reasoning ability.

Another promising direction has been seen in studies where students are taught strategies for diagram application that enable them to graphically portray their argumentation. For instance, Hughes and Lavery (2015) investigated a model that featured what they called T arguments, V arguments, and complex arguments. **T arguments** are used when the combination of two premises provides support for a conclusion. **V arguments** are presented when separate reasons are offered in support of the conclusion, while **complex arguments** refer to the situation in which a first premise supports the second premise.

In other research, Osborne et al. (2001) worked with middle school science teachers in the United Kingdom to develop interactive activities to strengthen argumentative thinking and reasoning. Students worked in groups exploring the truthfulness of data and evaluating the relevancy of data to claims and conclusions. Mason (1996) focused on students' collaborative work and peer interaction as they dealt with task structuring and modeling.

In China, there has been some recent research on argumentative writing, including an increasing focus on critical thinking. First, evidence shows that Chinese students often lack well-developed argumentation skills (Chen, Zou, Li, & Chen, 2016; Du, 2008), especially in effectively developing sound evidence and considering alternative arguments. Second, some scholars have examined the effects of certain kinds of instruction on students' argumentative writing, such as asynchronous debate used to enhance critical-thinking and writing ability (Liu, Wu & Shieh, 2015), scaffolding through collaborative study (Wu & Rubin, 2000), and training in audience awareness, logical fallacy identification, and correction (Li, 2011). The results of these studies showed that these approaches were somewhat effective in helping students improve their argumentative writing performance.

However, the primary focus of such research has been on college students; very little research has looked at how to improve students' argumentation in high school contexts. Although there is less emphasis on argumentative writing in high school compared to college in China, it is important to develop students' thinking through learning how to argue reasonably and logically. Thus, we decided to conduct an action research project aimed at fostering high school students' argumentative writing through a combined emphasis on teaching structure and reasoning while seeking to answer these research questions:

1. Can students' argumentative writing improve through an intervention featuring a structural orientation and an emphasis on informal reasoning? If so, how has their argumentative writing improved?

2. What specific knowledge about argumentation did the students gain? Were there differences in how students responded to the two elements of the intervention (emphasis on structure and emphasis on informal reasoning)? Was this an effective combination?

Methods

The 27 participants of the study were 16- and 17-year-old students in one class at a high school in Beijing. At the time this study was conducted, these students had just started the second semester of their first year in high school and one author (Wu) was their English teacher. Their average English proficiency was at an intermediate level among high school students in Beijing. Before the study, they had not been taught argumentation or reasoning, and this was their first chance to learn about it and to write argumentative essays in English.

At the initial stage of the intervention, students' argumentative writing abilities were tested and analyzed. Students were asked to write an argumentative essay at least 120 words in length outside class on the topic, *Is parental stress on academic achievement good for children or not? Why or why not?* The writing assignment was given on a Friday, and it was collected on the following Monday so that students had enough time to plan, organize, search for evidence, write, and revise. This was in essence a diagnostic as well as pre-test essay that allowed us to identify students' strengths and weaknesses. We analyzed students' writing and identified these problems in their writing: (1) the structure of students' writing was vague; (2) most students' reasoning process was not sound; (3) there was no linking of reasons with their claims; and (4) a lack of counterargument and rebuttal were common in nearly all the students' writing.

In the 11-week action research project that followed, and in response to the problems identified, we then implemented our intervention, which comprised two phases of instruction: how to reason and how to argue. The reasoning activities involved students in analyzing logic structures of English paragraphs; acknowledging claim, evidence, and explanation; and listing possible statements to strengthen or weaken an assertion. This stage occurred during the first three weeks of the instructional period. Following this emphasis on reasoning, there was instruction for eight weeks on how to argue—that is, how to construct an argument in writing. This included planning structure(s) for an essay, evaluating quality of evidence, and practicing counter arguments.

Soon after the instructional period ended, students were required to write an essay on the same topic as in the diagnostic test: *Is parental stress on academic achievement good for children or not? Why or why not?* Here, again, there was a minimum of 120 words, and the essay was written outside class. We believed that by comparing students' writing before and after the intervention and on the same topic, convincing conclusions could be obtained regarding the degree of students' improvement on argumentation.

Data gathered included individual interviews with ten students, teacher Wu's weekly journal entries, and students' essays. Based on Yeh's (1998) holistic scoring rubric to assess general argumentation, we rated students' essays with a relatively high inter-rater agreement (Cohen Kappa= 0.83, 95 percent confidence interval= 0.67, 1.00, P <0.001) with a total score of 6.0. Each essay was also content coded following Stapleton and Wu's (2015, pp. 18) analytic template of scripts, which included number of Toulmin-like elements, original sentences stating the key points, quality of data, and number of reasons at each quality level.

Implementation of the Action Research Plan

A more detailed description of our two-stage instructional intervention follows.

Learn How to Reason

During this initial three-week stage, students participated in reasoning activities to identify claim, evidence, and explanation based on the claim-evidence-explanation (CEE) model. In Week 1, sample paragraphs were extracted from textbooks, journals, and newspapers. After students read all these samples, they summarized features of good reasoning to strengthen their understanding of the CEE model. In addition to the CEE model, the teacher also introduced students to reasoning statements with more complicated structures in Week 2, such as the T structure, V structure, and complex structure mentioned in Hughes and Lavery's (2015) study. The students were also taught how to draw a tree diagram involving claim, evidence, and explanation. In Week 3, students were assigned to list possible statements to strengthen or weaken an assertion on various topics.

Learn How to Argue

During the second stage, comprising eight weeks of instruction, the students practiced argumentative thinking, or reasoning, and writing. In Week 4, a movie clip from "The Great Debaters" was used to reveal main features of an effective argument—logical coherency, factual accuracy, and emotional appeal. The students were also required to draw mind maps to present logic employed in the debates. In Week 5, students discussed two essays, "Can Television Be Considered Literature and Taught in English Classes?" and "The Rule of the Road," and analyzed the structure of argumentative essays— introduction, argument, counterargument, rebuttal, and conclusion. The teacher then provided detailed instruction concerning the structure of an argumentative essay from Week 6 to Week 9. Much of this time was spent on modeling writing (Mason, 1996), during which she used the method of think-aloud to present how she proposed claim, counterargument, and rebuttal; evaluated quality of data for each claim; and applied the CEE model to guide paragraph writing. The quality of data was assessed based on the relevance and acceptability of the reasons following Stapleton and Wu's (2015) research and was labeled as "acceptable," "weak or vague," "not acceptable," and "not relevant." In addition, to strengthen students' counterargument awareness, the teacher designed an "I Understand, But I Don't Agree" role-play activity. In this activity, which reflected some real-life situations, Student A presented a claim and gave supporting reasons, and then Student B restated student A's reasons by using the phrase *I understand that . . ., but I don't agree* followed by counterargument reasons.

In Weeks 3, 7, and 8, students also had argumentative writing practice based on these topics: *Is having a dream important? Which do you prefer, being a big fish in a small pond or being a small fish in a big pond? Is marriage good for you?* The teacher provided oral feedback on their writing. In Week10, students were assigned to write an argumentative essay after choosing a topic among 10 options, such as *Do Violent Video Games Contribute to Youth Violence?* or *Should Euthanasia or Physician-Assisted Suicide Be Legal?* The essay was to be at least 120 words in length. Before the students started to write, the teacher arranged group debates. Students chose one topic and formed groups with those who were interested in the same topic. To prepare for the debates, students formed their own stance on their topic, planned debating structures, and listed strong evidence to support their claims and rebut possible counterarguments. Thus, when they eventually shifted to writing on their topic after the debates, they were expected to feel confident, especially about their counterargument and rebuttal paragraphs. Before handing in the essays, students received Stapleton and Wu's (2015) analytic template for self-editing. After that, the teacher gave oral and written feedback on students' writing, including quality of structure, and the relevance, acceptability, and quantity of evidence used.

Data Analysis and Discussion

Results with respect to analysis of the students' argumentative writing are presented next, followed by an examination of the interview data.

Effects on Students' Argumentation in General

To assess students' argumentative competence, we used holistic scoring criteria adopted from Yeh's (1998) six-point rubric. The results are listed in Table 11.1, which compares students' essays before and after the project. The table shows that students' argumentation ability improved significantly ($p = .000$) after the instructional period, with an average score of 4.519, while students averaged only 3.685 points before the action research took place.

Table 11.1

Changes in Argumentation of Students' Writing before Research and after Research

		Average	Standard Deviation	Standard Error	t	sig. (2-tailed)
overall score of argumentation	before the study	3.685	.7984	.1537	−5.204	.000
	after the study	4.519	.7530	.1449		

To obtain a more fine-grained analysis of the results, based on students' English scores in the high school entrance examination, which is a very important test for senior high schools to select students with high validity and reliability designed carefully by experts and distributed by the city educational bureau, the 27 students were divided into three groups: lower-proficiency, medium proficiency, and advanced proficiency. The average improvement for each group was 0.833, 0.889, and 0.778, respectively. In other words, students of medium language proficiency and lower language proficiency showed more improvement compared with students of advanced English proficiency.

Effects on Students' Inclusion of Argumentative Elements

We also examined students' improvement in the inclusion of different argumentative elements. The four argumentative elements refer to claim, data, counterargument, and rebuttal, so the maximum score would be 4.0. As shown in Table 11.2, the average number of argumentative elements used before the intervention was 2.37, and it increased to 3.67 later (p= .000). Each student added 1.34 elements on average.

As for performance by groups, the average increase for the lower-proficiency group was 1, for medium proficiency it was 1.333, and for higher proficiency it was 1.556. The results indicate that students of advanced language proficiency and medium proficiency were more likely to add more argumentative elements, counterargument, and rebuttal in particular. However, these findings need to be treated with caution, as several students from the lower-proficiency group reported that compared with adding a rebuttal paragraph, they preferred to spend more time on revising their reasoning paragraphs. For instance, student MJ said that, "Miss Wu, we already have too much homework now, you know. So each time when I finished writing the reasoning paragraph, it was already over 120 words. I did not have motivation

Table 11.2

Changes in Numbers of Argumentative Elements before and after Research

		Average	Standard Deviation	Standard Error	t	sig. (2-tailed)
number of elements	Before the study	2.37	.742	.141	−6.310	.000
	after the study	3.67	1.155	.222		

to write more. Instead, I worried more about my vocabulary and grammar, and so I went back to review the reasoning paragraph." Accordingly, teacher Wu, in her reflective journals, noted that "the practice of building only one reasoning paragraph might be a good beginning for novice writers as it can bring students to the depth of relationship between adjacent sentences, among all the sentences in one paragraph, and then lead to other reasoning structures."

Effects on Students' Reasoning Ability

Reasoning ability was mainly measured in three ways: by sufficiency, acceptability, and relevance of reasons. **Sufficiency** was measured strictly by times students cited reasons. **Acceptability** refers to soundness of whether a reason can be reasonably accepted, and the term **relevance** means whether the reason supports the conclusion. By comparing average times students cited reasons and quality of reasons, we explored overall improvement in students' reasoning ability. Therefore, next sufficiency is examined.

Table 11.3 shows that before the intervention, the average number of times students cited reasons was 2.11, while after the intervention it rose to 3.41 (p= .000). Looked at another way, students cited reasons 57 times at the beginning, while after the intervention, the total number rose to 92 times. Here, it needs to be noted that the same reasons may have been used more than once by students either before or after the research, respectively, with 28 and 53 completely different reasons appearing in their essays. The data shows that students improved on not only quantity of times they cited reasons but also in variety of reasons they proposed.

The average increase of times students cited reasons for the lower-proficiency group was 1.556, for medium proficiency it was 0.667, and for higher proficiency it was 1.667. The results indicate that students at the advanced and lower proficiency levels tended to cite more reasons after the intervention compared with those at the medium level. More specifically,

Table 11.3

Changes in Numbers of Reasons before and after Research

		Average	Standard Deviation	Standard Error	t	sig. (2-tailed)
number of reasons	before the study	2.11	1.155	.222	–5.456	.000
	after the study	3.41	.797	.153		

the medium-proficiency students were more inclined to use reasons before the intervention: 2.7 reasons on average compared to 1.7 for the advanced group and 2.0 for the lower group in the diagnostic essay. The explanation for this difference was that the medium-proficiency students were inclined to think more about the issue of essay length—that is, the longer the essay, the better. In this way they could compensate for not having a higher level of proficiency. As a result, they had less need to increase their use of reasons after the intervention. For instance, medium-proficiency student RY said, "I used to write as many as possible because the reviewers might give me more scores on working so hard." On the other hand, her advanced group classmate, ZX, said, "It does not matter how much you say, but how well you say it. So I would only explain 1 reason with simply 120 words. Now even though I still hold the same idea, I tend to use more words and more reasons to make my essay more persuasive. That way I even wrote over 400 words."

In addition to times students cited reasons, significant changes were also identified in the quality of reasons assessed by the number of acceptable and relevant reasons used, as depicted in Table 11.4. To achieve this, we labeled all these reasons independently as "acceptable," "weak or vague," "not acceptable", and "not relevant" following Stapleton and Wu's (2015) study. Specifically, the relevance of the reasons refers to whether the data is relevant to the claim. The acceptability presents the degree to which the reason is logical in supporting the claim. We consolidated the content coding of all the reasons from inter-rater checks and discussion. The inter-rater reliability coefficient was 75 percent, and differences were resolved via discussion.

Before the intervention, 74 percent of the reasons provided (among the 57 cited) were deemed acceptable, and the average number of acceptable reasons in students' writing was 1.56, while after the intervention, the average of acceptable reasons rose to 81.5 percent among 92 reasons used.

Table 11.4

Changes in Numbers of Acceptable Reasons before and after Research

		Average	Standard Deviation	Standard Error	t	sig. (2-tailed)
number of acceptable reasons	before the study	1.56	.934	.180	–4.158	.000
	after the study	2.78	1.476	.284		

The average post-intervention number was 2.78 (p=.000). On average, each student added 1.22 acceptable reasons into their argumentative writing. The average improvement for the lower-proficiency group was 1.111, for medium proficiency it was 1.556, and for higher proficiency it was 1. In other words, the highest level of improvement was among medium-proficiency students. Improvement among all three groups suggests effectiveness of instruction about how to reason, including the CEE model, T structure and V structure, and logic strength.

Students' Gains in Knowledge about Argumentation

Based on the analysis of students' interviews, we examined the specific knowledge about argumentation and argumentative writing students gained. The frequency of elements mentioned by them was used to show what knowledge they remembered better and therefore indicate a positive effect of the project. The results are shown in Table 11.5, and the texts in the parentheses represent actual words from students.

In terms of notable comments, all the 10 interviewees mentioned counterargument. Students highly acknowledged the usefulness of counterargument and showed us how they benefited from learning about it. For instance, student RY said,

Table 11.5

Argumentative Writing Structure Knowledge

Category	No.
Argumentative Writing Structure	28
introduction (social phenomena, clear statement)	2
argument (introduction-Argument1-Argument 2-counterrebuttal-conclusion, word number)	2
counterargument (list pros and cons, evaluate, two spiritual figures in mind, more persuasive, subjective, from other side, more words, used at home)	10
rebuttal (hard to argue, word limit)	2
CEE model (easy to apply, better for thinking, different from Chinese model, explanation is important, no explanation is like robot, sometimes explanation is obvious)	8
other models (T model, V model, topic too simple for the models, good pattern for thinking)	4

Note: Each category is subdivided into specific codes used to analyze interview transcripts. The number column refers to the number of students who mentioned the code in the interview.

After this semester, I feel that I became dramatic when I was writing an argumentative essay. There were often two figures in my mind. One figure stated one point and the other said the opposite point. Usually the other figure would criticize what this figure said, and the figure found faults with the other one. I think this is a good sign and shows maybe I have a little bit critical awareness, and I no longer just say that this is good and why it is good. I can think about one problem from different aspects.

Another student, ZX, became more aware of counterargument through in-class discussion. She said "I often raise many reasons, but which one is more convincing? I will question myself for many times. For example, I will think in this way: if I say this, will our classmates argue with me? What will my teacher say when she gives me feedback?"

The other item that stands out is the Claim-Evidence-Explanation (CEE model), with eight students offering positive comments about it. It was a model the students were not familiar with before the study. As student CX said, "This model is reasonable. First you state your claim, then give your example, then you link your reasons with your claim. I wonder why I did not perceive the existence of such a model in the past." It should be noted that Chinese students would already know about reasoning patterns through Chinese traditional argumentative writing, but this would be quite complex reasoning both inductive and deductive in nature. What they lacked was such knowledge in English, and the CEE model gave them that knowledge. This matches Liu and Gan's (2019) finding that "neither Chinese paragraphs nor EFL ones are similar to the modern English rhetorical paradigm, and English rhetoric instruction will facilitate the introspection of the two kinds of rhetoric" (p. 431). Thus, the introduction of such a model directly presented argumentative thinking patterns that led to the path of argumentation in English.

Compared with structure (28), students mentioned informal reasoning less frequently (17), as Table 11.6 shows. Among the three elements of reasoning ability investigated, students commented most on their increased understanding of acceptability of reasons (9). They summarized their past experiences of writing arguments as "a flow of thinking—you write as you think" where "no logic" was necessary. For instance, RY said, "In middle school, our writing task such as invitation letter is very easy and even without logic, we can gain a relatively high score." After the intervention, however, the students sensed the importance of logic in English argumentative writing. This is shown by students' increased awareness of applying reasoning models. The students also began to evaluate the truthfulness of evidence. For instance, both student MH and CY mentioned that they spent more time

Table 11.6: Informal Reasoning Knowledge

Category	No.
Reasoning Ability	17
adequacy of reasons (2 arguments, self-witness, peer stories, celebrities, logic model)	4
acceptability of reasons (logic strength, T model, V model, arguing voice, sequence of their utterances, what to include)	9
relevancy of reasons (search for evidences, internet access, topic interest)	4

Table 11.7: Knowledge Sources

Category	No.
Knowledge Sources	47
sample paragraphs and essays	6
reasoning activities	12
think aloud modelling writing	8
I understand but I do not agree because activity	8
in-class group debate	5
feedback	8

Note: The code indicates argumentation knowledge sources to which students attributed their knowledge.

in selecting what reasons to include for their argument and the sequence of their utterances to make their writing more persuasive.

Another area we looked at was how the students responded to different ways in which information about argumentation was presented during the course. Their responses are displayed in Table 11.7, which shows a much higher number of responses than for the categories already discussed. Among different categories of instruction, what stood out was reasoning activities (12), teacher's modeling writing (8), counterargument activities (8), and feedback on students' writing (8). The reasoning activities included identifying logic structures of English paragraphs; acknowledging claim, evidence, and explanation; and listing possible statements to strengthen or weaken an assertion.

The frequency count for counterargument activities matches the interest shown in counterargument displayed in Table 11.5 and so is not surprising. What is interesting is the popularity of teacher modeling and feedback. The students appreciated her modeling writing because, said student HX, "when we read an essay, even though we know it is good, we still do not know how we can write as good as the writer. However, when you are thinking aloud, we are also thinking. It offers us an opportunity to compare our thoughts with your thoughts and reflect on our thinking process." This finding corresponds with other research on the positive effects of modeling writing (e.g., Mason, 1996). Feedback may have worked in a similar way, as students read or heard another voice putting their writing in perspective, and they received extensive feedback during the intervention.

Closing Thoughts

The action research described investigated the quality of Chinese high school students' written argumentation before and after an instructional intervention. In their diagnostic essays, these common problems in students' writing were identified: the structure of students' writing was vague, students' reasoning process was not sound, and alternative opinions were ignored. After the intervention, students' argumentation ability improved in general, with more inclusion of argumentative elements and better quality of reasons used. The study also provided insights into how students with different levels of writing proficiency responded to what and how they were taught. This does not mean the students mastered argumentative writing, but it appeared that the combined focus on structure and reasoning enabled them to make progress, especially with respect to counterargument.

The results of this study suggest that Chinese high school students are ready for and can benefit from meaningful instructional exposure to argumentation in English, especially a combined focus on ways of reasoning and then structures through which that reasoning can be expressed clearly. It is hoped that this study will lead to other studies on English argumentative writing instruction in Chinese high schools.

REFERENCES

Chen, Z. H., Zou, M., Li, X. F., & Chen, S. Y. (2016). Constructing the framework of thinking ability in English writing. *Chinese Foreign Language Education, 9*(3), 11–19.

Common Core State Standards Initiative. (2010). Common core state standards for English language arts and literacy in history/social studies science, and technical subjects. Retrieved from www.corestandards.org

Cottrell, S. (2017). *Critical thinking skills: Effective analysis, argument and reflection.* London: Macmillan.

Du, Y. (2008). The intervention study on the ability of writing essays of junior three students with learning disabilities. Unpublished doctoral diss., East China Normal University, Shanghai.

Erduran, S., Simon, S., & Osborne, J. (2004). TAPping into argumentation: Developments in the application of Toulmin's argument pattern for studying science discourse. *Science Education, 88*(6), 915–933.

Hirvela, A. (2017). Argumentation & second language writing: Are we missing the boat? *Journal of Second Language Writing, 36,* 69–74.

Hughes, W., & Lavery, J. (2015). *Critical thinking: An introduction to the basic skills* (5th Ed.). Peterborough, Canada: Broadview Press.

Kirkpatrick, A. & Xu, Z. C. (2012). *Chinese rhetoric and writing: An introduction for language teachers.* Fort Collins, CO: The WAC Clearinghouse and The Parlor Press.

Li, L. (2011). An action research on how to increase reader awareness and critical thinking. *Foreign Language in China, 8*(3), 66–73.

Liu, D. H., & Gan, Q. (2019). What characterizes Chinese students' exposition besides deduction and induction?: A Comparative rhetoric perspective. *Chinese Journal of Applied Linguistics, 42*(4), 431–448.

Liu, P. E., Wu, W. V., & Shieh, R. (2015). Enhancing EFL students' critical thinking and writing: An asynchronous debate instructional design. *English Teaching and Learning, 39*(3), 33–59.

Mason, L. (1996). An analysis of children's construction of new knowledge through their use of reasoning and arguing in classroom discussions. *International Journal of Qualitative Studies in Education, 9*(4), 411–433.

Means, M. L., & Voss, J. F. (1996). Who reasons well? Two studies of informal reasoning among children of different grade, ability, and knowledge levels. *Cognition and instruction, 14*(2), 139–178.

Mercier, H., & Sperber, D. (2011). Why do humans reason? Arguments for an argumentative theory. *Behavioral and Brain Sciences, 34*(02), 57–74.

National English Curriculum Standards. (2017). Chinese Education Bureau. Retrieved from http://www.xf5z.com/ueditor/php/upload/file/20200618/1592440933237363.pdf

Newell, G. E., VanDerHeide, J., & Olsen, A. W. (2014). High school English language arts teachers' argumentative epistemologies for teaching writing. *Research in the Teaching of English, 49*(2), 95–119.

O'Hallaron, C. L. (2014). Supporting fifth-grade ELLs' argumentative writing development. *Written Communication, 31*(3), 304–331.

Osborne, J., Erduran, S., Simon, S., & Monk, M. (2001). Enhancing the quality of argument in school science. *School Science Review, 82*(3), 63–70.

Piolat, A., Roussey, J. –Y., & Gombert, A. (1999). The development of argumentative schema in writing. In. G. Rijlaarsdam & E. Esperet (Series Eds.) & J. Andriessen & P. Coirier (Vol. Eds.), *Studies in writing: Vol. 5. Foundations of argumentative text processing* (pp. 117–135). Amsterdam. The Netherlands: Amsterdam University Press.

Perin, D., Lauterbach, M., Raufman, J., & Kalamkarian, H. S. (2017). Text-based writing of low-skilled postsecondary students: Relation to comprehension, self-efficacy and teacher judgments. *Reading and Writing: An Interdisciplinary Journal, 30,* 887–915.

Resnick, L. B., Salmon, M., Zeitz, C. M., Wathen, S. H., & Holowchak, M. (1993). Reasoning in conversation. *Cognition and Instruction, 11*(3–4), 347–364.

Sandoval, W. A., & Millwood, K. A. (2005). The quality of students' use of evidence in written scientific explanations. *Cognition and Instruction, 23*(1), 23–55.

Stapleton, P., & Wu, Y. A. (2015). Assessing the quality of arguments in students' persuasive writing: A case study analyzing the relationship between surface structure and substance. *Journal of English for Academic Purposes, 17,* 12–23.

Schwarz, B. B., Neuman, Y., Gil, J., & Ilya, M. (2003). Construction of collective and individual knowledge in argumentative activity. *The Journal of the Learning Sciences, 12*(2), 219–256.

Toulmin, S. E. (2003). *The uses of argument.* Cambridge, England: Cambridge University Press.

Wen, Q. F., & Liu, R. Q. (2006). Analysis of the characteristics of college students' abstract thinking from English argumentative papers. *Foreign Languages (Journal of Shanghai International Studies University), 2*(1), 49–58.

Wu, S. Y., & Rubin, D. L. (2000). Evaluating the impact of collectivism and individualism on argumentative writing by Chinese and North American college students. *Research in the Teaching of English, 35,* 148–178.

Yeh, S. S. (1998). Empowering education: Teaching argumentative writing to cultural minority middle-school students. *Research in the Teaching of English, 33,* 49–83.

12

The Argumentative Essay from Multiple Sources: Genre-Based Instruction to Foster Autonomy in EFL Academic Literacy

NATALIA VERONICA DALLA COSTA

Abstract

This chapter reports the results of a study conducted to foster autonomy in EFL academic literacy. The specific objective was to evaluate whether genre-based instruction in argumentative essay writing utilizing multiple sources has positive effects on students' performance, self-perceived abilities, and attitudes. A quasi-experimental design with quantitative and qualitative methods was employed. Participants were one instructor, two raters, and 79 advanced EFL students. The results reveal that genre-based instruction is an effective pedagogical tool in the context of the study to develop students' skills to draw from sources when generating argumentative essays.

Literacy in EFL, particularly the ability to integrate information obtained from reading into text production, is essential in academic contexts. So, too, is the ability to produce written arguments that make effective use of source text material. Consequently, there is a need to provide instruction that focuses on writing from sources, which enables students to justify their arguments and transform information into knowledge in an autonomous way. Nevertheless, many students find such tasks difficult, in part, because they are unaware of the genre conventions they are expected to follow. Thus, there is a need to build both genre knowledge and the ability to work with sources. This chapter elaborates a proposal for genre-based instruction in argumentative essay writing from multiple sources to foster autonomy in EFL academic literacy.

Writing from Sources

In a university setting, many tasks that require reading for academic purposes also involve writing based on that reading—that is, reading to write. Hirvela (2016) has used various terms to discuss the notion of moving from reading into writing, such as *reading for writing, reading while writing,* and *writerly reading.* They are all related to the belief that reading is the foundation for much of what takes place in academic writing. This, in turn, means that students must acquire various skills related to working with source texts, which Hirvela (2016) has described as one of the most challenging tasks students face as they develop their academic literacy abilities. This includes gaining command of four key operations: quoting, paraphrasing (i.e., indirect quoting), summarizing, and synthesizing sources. It also implies avoidance of the practice of copying sentences, clauses, or phrases from the original source without acknowledgment of the source.

The four operations that students are commonly taught can be defined as:

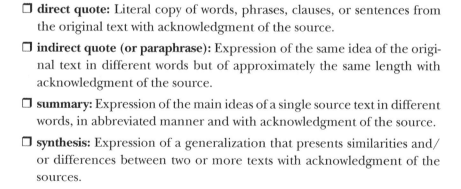

❑ **direct quote:** Literal copy of words, phrases, clauses, or sentences from the original text with acknowledgment of the source.

❑ **indirect quote (or paraphrase):** Expression of the same idea of the original text in different words but of approximately the same length with acknowledgment of the source.

❑ **summary:** Expression of the main ideas of a single source text in different words, in abbreviated manner and with acknowledgment of the source.

❑ **synthesis:** Expression of a generalization that presents similarities and/ or differences between two or more texts with acknowledgment of the sources.

Pecorari (2001) maintains that, when students use information obtained from reading in their writing by following the established conventions for these source text use operations, a strong relationship between these skills is built. This leads to the acquisition of autonomous academic literacy abilities. Learners who struggle with these operations and fail to adhere to conventions may engage in what is considered **plagiarism**, a violation of academic norms. To develop students' source use skills and prevent plagiarism, teachers can direct them to various strategies for successful source text use.

Researchers have identified several factors that contribute to students' struggles with source use techniques. These include language competence (Shi, 2004), knowledge of the topic (Chandrasoma, Thompson & Pennycook, 2004), reading skills (Angélil-Carter, 2000), an education system that favors imitation (Bloch & Chi, 1995), cultural attitudes (Pennycook, 1996), and unawareness of conventions (Ellery, 2008).While the problems students display are often labeled as *plagiarism*, a number of scholars argue that the use of inappropriate strategies should not be identified as dishonest behavior but rather attributed to lack of competence for the task (e.g. Abasi, Akbari & Graves, 2006). In this sense, some authors have found that L2 students resort to copying owing to their lack of familiarity with academic writing and limited language competence (Johns & Mayes, 1990; Keck, 2006), and to issues of culture, language and identity (Mott-Smith, Tomaš &, Kostka, 2017) and not out of an intention to deceive.

Bereiter and Scardamalia (1987) identify an additional dimension to students' use of sources—their purpose in using them. These authors distinguish between two possibilities: a **knowledge-telling model** in which students simply reproduce the information gleaned from the sources, and a **knowledge-transforming model** in which they evaluate what they read and then use it to create new meaning. In the same way as the source use operations described earlier, these two models can be taught in writing courses to further develop students' ability to write from sources.

Genre-Based Academic Literacy Instruction

Another major component of academic literacy instruction is genre. Introduced by Swales (1990) within the framework of ESP, it has since become important in EAP (or English for Academic Purposes) as well. It focuses on the analysis of the schematic structures that make up a genre and their lexico-grammatical realizations. Numerous genres have been analyzed, and these can be taught in academic writing courses that take into account the specific genre needs of students.

Genre-based pedagogies employ the notion of scaffolding that highlights the role of interaction with peers and experienced others in learning. The concept is mainly associated with Systemic Functional Linguistic (SFL) approaches. In the Sydney School, or the Australian SFL approach, it has been elaborated into an explicit model, the "teaching-learning cycle" (Feez, 1998, p. 28), which shows the process of learning a genre as a series of stages: **building the context, modeling, joint construction, independent construction,** and **linking related texts.** Some researchers (Belcher & Braine, 1995; Hyland, 2007) have reported that the genre-based approach is effective for literacy instruction, yet these studies have focused mainly on genres written by post-graduate students and professionals. Investigations of undergraduate students' genre use are less frequent. These include the teaching of the argumentative essay as perhaps the most dominant genre that learners encounter as they write across the curriculum.

Argumentative Essay Writing from Multiple Sources

An argumentative essay, often rooted in the well-known theory proposed by Toulmin (1958), generally has five sections in which it is possible to find the elements of Toulmin's model: **introduction** (claim), **arguments** (data and warrants), **counterarguments**, **refutation**, and **conclusion**. As part of the development of these sections, one of the techniques used in academic argumentation is **citation**—that is, the use of source text material. By referencing background reading texts, students support their own arguments and present and refute counterarguments. To carry out the task of writing argumentative essays from multiple sources, students have to put into practice effective citation strategies or operations such as quoting, paraphrasing, summarizing and synthesizing. They also follow the *knowledge-telling* or *knowledge-transforming* models as they arrange source material in their essays. For this reason, the effective use of sources and strategies to write from them is central to argumentative writing. Swales (2014) underscores that citations not only demonstrate knowledge of the literature on a topic, but also work "rhetorically to strengthen arguments" (p. 118). Thus, students cite sources so that their writing becomes more persuasive.

However, writing an argumentative essay from multiple sources is not an easy task. This has led some researchers (e.g., Barks & Watts, 2001) to recommend explicit instruction to help students overcome their dependence on source texts and acquire autonomous reading and writing skills. The study described in this chapter was rooted in the combined focus on genre-based instruction centered around the features of the argumentative essay and strategies to write from sources.

The Study

The motivations for undertaking this study grew out of the challenge many undergraduate students face when reading and writing in EFL at university, especially when writing argumentative essays drawing on source texts. Experience had shown that, in previous studies, the student subjects often found it difficult to integrate information from reading into their academic writing. They resorted to copying as the main method of source text use and/or tended to produce a collage of citations in which it was not easy to distinguish their own line of thought. The resulting essays seemed to be driven by the sources instead of being guided by the writer's arguments. This suggested a lack of autonomous literacy abilities, which may have been due to the absence of explicit citation and genre instruction. In fact, the skills of reading and writing at university differ from those acquired during previous schooling and cannot be learned implicitly (Carlino, 2006). As a result, it has been hypothesized that these students need explicit instruction to develop autonomous EFL academic literacy skills, which served as the basis for the present study.

Objectives, Hypothesis, and Methodology

The general aim of this investigation was to foster autonomy in EFL academic literacy among university students at an advanced level of language proficiency, with a particular interest in argumentative writing. The specific objective was to determine whether teaching argumentative essay writing utilizing multiple sources within the framework of the genre-based approach would have positive effects on students' performance, self-perceived abilities, and attitudes. In pursuing this objective, the study sought to contribute to scholarship on teaching argumentative writing from a *learning to argue* perspective.

The hypothesis formulated was that genre-based instruction is an effective pedagogical tool to improve argumentative essay writing from multiple sources on the part of EFL university students at an advanced level of language proficiency.

To test its hypothesis, this study employed a multimethod approach to collect and analyze the data. A quasi-experimental design (one-group pre- and post-test) was employed, and data were analyzed both quantitively and qualitatively.

Context and Participants

The setting for this study was a School of Languages in an Argentinian university. This institution offers five-year EFL Teaching, Translation, and Licentiate programs. Each academic year includes an English Language course running from April to October that students are required to complete independently of the program in which they are enrolled. In this five-level course, the four language skills are developed by means of content-based instruction. Students are expected to make progress from an intermediate to a proficiency level of English.

The study was carried out during the second term of the 2014 academic year, and the participants were 79 students enrolled in English Language IV, the course in which argumentative essay writing from multiple sources is taught. These students were 23 years old on average and were at a level equivalent to C2 of the Common European Framework of Reference for Languages. They attended 80-minute class sessions held in English twice a week from August to October. The rest of the participants were the course instructor and two raters.

Materials

The materials used were an instructor course pack, a raters' pack, and a set of genre-based classroom materials for students. The sources of data were two argumentative essay writing tasks (pre- and post-test) and student surveys.

The instructor pack provided guidelines for following the genre-based instructional approach. The raters' pack provided instructions for assessing students' performance using an analytic scoring scale with five descriptors designed for this study. The genre-based classroom materials were based on the "teaching-learning cycle" (Feez, 1998, p. 28), which informed the design of the activities carried out during the treatment and aimed at:

❑ **building the social context**, which sought to promote understanding of the argumentative essay from multiple sources by analyzing how it is organized in terms of purpose, audience, reader-writer relationships, and register.

❑ **modeling**, which focused on deconstructing the genre to provide its schematic structure and lexico-grammatical features through language scaffolding tasks, such as text- and language-level familiarization tasks, model manipulation, and controlled and guided composition tasks.

☐ **joint construction**, which had as its aim to produce the genre in collaboration with the teacher and peers. Learners were guided by means of strategies for generating content, planning, drafting, writing, revising, and editing their texts. The teacher gradually relinquished responsibility to the students as they gained control of the genre.

☐ **independent construction**, which focused on removing scaffolding and allowing students to write by themselves. This shifted responsibility to the learners, who produced texts on their own and evaluated their progress.

☐ **linking related texts**, which sought to relate the argumentative essay from sources to other texts and contexts, comparing the use of other genres in the same context–such as summary responses, literary essays, annotated bibliographies, and literature reviews—and the same genre in other contexts. This provided opportunities for critiquing and manipulating the genre.

The pre- and post-test consisted of two similar but not identical argumentative essay writing tasks to avoid pre-test bias. The pre-test was related to Unit 1 of the course syllabus, Educational Challenges in Today's World, while the post-test was related to Unit 3: Art: The Role of Artistic Expression in (Post-) Contemporary Society. Students were given this prompt in both testing situations (see Figure 12.1):

Figure 12.1
Writing Prompt Used in the Study

READ THE INTRODUCTORY MATERIAL AND WRITE AN ARGUMENTATIVE ESSAY OF ABOUT 600 WORDS BASED ON THE FOLLOWING:
[Quote from compulsory reading material related to the purpose of education (pre-test) and the role of art (post-test)]
Examine this view and argue in favor of or against it building a convincing case to demonstrate your personal understanding of the topic. In the course of the development of your argument, establish meaningful connections with and make explicit references to background reading and audiovisual texts included in the course materials that you have explored in depth.

The pre- and post-study surveys collected demographic information about the student participants, and information about their ability to produce the genre and their attitudes to genre-based instruction.

Data Collection and Analysis

To evaluate whether genre-based instruction in argumentative essay writing from multiple sources had positive effects on students' performance, a pretest was administered in a 120-minute session at the beginning of the second term in August. The post-test was also administered in a 120-minute session at the end of the second term in mid-October, after a ten-week period of instruction. Forty minutes of every 80-minute session were devoted to genre-based instruction in argumentative essay writing from multiple sources. The instructor raised students' awareness of the schematic structure of the argumentative essay by focusing on its sections, the moves within them, their lexico-grammatical features, and the strategies available to write from sources, including the functions and patterns of such strategies. In addition to drawing students' attention to the rhetorical dimensions of the genre, there was an emphasis on the roles of the writer, reader, and context. To carry out the pre- and post-test tasks, students were allowed to use a bank of quotes which they had previously elaborated from the sources included in the compulsory course reading and audiovisual materials.

The analysis of students' essays was carried out using two statistical tests: Cohen's Kappa (simple unweighted coefficient) to measure interrater reliability and Wilcoxon Rank Sums (matched pairs) to compare pre- and post-test performance. Two raters scored the tests using the analytic scale described earlier. They assessed each of these aspects of the essays: content, organization, lexico-grammatical features, contextual appropriateness (purpose, audience, register), and formal aspects on a scale ranging from 0 to 100 percent. The final mark was obtained by adding the scores assigned to each aspect and dividing the resulting number by five, that is, the total number of aspects. This percentage was transformed into a score on a scale from 1 to 10 (passing mark: 4=60 percent).

The strategies to write from sources students made use of were identified by means of textual analysis of the content of the essays. The data were segmented employing the sentence as the unit of analysis. Each segment was assigned a pre-determined category that represented a strategy. In some cases, consecutive sentences were classified as belonging to the same category (i.e., summary and synthesis). The strategies were detected by means of comparisons of the textual segments with the source texts and the students' banks of quotes. The resulting nominal variables were tabulated, and the relative frequency of each category was shown as a percentage. There were reliability checks by means of peer checking. To this end, 33 percent of the data were randomly selected (26 pre-test and 26 post-test essays) so that the strategies were classified by a second rater. This process yielded an interrater reliability percentage of 78 percent. The categories over which there was less agreement were discussed and revised. The organization of the essays and the functions and patterns of the strategies were examined by means of content analysis, too.

The pre- and post-study surveys were administered together with the pre- and post-test respectively and analyzed quantitatively.

Results and Discussion

The results of the study are presented first by considering overall student performance, then by examining the strategies to write from sources employed and the organization of the essays, and finally by looking at students' self-assessed abilities to carry out the task and attitudes to genre-based instruction.

Overall Student Performance

When analyzing the agreement between the raters on the scores of students' performance in the pre- and post-test, Cohen's simple unweighted coefficient determined statistically significant values of 0.600 ($p < 0.0001$) and 0.631 ($p < 0.0001$), respectively. After establishing a good level of interrater reliability, the average of pre- and post-test scores assigned by both raters was considered. A non-parametric test, Wilcoxon Rank Sums (matched pairs), was used to compare the scores before and after the treatment. Results indicate that the pre-test mean was 2.25 and the post-test mean was 6.25, so the mean difference between pre- and post-test scores was 4 points, which is statistically significant ($p < 0.0001$). Figure 12.2 shows the percentage of students according to pre- and post-test scores. In the pre-test, it is possible to observe a similar percentage (around 30%) for the marks 1, 2 and 3, and a much lower percentage for the passing mark (4=60%), while, in the post-test, the highest percentages can be observed for the marks 5, 6 and 7.

Figure 12.2 shows, along the upper line with grey squares, students' average post-test scores according to the pre-test scores before receiving genre-based instruction. The lower line with black circles reveals the score gainsafter genre-based instruction (obtained subtracting the pre-test score from the post-test average).

Figure 12.2

Percentage of Students According to Pre- and Post-Test Scores

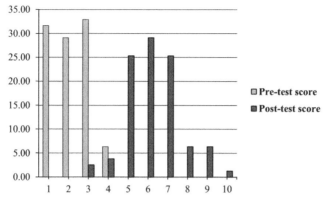

In conclusion, significative mean differences between students' pre- and post-test scores, and post-test score gains could be considered evidence for the positive effect of genre-based instruction.

Strategies to Write from Sources, Functions, and Patterns of Task Performance

The analysis of the strategies to write from sources in the pre- and post-test indicates that students employed more effective strategies in the post-test. Such strategies improved both quantitatively, in terms of the number of strategies used (410 in the pre-test and 533 in the post-test), and qualitatively in relation to judgments of use of more effective strategies. As Figure 12.3 shows, the only case in which the percentage decreased was the use of Copy whereas, for the rest of the strategies, the percentage increased in the post-test.

The pre-test was characterized by the use of strategies to write from sources that were ineffective in the context of the task, which required integration of multiple sources: Copy, which represented 46.09 percent of the total of pre-test strategies, and Direct Quote (38.29 percent). These strategies implied local, microstructural reformulations or reproduction, that is, **knowledge-telling**. The rest of the strategies used, in order of frequency, were Synthesis (5.6 percent), Summary (5.12 percent), and Indirect Quote (4.87 percent). These strategies, which were more effective than Copy and over-

Figure 12.3

Strategies to Write from Sources

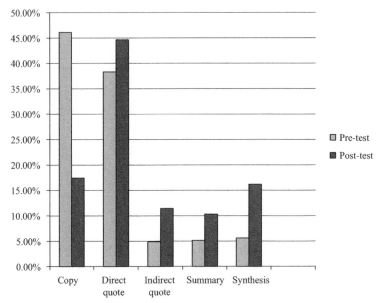

use of Direct Quote because they contributed to **knowledge-transforming**, accounted for much smaller percentages of the total of strategies employed. Therefore, the resulting essays were mostly literal reproductions of the sources. In general, pre-test argumentative essays from multiple sources seemed to reflect either lack of the comprehension of the main ideas of source texts or lack of the linguistic resources necessary to express them using appropriate citation strategies.

On the other hand, the post-test was characterized by the greater use of strategies that were more effective in the context of the task, such as Synthesis, Indirect Quote, and Summary, which suggested global or macrostructural reformulations, or increased **knowledge-transforming**. The most frequent strategy employed was now Direct Quote, which represented 44.65 percent of the total of post-test strategies, or nearly half. Copy, the most frequently used strategy in the pre-test, decreased to 17.44 percent. The remaining 37.91 percent of citation strategy use consisted of Synthesis (16.13 percent, up from 5.6 percent), Indirect Quote (11.44 percent, up from 4.87 percent), and Summary (10.31 percent, up from 5.12 percent). The decline in the use of Copy from 46.09 percent to 17.44 percent total use revealed a significant shift in the students' approach to citation, as did the increase in Synthesis, Indirect Quote, and Summary from 15.59 percent (total) to 37.91 percent (total). Relative to this context, the increased use of Direct Quote could mean that students became aware of what constitutes plagiarism and tried to avoid it following conventions for source text use when reproducing background reading or audiovisual materials literally. It might also mean that they simply continued to view it as the most appealing citation strategy given their relatively new awareness of conventions and incipient ability to put more effective strategies to write from sources into practice. In general, post-test essays were a reflection of a major shift in how the students viewed citation in the development of their argumentative essays.

Together with the use of mostly ineffective citation strategies to write from sources, several pre-test argumentative essays exhibited an inappropriate schematic structure. More than half of the essays, 61 percent (48), followed the traditional method of development that presents an introduction, arguments, counterargument, refutation, and conclusion. Nine essays (11 percent) followed less traditional methods that present the counterargument and refutation before the arguments, or develop argument, counterargument and refutation in a single paragraph and repeat this pattern for each of the arguments. Nonetheless, in 28 percent (22) of the essays, there was inadequate organization and development—for example, introduction, arguments, and conclusion without counterargument or refutation. Furthermore, 38 percent (30) of the essays did not propose an adequate thesis. Finally, most essays (91 percent=72) evidenced problems in arguments, counterarguments, and/or refutation, which were unsuitable or underdeveloped.

Together with the use of more effective strategies, most post-test essays exhibited improvement in terms of an appropriate and logical generic structure. Only nine essays (11 percent) followed the traditional method of development, and 60 essays (76 percent) followed less traditional methods. This revealed manipulation of models to use alternative rhetorical patterns that varied according to the strength of arguments and communicative intention. Only 10 (13 percent) essays exhibited inadequate organization. Moreover, most of the students (70=89 percent) proposed an adequate thesis. Lastly, more than half of the essays (66 percent=52) did not evidence problems in arguments, counterarguments and/or refutation, which were suitable and well developed.

The strategies used to write from sources should not be seen as ends in themselves but as means to incorporate information from reading into text production. Indeed, these strategies often serve functions in the new text by means of which the writer's stance is constructed and the argument is

Table 12.1
Functions of Strategies to Write from Sources in Argumentative
Essays

Functions of Strategies	Pre-Test	Post-Test
Providing an introduction	90 (21.95%)	41 (7.69%)
Presenting the thesis	27 (6.58%)	5 (0.93%)
Presenting arguments	42 (10.24%)	14 (2.62%)
Providing evidence for arguments	146 (35.60%)	292 (54.78%)
Presenting counterarguments	10 (2.43%)	20 (3.75%)
Providing evidence for counterarguments	13 (3.17%)	44 (8.25%)
Presenting a refutation	13 (3.17%)	15 (2.81%)
Providing evidence for refutation	33 (8.04%)	70 (13.13%)
Presenting a conclusion	36 (8.78%)	32 (6.00%)
Total of strategies	410 (100%)	533 (100%)

developed. The functions of the strategies in students' essays are presented
in Table 12.1.

Both in the pre- and post-test, most strategies to write from sources
(35.60 and 54.78 percent, respectively) served the function of providing
evidence for arguments, with a significant increase in the post-test situation.
In the post-test, there was a decrease in the use of citation strategies to serve
functions that might not be effective, such as providing an introduction,
presenting the thesis, putting forward arguments, presenting a refutation
and a conclusion (usually as topic sentences of paragraphs whose method
of development is deductive rather than inductive). In contrast, there was
an increase in the use of strategies to serve more effective functions in the
context of the task, such as providing evidence for arguments, counterarguments, and the refutation. This may be due to the fact that, following the
instruction they received, students became more aware of the functions
of such strategies in the argumentative essay. Additionally, they no longer
privileged the source authors' positions but adopted a more critical stance
where their own views emerged. These results coincide with Abasi et al.'s
(2006) findings concerning the functions of source use strategies among
less and more proficient student writers.

These strategiesand their functions lead to different patterns of performing the task of writing an argumentative essay from multiple sources.

These patterns, which represent typical ways of carrying out the task, have been classified into:

☐ **failed attempts at source integration:** Use of Copy, Direct, and/or Indirect Quote in a process of verbatim reproduction of sources while disregarding conventions, following conventions through Direct Quote, or carrying out microstructural reformulations through paraphrase without integration with other sources.

☐ **integration of single source texts:** Use of Summary (with or without Copy, Direct Quote, and/or Indirect Quote) in a process of reformulation through selection of main ideas, omission of details and generalization, construction, and integration of ideas from a single source text without integration with other sources.

☐ **integration of multiple sources:** Use of Synthesis (with or without Copy, Direct Quote, Indirect Quote, and/or Summary) in a process of reformulation of sources through selection of main ideas, omission of details and generalization, and construction and integration of ideas from two or more sources.

As Figure 12.4 shows, failed attempts at source integration, the most ineffective pattern, decreased significantly, from 68.35 percent in the pre-test to 32.91 percent in the post-test, whereas integration of multiple sources, the most effective pattern in the context of the task as it can result in richer argumentation, increased notably from 24.05 to 58.22 percent. The integration of single source texts increased very slightly from 7.59 to 8.86 percent. Here, too, there is strong evidence for the effectiveness of the combined source use/genre-based instruction.

In light of the analysis of the strategies used to write from sources, their functions, and their patterns, it is possible to state that such strategies improved in the post-test, thus revealing the value of the treatment. The pre-test strategies are consistent with the ineffective strategies reported by other studies (Johns & Mayes, 1990; Keck, 2006), which show that L2 students often use Copy as the main method of text integration. The reasons for this may be related to students' efforts to construct their stance and, at the same time, avoid distorting the meaning of sources and imitate academic language.

To put this in another light, although in the pre-test students seem to have written mostly following the knowledge-telling model of merely reproducing source text content, when it came to the post-test, they reformulated

Figure 12.4
Patterns of Task Performance

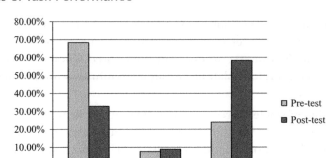

it according to the knowledge-transforming model (Bereiter & Scardamalia, 1987). On the whole, the strategies to write from sources, their functions and patterns constitute a continuum that ranges from writing "dependent on literalness" (Ruiz Flores, 2009) to an independent or autonomous way of writing. This suggests that providing instruction in effective citation strategies fosters autonomy in EFL academic literacy.

Students' Abilities and Attitudes

The students were required to evaluate their ability to write an argumentative essay (i.e., presenting the thesis, arguments, counterargument, refutation, and conclusion) and their ability to write from sources (e.g. quoting, paraphrasing, summarizing, and synthesizing). The results demonstrate that, in the pre-study survey, even though slightly more than 50 percent of the students considered that their abilities to write an argumentative essay and to write from sources were good (52 and 59 percent, respectively), a percentage also near 50 percent (47 and 41 percent, respectively) stated that such abilities were only fair or weak. Surprisingly, only one student assessed their ability to write an argumentative essay as very good, and none evaluated their ability to write from sources in that way. This may be due to their lack of knowledge of genre conventions. On the other hand, in the post-study survey, the percentage of students that regarded their ability to write an argumentative essay as good or very good increased to 64 and 19 percent, respectively. The percentage of students that considered their ability to write from sources as good diminished slightly to 56 percent (from 59 percent), but 26 percent of the students assessed this ability as very good, as opposed to none in the pre-test. In like manner, fewer students judged such abilities as fair or weak (16 and 17 percent, respectively).

Interestingly, although 42 percent of the students denied having used Copy, this was the most frequently used strategy in the pre-test, as previously mentioned. The most plausible reason for their use of Copy, reported by 38 percent of the respondents, was unawareness of the conventions, which coincides with the main cause identified by Ellery (2008). The next three reasons given were (1) limited knowledge of the topic, (2) an education system that favors imitation, and (3) a necessary stage to acquire effective strategies, reported by 23, 20, and 18 percent of the students, respectively. Other reasons cited were lack of reading skills (14 percent), limited language competence (9 percent) and knowledge of the task (9 percent).After receiving genre-based instruction, 80 percent of the students maintained that their ability to write an argumentative essay from multiple sources improved.

Regarding students' attitudes to genre-based instruction, in the post-study survey, 82 percent of the students responded that the way in which they learned to write the genre was effective and fosters independence from literalness as well as autonomy in EFL academic literacy. In addition, even if 14 percent of the students answered that the approach limited their creativity, 86 percent affirmed that it increased their confidence. These results indicate that, in spite of the fact that the criticism often leveled at genre-based instruction—that models stifle creativity—is reflected in the survey, its benefits are perceived by most students.

In sum, the survey shows that students' self-perceived abilities to write an argumentative essay from multiple sources and their attitudes toward genre-based instruction improved after the treatment.

Closing Thoughts

The triangulation of results confirms the hypothesis that genre-based instruction was an effective pedagogical tool to improve argumentative essay writing from multiple sources on the part of the EFL students that participated in this study, since it had positive effects on their performance, self-assessed abilities, and attitudes.

The main pedagogical implication arising from this investigation is that advanced EFL university students still need explicit instruction in academic genres, especially those that require argumentation and writing from sources. These findings contribute to improving the teaching of academic reading and writing in this and other English language courses offered at the institution where this study was carried out and suggest application of the treatment in other settings.

To foster autonomy in EFL academic literacy and strengthen argumentative writing ability, students should develop skills to write from sources. It is also clear that university teachers should adopt adequate literacy theories, such as genre-based approaches, that underline not only the linguistic products or mental processes of reading and writing but also the social contexts of academia. They should adopt a social practices orientation. On the basis of such theories, teachers should provide training in strategies that allow students to quote, paraphrase, summarize, and synthesize sources in their own arguments, and assign reading and writing tasks that require transforming information into knowledge.

As regards the caveats of this study, its results may not be generalized to a population outside the context of the research site. Moreover, similar longitudinal studies with larger groups of students should be conducted. Further research could evaluate the effect of genre-based instruction in argumentative essay writing from multiple sources in similar contexts (other universities and teacher training colleges) and different contexts (secondary and graduate school). Likewise, future lines of research could focus on the transference of genre knowledge to other courses, on related genres, and on the correlation between teacher training in genre theory and its effectiveness.

All in all, genre-based instruction should be exploited to help learners find their way successfully through the intricate paths of reading, writing, and argumentation at university. They should become aware that writing from sources is vital to construct their own stance and build knowledge in their discipline. To that end, they need to acquire effective strategies to avoid reproducing texts and elaborate the information they read critically. The responsibility for fostering autonomy in academic literacy should be shared by the whole academic community. Thus, teachers set the foundations for lifelong text comprehension and production practices that continue throughout students' academic and professional development. It is hoped that this study will be conducive to a greater understanding of how EFL academic literacy might most appropriately be taught and shed some light on the argumentative essay from multiple sources, a complex genre that merits further consideration both as a linguistic activity and a cognitive process to construct knowledge in particular social contexts.

REFERENCES

Abasi, A., Akbari, N., & Graves, B. (2006). Discourse appropriation, construction of identities and the complex issue of plagiarism: ESL students writing in graduate school. *Journal of Second Language Writing, 15*, 102–117.

Angélil-Carter, S. (2000). *Stolen language? Plagiarism in writing.* London: Routledge.

Barks, D., & Watts, P. (2001). Textual borrowing strategies for graduate level ESL writers. In D. Belcher & A. Hirvela (Eds.), *Linking literacies: Perspectives on L2 reading-writing connections* (pp. 246–267). Ann Arbor: University of Michigan Press.

Belcher, D., & Braine, G. (1995). Introduction. In D. Belcher & G. Braine (Eds.), *Academic writing in second language: Essays on research and pedagogy* (pp. iii–xxix). Norwood, NJ: Ablex.

Bereiter, C., & Scardamalia, M. (1987). *The psychology of written composition.* London: Lawrence Erlbaum.

Bloch, J., & Chi, L. (1995). A comparison of the use of citations in Chinese and English academic discourse. In D. Belcher & G. Braine (Eds.), *Academic writing in a second language: Essays on research and pedagogy* (pp. 231–247). Norwood, NJ: Ablex.

Carlino, P. (2006). Concepciones y formas de enseñar escritura académica. Un estudio contrastivo. *Signo y Seña. Revista del Instituto de Lingüística Facultad de Filosofía y Letras, Universidad de Buenos Aires. Procesos y Prácticas de Escritura en Educación Superior, 16*, 71–117.

Chandrasoma, R., Thompson, C., & Pennycook, A. (2004). Beyond plagiarism: Transgressive intertextuality. *Journal of Language, Identity and Education, 3*, 171–193.

Ellery, K. (2008). Undergraduate plagiarism: A pedagogical perspective. *Assessment and Evaluation in Higher Education, 33*(5), 507–516.

Feez, S. (1998). *Text-based syllabus design.* Sydney: McQuarie University/AMES.

Hirvela, A. (2016). *Connecting reading and writing in second language instruction* (2nd ed.). Ann Arbor: University of Michigan Press.

Hyland, K. (2007). *Genre and second language writing.* Ann Arbor: University of Michigan Press.

Johns, A., & Mayes, P. (1990). An analysis of summary protocols of university ESL students. *Applied Linguistics, 11*(3), 253–272.

Keck, C. (2006). The use of paraphrase in summary writing: A comparison of L1 and L2 writers. *Journal of Second Language Writing, 15*(4), 261–306.

Mott-Smith, J., Tomaš, Z. &, Kostka, I. (2017). *Teaching Effective Source Use: Classroom Approaches That Work.* Ann Arbor: University of Michigan Press.

Pecorari, D. (2001). Plagiarism and international students: How the English-speaking university responds. In D. Belcher & A. Hirvela (Eds.), *Linking literacies: Perspectives on L2 reading-writing connections* (pp. 229–245). Ann Arbor: University of Michigan Press.

Pennycock, A. (1996). Borrowing others' words: Text, ownership, memory and plagiarism. *TESOL Quarterly, 30*(2), 201–230.

Ruiz Flores, M. (2009). *Evaluación de la lengua escrita y dependencia de lo literal.* Barcelona: Editorial GRAÓ.

Shi, L. (2004). Textual borrowing in second language writing. *Written Communication, 21,* 171–200.

Swales, J. (1990). *Genre analysis. English in academic and research settings.* Cambridge, England: Cambridge University Press.

Swales, J. (2014). Variation in citational practice in a corpus of student Biology papers: From parenthetical plonking to intertextual storytelling. *Written Communication, 31*(1), 118–141.

Toulmin, S. (1958). *The uses of argument.* Cambridge, England: Cambridge University Press.

13

Argumentative Writing at the Tertiary Level: Students' and Teachers' Perceptions of a Hybrid Approach

LUCAS KOHNKE AND FRANKIE HAR

Abstract

This qualitative study explores pedagogical approaches to teaching argumentative writing in a first-year undergraduate EAP course at an English-medium instruction (EMI) university in Hong Kong. 16 undergraduate freshmen students were interviewed in the study. The findings indicate that the adoption of a hybrid approach over a traditional teacher-led class assisted students in developing an understanding of argument and the concept of argumentation. Our study suggests that integrating several input methods (videos, quizzes, reflections, peer review, face-to-face instruction) provided multiple explanations that helped develop students' argumentative writing skills.

The ability to formulate a sound argument is a crucial skill, yet both L1 and L2 writers find this skill particularly challenging. Formulating arguments requires advanced reasoning skills and an academic vocabulary to explain the claims and counterclaims of a well-considered argument (Liu & Stapleton, 2014). Learners must take and justify their stance, anticipate opposing positions, and consider alternatives. The cognitive demands of writing an argumentative essay for L1 and L2 learners are high; therefore, this writing is often very challenging to first-year undergraduate writers. Previous studies have demonstrated that with explicit and relevant instruction, ESL/EFL students can overcome such difficulties (Hirvela, 2013; Hyland, 2003).

Much has been written on argumentative writing pedagogies, which tend to rely on one primary method or approach to enhance students' learning (Helms-Park & Stapleton, 2003). However, less attention has been paid to a multiple-method input approach consisting of small, focused learning units in teaching argumentative writing and whether such an approach can enhance students' learning. This is surprising, given the importance of composing argumentative essays for undergraduates.

This chapter discusses a hybrid approach to teaching argumentative writing. "Hybrid" here means a multimodal pedagogy, combining online and face-to-face teaching while using multiple input sources, including videos, quizzes, reflections, peer reviews, and face-to-face (F2F) instruction for tertiary-level learners that enables students to understand and practice various argumentative writing elements. This contrasts with more traditional, or non-multimodal, teaching methods (e.g., only F2F), that may limit students' exposure to relevant input. In the study described, we sought insight into how English for Academic Purposes (EAP) students at a Hong Kong English-medium university responded to this hybrid approach.

These questions guided this explorative study:

1. What were students' perceptions concerning the various online and in-person methods of learning argumentative writing in a hybrid class?
2. Which method(s) provided students with a more in-depth understanding of argumentative writing?

Literature Review

Academic writing skills are essential for academic success (Hyland, 2013). Many researchers have investigated the academic writing practices of higher education students in diverse settings, leading to the emergence of different approaches to writing in higher education. L2 students entering their first year in an English-medium university are expected to compose well-written essays in their L2, so they must learn and adjust their writing quickly to produce satisfactory academic writing using discipline-specific registers and rhetorical structures. This is often quite different from their high school experience and poses an additional burden for L2 learners (Hyland, 2013). Hirvela (2011) noted that the time commitment and patience necessary for students to develop their L2 writing proficiency is high. In higher education, L2 students' academic achievement often depends on texts they produce in English. Consequently, L2 students must reach a specific level of competency and fluency in academic writing to succeed in their studies (Hyland, 2013) and thus should focus on "specific, purposeful uses of language" (Hyland, 2016, p. 17).

At university, both L1 and L2 writers face challenges producing successful argumentative writing. Felton, Crowell, and Liu (2015), as well as Toplak and Stanovich (2003), found that L1 college students often neglected opposing viewpoints when debating with their peers. Generally, previous research in L1 contexts indicated that the main challenge for students is a lack of support for reasons, counterclaims, and supporting reasons for counterclaims. L2 learners face similar challenges, but as language learners, they also face more significant micro- and macro-level pragmatic-linguistic challenges. For instance, Liu and Stapleton (2014) found that EFL students in China often omitted the counterargument section due to insufficient knowledge of argumentative structure. They also omitted rebuttals. Thus, the challenge L2 undergraduate students face in producing written academic arguments, the most common genre undergraduate students write (Wu, 2006), is significant. Appropriate teaching and learning approaches are necessary to address any deficiencies.

The literature has established that both teachers and students are uncertain about the term *argument* and the concepts of argumentation (Wingate, 2012). The primary elements of argumentation are the development of a position/stance, the building and presenting of evidence in a logical sequence, and selection of relevant evidence (Andrews, 1995; Toulmin, Reike, & Janik, 1984; Wu, 2006). Various pedagogical methods have facilitated students' argumentative writing development, including model pieces of writing (Knudson, 1992), question prompts (Jonassen, Shen, Marra, Cho, Lo, & Lohani, 2009), constraint-based argumentation scaffolding (Cho & Jonassen, 2002), and blended learning approaches (Lam, Hew & Chiu, 2018). Because of how critical it is for undergraduate L2 writers to successfully develop argumentative writing skills, exploring a multi-method approach seems worth pursuing. This chapter investigates which pedagogical approach(es) students perceive as the most useful in teaching and learning argumentative writing.

Study Context

Course Description and Instruction

This study took place at a Hong Kong EMI university where all first-year students complete a compulsory three-credit EAP course. This course runs three hours face-to-face each week for 13 weeks. Students complete independent learning activities, two written tasks, and one academic presentation. The course aims to equip them with academic writing knowledge and practice along with disciplinary-specific research skills to prepare them for their major studies. Approximately 3,000 students attended sections of the course when this study was conducted. Students enter EAP courses/classes according to their majors (e.g., nursing students study with other nursing students in the same EAP group). The course learning outcomes are to (1) refer to sources in written texts and oral presentations; (2) paraphrase and summarize materials from written and spoken sources; (3) plan, write, and revise expository essays with references to sources; and (4) deliver academic presentations. The course begins by introducing language appropriate for academic writing and expressing ideas and views in tentative rather than assertive language, where appropriate. Then the focus turns to locating relevant academic sources, selecting appropriate reporting verbs, summarizing and paraphrasing, developing citation skills, and writing coherent paragraphs. The third unit introduces argumentative writing and focuses on two assessed tasks of (1) writing a problem-solution essay (500 words), and (2) writing a for-and-against essay (800 words).

For the in-class problem-solution essay, students were given four academic articles on an assigned topic (e.g., water scarcity, healthy eating) to read and discuss with their classmates and teacher over five weeks. In the assignment, students were given a set of pre-writing task questions relating to one or more aspects of the problem/topic, extracts from at least two of the four articles, as well as some additional extracts. Students then wrote the essay, incorporating the extracts provided as source materials and their own views.

The second written assignment involved writing an out-of-class 800-word argumentative essay analysing one of two given topics. Each semester, all students enrolled in the course across all majors write on the same topic (e.g., medical services in Hong Kong, air or light pollution in Hong Kong), which is not related to their major. In the study, students submitted a detailed outline to their teacher and peers for feedback. Their final draft included a minimum of four different academic sources demonstrating integral and non-integral citation skills.

The fourth unit concentrated on delivering academic presentations following a problem-solution and for-and-against structure.

High schools in China and Hong Kong, Chinese-medium and English-medium, often do not explicitly teach argumentation, or if they do, students may learn very different argumentative writing concepts than at university. In the high school context, argumentative essay writing approaches often emphasize direct instruction, providing lexical items and prescriptive essay structures for students to follow (Lam et al., 2018). In our experience of teaching academic writing in Hong Kong, we have observed that students (1) often lack background knowledge about topics and concepts that their instructors take for granted; (2) cannot construct evidence-based arguments, including organizing their ideas logically; and (3) lack critical-thinking skills. Before their university studies, Hong Kong students often compose only relatively simple argumentative essays, often not incorporating academic citations as evidence. Thus, when embarking on this EAP course, students encounter discursive culture shock, as they must construct evidence-based arguments incorporating academic citations using complex structures, such as complex noun phrases and nominalization, as well as employ an academic register. Previous research has focused on academic writing in general, structures of arguments, or rhetorical features. Surprisingly, given the importance of academic writing as a gatekeeper for academic achievement (Hyland, 2013), few researchers have investigated which pedagogical approach tertiary learners perceive as the most useful in discursive writing.

Hybrid Approach

We believe a hybrid and eclectic teaching approach would be a pedagogically sound approach when students are moving from one educational context to another (e.g., secondary to tertiary). A central component in this approach is its use of input to prepare students to write argumentatively. In our hybrid approach, five input methods work together (videos, quizzes, reflections, peer review, and F2F instruction) with the aim of stimulating better recall, retention, and comprehension, thereby leading to a more productive learning environment. Short out-of-class online activities motivate learners to work through the activities multiple times to deepen learning. These function as part of a broader integrated learning experience to increase flexibility and lead to higher levels of engagement among learners. It is hoped that the variety of input methods will lead to a better understanding of argumentative writing and improved student performance. The five input methods are outlined next.

❐ **Videos:** Videos relating to argumentation provide and reinforce input before and after F2F sessions. Generally, learners find videos more inter-active than other media, and the videos stimulate better levels of recall and retention (Hung, Kinshuk, & Chen, 2018). In our course, videos are especially useful for offering "just-in-time" learning on topics such as learning academic style, discovering reasons to reference, reading academic articles, narrowing down topics, and planning an argumentative essay. Students can pause and re-watch the content multiple times to ensure full understanding of the video content. These videos produced by the subject leaders are short (e.g., 1–5 minutes) and presented in plain English. Each video focuses on one learning outcome at a time to optimize students' engagement and maximize learning impact.

☐ **Quizzes:** Low-stakes online formative quizzes can assess students' progress in learning elements of argumentation. The quizzes used in this study consisted of drag-and-drop, true/false, multiple choice, and open-ended answer options. Students can retake each quiz multiple times, review their answers, and evaluate their progress. Teachers can use this immediate feedback to inform further learning activities, fill knowledge gaps, and address misunderstandings in F2F follow up.

☐ **Reflections:** Reflections enable students to consider how they are learning and, equally important, what they are learning by following a checklist. Students write weekly reflections, 50–100 words in length, which lead them to gain insight into their thinking and the development of criticality and argumentative writing. Reflections encourage learners to further engage in their learning and reflect on their progress.

☐ **Peer review:** We encourage students to read each other's work, give advice, and suggest improvements. This review is an essential element of the writing process, as students evaluate and critique each other's work and collaboratively develop their ability to act as critics. In the context of argumentation, it is sometimes difficult for students to see their logical fallacies, and teachers' comments may be difficult to understand. In contrast, peer review provides a valuable opportunity for students to develop critical-thinking skills and rely less on teacher input.

☐ **F2F instruction:** Face-to-face instruction takes place for three hours per week. These sessions focus on reinforcing the knowledge students acquire before the session, as well as introducing new information. For example, the content consists of reading passages and identifying style problems (informal verbs, clichés, informal sentence starters); identifying citations; using sources in academic writing and referencing styles; and breaking down academic essays to identify the structure, topic sentences, as well as describing cause and effect. Second, academic articles on the assigned topic are used to analyze arguments by identifying common moves, such as illustrating, authorizing, borrowing, extending, and countering. This helps students develop an understanding of sound argumentation and envision the kind of writing they are expected to produce.

Figure 13.1

Hybrid Model for Teaching Argumentative Writing

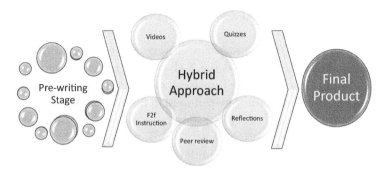

Figure 13.1 illustrates the hybrid approach for the EAP course.

To fully engage students in their argumentative writing learning journey, during the pre-writing stage we ask students to generate ideas using journalistic questions (e.g., who, what, where, when), clustering, listing, and looping. Looping is a freewriting technique that allows the student to focus their ideas to discover a writing topic. The aim here is to help them generate and organize ideas, thus aiding them in developing topics for their writing at a later stage. Providing a multimodal approach combining online and F2F teaching while using multiple input sources, including videos, quizzes, F2F instruction, followed by reflections and peer reviews together, is the cornerstone of our pedagogical framework. We ask students to include a minimum of four different academic sources and demonstrate integral and non-integral citation skills in developing their argument in their final product.

Methodology

Participants

This study took place with 16 undergraduate first-year students (six women and ten men), studying land surveying and geo-informatics at a Hong Kong EMI university. The aim was to acquire a rich and holistic understanding (Creswell, 2008) of the teaching, or input, method(s) that participants believed most helped them understand argumentative writing. Participants were from both mainland China ($n = 8$) and Hong Kong ($n = 8$), and so were from different educational systems. Pseudonyms protected participants' anonymity, and participants could withdraw from the study at any time.

Methods of Data Collection and Data Analysis

The data came from 16 semi-structured recorded and transcribed interviews with students enrolled in the EAP course; interview length varied from 23–38 minutes. We chose interviews to yield rich responses in a nonthreatening and comfortable environment in English, and we explored the participants' experience of all five sources of input (i.e., videos, quizzes, reflections, peer review, and F2F instruction), particularly the approaches participants felt provided a better understanding of argumentative writing. We used member checks to establish the trustworthiness of the data (Merriam, 2017). Each participant approved the interview transcripts without any revisions.

As the sample size was relatively small, we analyzed the data manually using Braun and Clarke's (2006) six-step thematic analysis framework. Thematic forms of analysis are flexible, and key ideas and viewpoints of the researchers guide the process (Braun & Clarke, 2006). Participants completed a second member check when they received the final results and a discussion (themes and representative quotes) of the research. Participants verified that the information accurately represented their learning experiences, and they did not request any further changes.

Results and Discussion

RQ 1. *What were students' perceptions concerning the various online and in-person methods of learning argumentative writing in a hybrid class?*

The first aim of the study was to investigate students' perceptions of various online and in-person methods to establish a general understanding of argument and the concept of argumentation. Students found three sources of input (videos, quizzes, and F2F instruction) particularly helpful in learning about argumentative writing, while they had mixed reactions to peer review and reflection.

The students felt that their unlimited access to **videos** and **online quizzes** reduced the direct pressure to learn and that the material enhanced their knowledge and skills. Mariyam, one of the interviewees, clarified this idea:

I think it is very helpful to be able to view the videos before and after class to review the content. I can watch the videos multiple times, stop and take notes, and press play again. I feel more prepared and comfortable participating in class activities and asking questions.

Another student, Jonathan, stated:

The videos and quizzes make learning easier; I can watch them when I have time and then take a quiz to see how well I have understood. I particularly like that I have multiple opportunities for each quiz. I just feel that this fits me better, and I have less pressure compared to my other classes.

Fredrick agreed with both Mariyam and Jonathan, adding, "I'm able to watch the videos on my phone while I commute to school or my home, which helps with my studies." These predominantly positive attitudes suggested that videos and online quizzes assist students in preparing for class and reviewing class objectives. Students perceived that the course fit well with today's learners and their preferred modes of learning. The student comments reflected what other research has found: today's students are tech-savvy, and they expect to see or to use technology in everyday lessons (Kessler, 2018). This, in turn, could open them to learning about argumentation.

The students thought that providing **online quizzes** could help them evaluate their learning progress toward effective argumentative writing. For example, Peter found online quizzes effective in self-directed learning to track learning progress and test his understanding of arguments and the concept of argumentation. He commented:

Online quiz is really a good tool to motivate me to learn. It's hard for me to understand how much I understand how to present my arguments. As long as there's an online quiz available together with videos, this can help me remember what I've learnt.

Mariyam agreed with Peter and added:

I can make several attempts to complete online quizzes which can help me check my learning progress and how far I understand the concept of argumentation. If I just watch videos without doing any corresponding quizzes, it will be a bit useless.

These positive comments suggested that online quizzes are very useful in helping students review what they have learned and gauge how much they have understood, which can in turn increase their confidence. The online quizzes helped students learn how to present arguments and understand the concept of argumentation. They also helped teachers allocate significantly more time for in-class, follow-up active learning activities (e.g., debates) and generate more lively and in-depth class discussions (Hillman, 2012).

The students felt that having **F2F instruction** could help them reinforce the knowledge they had acquired previously prior to introducing new concepts and information in the session, which could be especially important for something as complex as argumentation. Christian, for example, described F2F instruction as bringing everything physically together:

> *When we come to class, we have watched the videos, completed the quizzes, so we have a good idea of what we will discuss. Before, when I came to class, I often felt clueless and didn't really know what was going on. But now, it is like the class reinforced what we have done so it is easier to see how it all fits.*

The participants described the F2F sessions as engaging and motivating because the sessions supplemented their background knowledge. This result is in accordance with the trend that motivating students often leads to better learning outcomes and better critical writing skills, and this critical faculty is essential to quality argumentation. As Lucy explained:

> *I feel like I can do this. I don't have to give up. It's so much easier to ask questions and explain my ideas, as I have already seen it being explained in the video. Yes, it's better to learn this way and more helpful.*

While all the students noted the benefits of videos, quizzes, and F2F instruction in learning argumentative writing, several students felt that two other course components—peer review and self-reflection—were less beneficial to their learning.

Nicole expressed a commonly held belief among the students: that **peer review** was potentially valuable; however, she noted that even though the teacher gave detailed instructions on how to conduct these reviews, she and her peers found it challenging to establish whether their arguments were well developed and sound. She commented:

> *It is good to read what my classmates have written, and when we compare, we can help each other and give ideas. But how do we know our argument is good? Even if we follow the checklist, I feel that I might be missing something. I just feel that it is good as an initial brainstorm idea, but I'd rather have the teacher's help.*

This sentiment was common among the participants. It can be difficult for students to evaluate each other's work due to a limited understanding of how to build an argument.

Reflection also elicited mixed responses. On the plus side, Jim stated:

> *During weekly reflection writing, I can reflect what I put down in my drafts which may help me think one step further.*

Nicole concurred:

> *Writing reflection is a good way to help me have deeper learning. It helps me think about how to avoid any logical problems and how to make more complex and integrated knowledge structures.*

On the other hand, Mariyam, though appreciative, showed a lack of commitment that worked against the goals of reflection:

> *My argumentation can be clearer through writing reflections, but I'll do them in the very last second, just before the next class begins.*

Another student, Peter, saw both sides:

> *At first, I thought, what is the point? . . . It seems such a waste of my time, but after a couple of weeks, I found it to be OK, as I could go back and review what I had written and why.*

The mixed responses of Mariyam and Peter suggest that student buy-in to reflection, despite its contribution to learning how to write arguments, is something that teachers may need to work on to achieve its full potential as a form of beneficial input.

To summarize the answer to the first research question, students were comfortable with and saw value in videos, quizzes, and F2F instruction but were less confident in and less convinced of the value of peer review and reflection. This less positive appreciation could be due to the increased language demands that these methods entailed, though these students' limited exposure to a learning culture other than what the teachers provided may have engendered a lack of experience with and confidence in these methods.

Overall, the participants acknowledged that each method brings unique benefits and, in our experience, collectively these methods provide a productive holistic model method of learning about argumentative writing. As teachers strive to develop students' argumentative writing skills, our study suggests that teachers should incorporate different methods of delivering multifaceted learning to reach all students. The methods we employed can provide practical learning opportunities that, together, teach students how to develop and write high-calibre academic essays. Thus, the delivery of material through various methods appears to provide students with convenient, engaging, and stimulating learning.

RQ 2: *Which method(s) provided students with a more in-depth understanding of argumentative writing?*

The second aim of this study was to explore which input method could improve students' confidence toward producing argumentative writing. The participants felt that composing quality academic essays, including arguments, is an essential skill for them to acquire if they want to succeed in university studies. Participants indicated that the input methods, on the whole, provided an organized and clear picture of argumentative writing and increased their understanding of argumentative essays. They also said that the various teaching methods helped them develop multiple views of their argument and ways to present an argument in writing. These findings are discussed in response to concerns students expressed about argumentative writing.

When **analyzing and evaluating evidence and developing positions,** the writer must take a position, anticipate the audience's position, rationalize his or her position, and consider alternatives. These elements are at the core of argumentative writing (Wingate, 2012). It is, therefore, not surprising that the participants noted the challenges of supporting their stances in their essays. Matthew spoke for many, stating, "My teacher kept saying my position was too simple." Similarly, George commented:

> *My essay lacks criticality. I'm supposed to discuss the ideas and convince the reader of my position, which I have done, but still, the feedback from my teacher is that I merely report and not discuss.*

Students considered this aspect of criticality both very difficult and very important. In response to this situation, they indicated that the instructional videos had helped to explain how to select and integrate information. Ola, for instance, stressed that the visual element plus supporting text in the videos broke down the components and illustrated how to construct a paragraph:

> *The video that the teacher created is really helpful. It discusses the article we have all read and then goes through how to read an academic article, highlighting the elements, and it*

shows how the position is being built sentence by sentence. Usually, in class, the teaching is very general, so this is more useful. And I can watch the videos as many times as I like.

Monica expressed a similar view while also acknowledging value in f2f instruction:

So, I like the videos and the quizzes, as I can take my time to figure out what sentence is the claim, counterclaim, and think about the process. But I still prefer when the teacher shows us how to develop the claim in class, as it is easier to ask questions.

As these quotations suggest, videos were especially well received in terms of learning input, but it was also interesting to note that some students preferred F2F teacher time to check their understanding of the input, to make them more confident about the process, and to help them think of the learning in a stepwise manner.

Another concern expressed about argumentative writing was a feeling of **insecurity and inferiority**. Participants found it very difficult to produce something new, regardless of multiple views on one idea. Elizabeth, for instance, asked:

How can I be expected to develop a brand-new idea? There's so much written already, on every angle: it's almost impossible to know what side I should write. And how am I supposed to criticize something that is published in an academic journal?

This comment shows that some students may have lacked criticality in selecting and evaluating sources, and they felt their views were less valuable as a result. In this context, four participants pointed out that F2F instruction was useful in illustrating that their ideas were valuable and worthwhile. Jim explained that:

In the class, the teacher was really supportive and explained that it isn't about if the idea is new or not; it's about how we present it.

Adam added that:

I feel more confident that I know how to pick an angle for the essay after our class discussion. It really helped me understand that I don't have to write something new, but I need to present my ideas in a new way with supporting evidence.

At the same time, several interviewees felt that peer review can provide support in developing their criticality. This observation corroborates previous studies that have found learners receptive to peer feedback (Maas, 2017). This feedback was particularly useful for Anna, Marcus, and Christian, who found that discussing their ideas helped them select a peer-reviewed article and develop a critique. However, some other students indicated that they lacked confidence to critique published research, making it difficult for them to take a position in an academic debate.

> **How to organize an argumentative essay** effectively was another concern commonly expressed among the students. Nicole said, "I was told my argument is hidden, and one needs to search for it." George added: "My conclusion isn't linked with the introduction. But I can't see why it isn't." Finally, Mariyam captured the situation this way: ". . . ah . . . I really don't understand how to write good topic sentences."

In response to that concern, the participants were motivated by combined input methods, especially videos and F2F teaching. Most participants agreed that the interactive videos supplemented the F2F teaching and provided useful learning input while also noting that the teacher in the F2F mode often pointed out their lack of knowledge of how to structure their argumentative essays. Thus, this input combination was valued. So, too, was videos in tandem with drag-and-drop activities. After watching the instructional videos on how to organize and position the material in their essays and completing drag-and-drop activities such as quizzes, the students appeared more positive and knowledgeable about how to proceed. For example, Peter said, "I really find the drag-and-drop activities to be helpful in learning how to organize the essay."

Overall, in response to the second research question, the students appeared positive about the hybrid approach in addressing the concerns they felt. Input coming from more than one direction seemed to enrich their learning. Moreover, the various layers of input appeared to help students gain confidence in their writing abilities.

Pedagogical Implications and Closing Thoughts

We have investigated how L2 students perceive writing instruction in an EAP course that adopted a hybrid approach class for teaching argumentative writing. This chapter highlights the importance of providing multiple sources of instructional input to help novice (L2) writers develop criticality and argumentative writing skills. Overall our study revealed a very positive student response to this hybrid pedagogical approach to learning how to write an argumentative essay.

Based on our findings, this hybrid approach's effectiveness depends on numerous elements, including using videos in combination with one or more other input methods: quizzes, F2F instruction, peer review, and students' reflections. Students viewed the use of illustrative videos that broke down the writing process in a step-by-step manner as particularly useful, because these videos provided multiple explanations and interactive quizzes where they could practice and self-correct their skills. The students recognized that the quality of an academic essay depends on the development of an argument. It was encouraging to see that the students found incorporating various input methods valuable in that regard.

In our course, subject leaders send suggested in-class and out-of-class activities in weekly emails that teachers can integrate into their instruction, and those teachers have systematically integrated the five sources of input into their courses not only to focus on surface features (Lea & Street, 1998) but also to make it clear that developing an argument is the objective. This hybrid approach suggests that no single method is optimal for teaching critical thinking and argumentative writing. Instead, a combination of closely interlinked input methods could better assist students in developing an understanding of argument and the concept of argumentation.

However, implementing a hybrid approach like the one introduced requires a great deal of time and effort. For instance, a teacher will need to create short videos with connected quizzes, create peer review sheets, read reflections, and prepare for in-class instruction. This is time- and labor-intensive work. We found that asking questions such as "What does the learner need to know or learn?" and "Will the learner find this resource useful?" before choosing the medium for the activities was a good starting point, but we also found that making final decisions on what will work was not easy. Incorporating various input methods into courses can initially seem time-consuming and challenging. However, as our study showed, the process is well worth it, as students then have the flexibility to choose their preferred input method, which can facilitate learning. We suggest that non-F2F input methods should be fairly short (8–15 minutes) and convey learning messages in simple and clear ways that enable learners to receive and interact with the relevant content actively.

This small-scale study cannot represent all Hong Kong EAP learners or L2 students entering academia in other settings. However, we hope that these findings may contribute to discussion of the appropriateness of providing multiple input methods to teach students critical-writing skills by explaining what students perceive as useful. While the current results illuminate students' perceptions, the perspectives of more participants, as well as evaluations of students' writing, would add more breadth to this study. Still, this qualitative study can contribute to the growing body of scholarship regarding hybrid approaches to teaching argumentative writing, as the results yield up-to-date information on students' perceptions of methods and understanding in their eyes, which all add to the still limited body of literature on best practices of argumentative writing instruction in Hong Kong and beyond.

REFERENCES

Andrews, R. (1995). *Teaching and learning argument.* London: Cassell.

Braun, V., & Clarke, V. (2006). Using thematic analysis in psychology. *Qualitative Research in Psychology, 3*(2), 77–101.

Cho, K. L., & Jonassen, D. H. (2002). The effects of argumentation scaffolds on argumentation and problem solving. *Educational Technology Research and Development, 50*(3), 5–22.

Creswell, J. W. (2008). *Educational research: Planning, conducting, and evaluating quantitative and qualitative research* (3rd ed.). Upper Saddle River, NJ: Pearson Education.

Felton, M., Crowell, A., & Liu, T. (2015). Arguing to agree: Mitigating myside bias through consensus-seeking dialogue. *Written Communication, 32*, 317–331.

Helms-Park, R. & Stapleton, P. (2003). Questioning the importance of individualized voice in undergraduate L2 argumentative writing: An empirical study with pedagogical implications. *Journal of Second Language Writing, 12*(3), 245–265.

Hillman, J. (2012). The impact of online quizzes on student engagement and learning report. Penn State Berks. Retrieved from http://berks .psu.edu/sites/default/files/cam-pus/Hillman_TLI_report.pdf

Hirvela, A. (2011). Learning to write: Issues in theory, research, and pedagogy. In R. M. Manchon (Ed.), *Learning-to-write and writing-to-learn in an additional language* (pp. 37–59). Amsterdam: John Benjamins.

Hirvela, A. (2013). Preparing English language learners for argumentative writing. In L. C. de Oliveira & T. J. Silva (Eds.). *L2 writing in secondary classrooms: Student experiences, academic issues, and teacher education* (pp. 67–86). New York, NY: Routledge.

Hung, I-C., Kinshuk, & Chen, N.-S. (2018). Embodied interactive video lectures for improving learning comprehension and retention. *Computers & Education, 117*, 116–131.

Hyland, K. (2003). *Second language writing.* Cambridge, England: Cambridge University Press.

Hyland, K. (2013). Writing in the university: Education, knowledge and reputation. *Language Teaching, 46*(1), 53–70.

Hyland, K. (2016). General and specific EAP. In K. Hyland & P. Shaw (Eds.), The *Routledge Handbook of English for Academic Purposes* (pp. 41–53). London: Routledge.

Jonassen, D. H., Shen, D., Marra, R. M., Cho, Y. H., Lo, J. L., & Lohani, V. K. (2009). Engaging and supporting problem solving in engineering ethics. *Journal of Engineering Education, 98*(3), 235–254.

Kessler, G. (2018). Technology and the future of language teaching, *Foreign Language Annals, 51*(1), 205–218.

Knudson, R. E. (1992). Analysis of argumentative writing at two grade levels. *Journal of Educational Research, 85*(3), 169–179.

Lam, Y. W., Hew, K. F., & Chiu, K. F. (2018). Improving argumentative writing: Effects of a blended learning approach and gamification. *Language Learning & Technology, 22*(1), 97–118.

Lea, M. R., & Street, B. V. (1998). Student writing in higher education: An academic literacies approach. *Studies in Higher Education, 23*, 157–172.

Liu, F., & Stapleton, P. (2014). Counter argumentation and the cultivation of critical thinking in argumentative writing: Investigating washback from a high-stakes test. *System, 45*, 117–128.

Maas, C. (2017). Receptive to learner-driven feedback in EAP. *ELT Journal, 71*(2), 127–140.

Merriam, S. B. (2017). *Qualitative research: A guide to design and implementation* (2nd ed.), San Francisco: Jossey-Bass.

Toplak, M. E., & Stanovich, K. E. (2003). Associations between myside bias on informal reasoning task and amount of post-secondary education. *Applied Cognitive Psychology, 17*, 851–860.

Toulmin, S., Rieke, R., & Janik, A. (1984). *An introduction to reasoning* (2nd ed.). New York: Macmillan

Wingate, U. (2012). "Argument!" Helping students understand what essay writing is about. *Journal of English for Academic Purposes, 11*(2), 145–154.

Wu, S. (2006). Creating a contrastive rhetorical stance: Investigating the strategy of problematization in students' argumentation. *RELC Journal, 37*, 329–353.

Analysis of Pre-Service Teachers' Reflective Journals: Learning-to-Argue through Writing about Writing

LISYA SELONI AND NUR YIĞITOĞLU APTOULA

Abstract

This chapter focuses on how pre-service teachers in a foreign language education program at a Turkish university enhanced their learning-to-argue ability through writing-about-writing journaling (WWJ) practices within their first-year writing (FYW) courses. In this chapter, we discuss the importance of writing-about-writing journals for learning-to-argue as L2 writers are acclimated to different forms of critical thinking and gain new academic writing practices. The chapter ends with a discussion of how a close look at pre-service teachers' learning-to-argue process through WWJs could give writing instructors and teacher educators additional pedagogical insights about pre-serve teachers' growing learning-to-argue abilities in their local contexts.

Achieving a "comprehensible agenda" (Hirvela, 2017) in L2 argumentation scholarship and searching for inclusive pedagogical insights is not possible without systematic consideration of how student writers across cultures and languages build argumentation and how these arguments are taken up. While scholarship on L2 argumentation within the North American contexts has "firm institutional footing in writing and rhetoric programs" (Kibler, 2017, p.75), the way argumentation is understood and taught in diverse EFL settings with English language learners and their instructors may include different forms of linguistic, cultural and institutional complexities. Learning and teaching argumentation might look quite different for teachers who exclusively work in such contexts. Additionally, while there is some scholarship on teaching argumentation across disciplines in various EFL settings (e.g., Miller & Pessoa, 2016), much of this body of research has been devoted to understanding the experiences of various student writer populations rather than the current or future teachers of these L2 writers (e.g., Hirvela & Belcher, 2007; Seloni & Henderson Lee, 2020). As the L2 writing field evolves and becomes more internationalized, understanding how practicing teachers and pre-service teachers across cultures engage in new writing practices, including diverse forms of argumentation, is important for the development of L2 writers and L2 writing teachers in non-English dominant contexts.

While there is a growing body of research on how EFL teachers learn to teach writing, this knowledge base is still quite limited compared to what is known about how writing teachers in English-dominant countries learn to teach L2 writing. The social and educational landscape highly shape the metaknowledge about writing knowledge affecting EFL teachers' writing instruction as well as L2 writing skills. In countries where there is limited access to and use of English in daily, professional, or academic life, it is no surprise that practicing teachers and teacher candidates might have fewer opportunities and resources to engage in the acts of reading and writing in their second language. As revealed in multiple chapters in Seloni and Henderson Lee's (2020) collection on L2 writing teacher preparation, writing is not a stand-alone course in such contexts but is often taught in combined skills courses alongside reading, listening, and speaking.

While both in-service and pre-service language teachers might not see the immediate need to use L2 writing as an act of communication, reading and writing are seen as important tools for learning the language in many non-English dominant contexts (Manchón, 2009). Therefore, first year L2 writing courses, like the ones offered in some language teacher education programs in Turkey, can be important spaces to understand how teacher candidates form their knowledge base about L2 writing and L2 writing instruction. While the language learning potential of writing courses should not be diminished, these courses can also be perceived as the rare spaces where pre-service teachers' perceptions of L2 writing in various text types, including argumentative writing, can be enhanced, and where they develop their evolving understanding of how to teach L2 writing.

In these writing courses, it is crucial for EFL writing instructors to consider the dichotomy between *arguing to learn* and *learning to argue* (Hirvela, 2017) rather than seeing argumentative writing instruction simply as teaching an essay form in a formulaic way. As Hirvela (2017) explains in his seminal article on argumentation and second language writing, writing instructors focusing on *learning to argue* aim to further their students' understanding and awareness of how to construct arguments. Whereas, in *arguing to learn*, the concept of argument is considered as a way of arriving at a deeper understanding of a topic through an analytical process. While the focus of this chapter is how language teacher candidates enhance their learning-to-argue abilities, it is important to include both kinds of analytical thinking in the development of pre-service teachers' writing development because, as Yigitoglu and Belcher (2014) also propose, writing experiences may play varying roles in writing teachers' instructional decision-making processes. As part of that process, these pre-service teachers will first need to know how to use argumentation as student writers; this is a background they can draw from later as writing teachers.

This chapter discusses the significance of learning to argue in the writing-to-learn framework in the context of EFL teacher development in Turkey. Through analyzing the content as well as textual elements in pre-service teachers' journal entries about writing, their attempts to understand the rhetorical expectations of academic writing, in particular practices needed to produce written arguments, are explored. This analysis is used to show how and why pre-service teachers' writing about writing can enrich their understanding of argumentation and better prepare them to teach such writing. Here, 'writing about writing' is used to mean students' written reflections about what they learn concerning writing in a writing course as a way of deepening their understanding of that learning.

Theoretical Framework

Pre-service language teachers in the Turkish context generally have limited opportunities to practice L2 writing, thus making a conscious transfer from one writing situation to another challenging. What takes place in writing courses may be limited in terms of content, plus there is a heavy emphasis on composing five-paragraph essays as a result of an examination-dominated education system where formulaic writing is emphasized. As a result, these teachers receive minimal, if any, exposure to other kinds of writing that could expand their awareness of the possibilities in L2 writing. Thus, it is important for university writing instructors to help student writers move from familiar writing situations like the five-paragraph essay to unfamiliar writing situations where students learn how to see writing as a communicative act. One way of doing this is **writing-about-writing** activities, which can be a useful writing exercise in first-year writing (FYW) courses (if such courses are offered by the institution), where pre-service teachers are usually introduced to various academic genres and academic writing practices.

Writing about Writing and Writing to Learn

Instead of teaching abstract writing skills in FYW courses, Downs and Wardle (2007) propose a writing-about-writing approach, which moves beyond the idea of teaching writing as an isolated skill. In this view, rather than assuming teaching selected genres and text types will automatically transfer to different writing situations, students are encouraged to read and write about writing research "identifying writing related problems that interest them" (p. 558) and report on them orally or in writing. As they state, "instead of teaching situational skills often incorrectly imagined to be generalizable, first year composition courses could teach about the ways writing works in the world and how the tool of writing is used to mediate various activities" (p. 558). In such an approach, students are encouraged to understand activities and practices related to writing rather than paying attention to the conventions and universal rules about writing and are taught that conventions within each discipline are context-specific.

Similar to this approach, the facilitative role of writing on learning and thinking has been discussed in several important studies in the general field of education (e.g., Bangert-Downs, Hurley, & Maniee, 2004; Langer & Applebee, 1987; Newell, 1984). In these studies, writing has been found beneficial to learn content compared to short-answer questions and conventional ways of assessing student learning. As stated by Bangert-Downs, Hurley, & Maniee (2004), "Writing can be a tool of self-reflective monitoring of comprehension, thus creating opportunities for students to evaluate their own understandings, confusions, and feelings about a topic" (p. 32). While it has been argued that it is unrealistic to expect student writers to develop learning strategies through every writing task, the nature of writing and its frequency could be important factors to trace the effects of writing on learning. For example, analytic writing in which students are engaged in arguing a viewpoint and investigation of relations about different ideas has been shown to help them retain information (Durst & Newell, 1989). Similarly, Bangert-Downs, Hurley, & Maniee (2004), in their meta-analysis of studies on the effectiveness of school-based writing-to-learn programs, found important relationships between learning, school achievement, and writing. Their review of these studies suggests that "writing interventions in which students were asked to reflect on their current understanding, confusions, and learning processes typically yielded more positive results" (p. 52).

Journal Writing

Journals have been used in L2 writing courses for many years. Among the benefits of journal writing are (1) increased awareness of the learning processes and (2) a better understanding of one's thinking as students engage in a dialogue with the teacher or respond to a reflective prompt. Casanave (2011) states that one of the purposes of journal writing is "to help learners engage with ideas, reflect on self and issues, and practice expressing ideas in written language to a real audience (teacher, peer, self)" (p. 5). Because journal writing can help create self-autonomous and reflective learners, it has been implemented in the field of L2 studies both as a tool for teacher candidates' reflection on their pedagogical development and for learners to observe their ongoing development as writers at various levels of education (e.g., Connolly, 2006; Trites, 2001) and in diverse contexts such as Malaysia (Kabilan, 2007), Korea (Yi, 2005), and Japan (Duppenthaler, 2004).

Taking this combined framework of writing for learning and journaling as our frame of reference, we argue that incorporating writing-about-writing and writing-to-learn practices through daily journal writing in a FYW course designed for teacher candidates could offer an alternative instructional model where student writers develop abilities to reason and to learn to think critically while also deeply reflecting on their current knowledge and learning processes concerning L2 writing. We further argue that this will be especially beneficial for pre-service English teachers in their preparation to teach L2 writing.

Writing-about-writing journals (WWJs) of 50 first-year pre-service teachers were analyzed. These teachers were enrolled in two sections of a compulsory FYW course during the 2016–2017 academic year at a Turkish university. This content analysis focused on what the pre-service teachers wrote in relation to their journey with academic writing. These entries involved topics related to writing style, learning of argumentation, and transfer of prior knowledge.

The Study

Context

The study took place in two sections of the same writing course in a foreign language teacher education program in a research-intensive university in

Istanbul, Turkey. Each year, approximately 90 students are placed in this teacher education program based on their nationwide university exam scores. Due to the lack of writing emphasis during secondary education in many public schools in Turkey, many students who are accepted into this program are exposed to their first formal writing instruction in a language program for pre-matriculated students, where they only study English as a foreign language (for more information on the higher education system, see Unaldi et al., 2020). After completing this pre-matriculation program, they are allowed to take their discipline-specific courses a well as a two-course writing sequence in their first year. The setting from which this data comes are two sections of one of the FYW courses, Critical Thinking into Writing, which "aims to develop freshman students' critical thinking and writing skills, with an emphasis on argumentation exercises as well as finding, storing, and evaluating sources" (taken from course description). As students moved through the course, they wrote short reflections (of half a page to one page in length)—that is, journal entries—on what they were learning each week.

The Focus and Research Questions

The study is part of a broader ethnographic study that aimed to investigate the L1 and L2 writing experiences and genre knowledge of first year pre-service teachers. For this broader version, data were collected from student and faculty interviews, participant observation, and artifacts, such as assessment tasks, including writing exams given to teacher candidates during their participation in the FYW course sequence. While this ethnographic orientation helped provide contextual knowledge, the focus here is on some of the written artifacts in the data corpus, namely writing-about-writing journal entries related to argumentative writing. The primary research question addressed in this chapter is: *How do pre-service teachers conceptualize argumentative thinking and learning in writing-about-writing journals?* The answer to this research question provided a deeper understanding of how student writers in this writing course enhanced their learning-to-argue ability through writing-about-writing journaling.

Data Collection and Analysis: Critical Analysis of WWJs

As part of the course requirement, the first-year pre-service teachers were asked to keep a writing journal throughout the semester where they documented their evolving understanding of different writing skills and genres they learned about in the writing course. The goal of this weekly writing assignment was to encourage pre-service teachers to explicitly think about and discuss the kinds of connections they were making between their prior writing knowledge/experiences and the new academic writing knowledge they were acquiring. Each class participant kept a handwritten journal where they composed a short response to the assigned academic readings on writing and the various writing genres they were learning about and practicing in class. Some of the guiding questions for these journals included: "What was your assumption about this writing skill/genre?" "What have you learned about this particular skill/genre this week?" "How has your previous knowledge helped you to make sense of this skill/genre?" For the purpose of this discussion, only what they wrote regarding learning to argue is analyzed. The pre-service teachers who agreed to participate in the study were given consent forms. Before the data analysis, pseudonyms were assigned to all participants.

The corpus generated during the study consisted of a total of 40 journals comprising approximately 400 handwritten pages of reflective writing. Of that writing, approximately 60 handwritten pages focused on comments related to argumentative writing. Summative content analysis was used to analyze the journal entries. Researchers adopting summative content analysis identify and quantify the key word counts, which is followed by a second layer of analysis that includes the close examination of context(s) in which they are used. For the purposes of this study, summative content analysis was especially important, since we primarily wanted to learn about some of the key writing habits, experiences, and knowledge that teacher candidates developed around various L2 writing skills. Only our summative content analysis findings as related to learning to argue via representative samples of the students' journal writing are discussed here.

Findings and Discussion

Based on the main research question, we were interested in how teacher candidates' learning of argumentation and argumentative writing skills was reflected within their weekly journals and thus how the writing-about-writing activity facilitated their argumentative learning. At a broader level, the findings revealed that WWJs provided the students with an informal but valuable space to reflect on and to raise questions about their learning process and L2 writing habits, including argumentation. More specifically, we found that journal writing functioned as a beneficial metacognitive tool to raise students' awareness of and intentionality regarding how argumentation works and what academic practices can enhance one's argumentative writing skills.

Documentation of Increased Awareness and Intentionality on How Argumentation Works across Contexts

Since many students in the Turkish educational context do not have much experience with writing, let alone writing about writing, we had pedagogical advantage when introducing WWJs as a weekly reflective writing task, and many of the pre-service teachers were quite open to and enthusiastic about exploring their L2 literacy practices and how those practices related to their current understanding of argumentation. While our student population primarily engaged in writing in the form of five- paragraph essays and formulaic writing in their earlier English language studies, the kinds of writing they were asked to do in the Critical Thinking into Writing course required them to move beyond essay-format argumentation. We found that even though students' earlier exposure to writing (both L1 and L2) was limited to five-paragraph essays and short-answer texts, in their journal entries many mentioned that they had experienced other kinds of writing in everyday life that resembled formal types of writing. For instance, in one of her earlier entries, Nil reflected on a class activity where students were studying the rhetorical moves and genre features of complaint letters. Here she exhibited some of her argumentative learning skills:

> This week's task was writing a complaint letter. I have never written a letter of complaint before but in my opinion, it was the easiest task for me because no longer ago than last week I had a problem with an e-commerce company which sells products that come from abroad. Although it [today's in-class writing] was a simple task, explaining the situation and what I want from the other person by using a neutral, non-blaming and descriptive language was effortful. I think using evidence to support my case was an exercise for composing our own arguments. It was a helpful experience.

As Nil stated in her journal, she had previously encountered a problem with a company where she purchased a product from abroad. While complaining as a customer was a familiar communicative act due to this prior experience, she said that she learned from her in-class writing activities specific argumentative skills (e.g., using evidence to support her argument) and rhetorical moves (e.g., inclusion of non-blaming language) to be a more effective communicator in this particular genre. Her words in this entry reveal to us the increased awareness and conscious thinking about the language used in the message she wanted to give in this particular communicative action where she builds an argument for why something is not her fault. Nil's use of words like *neutral, non-blaming,* and *descriptive* demonstrates that she understands that the complaint letter as a genre requires a specific kind of language, style, and register while making a claim that certain things may not be the customer's fault. This entry illustrates Nil's evolving knowledge of how certain word choices and rhetorical strategies can move people toward change.

Similarly, the writing-about-writing journal entries illustrated teacher candidates' increased awareness of the social situatedness of academic writing as well as its role in the language teaching profession. For instance, according to Seda's entry, different genres require different rhetorical strategies, such as the inclusion of one's opinion. She reports that relying predominantly on one's opinion in argumentative writing isn't a strong rhetorical pattern, and that she's learning how to "keep her views back":

> *I learned a lot of things about academic writing and critical thinking. They have great importance to me because we are going to be teachers. So, we have to know how to analyze a paragraph or a text, what the purpose is, what the hidden sides are. . . . Having an ability to answer these questions makes us more equipped as teachers. For example, we are not allowed to reflect on ourselves freely in all of our writing because some genres (like argumentative writing) don't have a base for it. I still have difficulties in terms of keeping my views back and just saying what's going on. In the past, (I mean only university language preparation term because in high school we didn't do anything to improve our writing), I was out of organization. I didn't care much about outlines or coherence. And now, I know that without a proper map, a planned way, our words may seem inappropriate.*

Here, Seda seems to perceive the process of learning how to write academically and critical thinking as important contributors to her development as a future language teacher. Because many student writers in our courses lack experience with argumentative genres, they usually deploy narrative writing discussing their opinions with limited integration of sources when asked to create an argumentative text. Feeling "more equipped," Seda reports that certain genres in academic writing, such as argumentative writing, require a specific way of composing (as opposed to freewriting) as well as critical-thinking skills. Her statement on not being allowed to reflect on her own ideas "freely" and her supporting argument for this ("some genres don't have a base for it") demonstrate her evolving awareness of diverse genre expectations she's encountering in college courses.

Moreover, we observed that students in our course were able to create claims and state their point of views for their arguments, but many of them had difficulties with synthesizing the arguments in the source texts to create some context for their opinions and claims. They needed practice, especially in integrating sources and evaluating ideas they read. Therefore, a regular practice in our classes was to ask students to read critically and combine sources on diverse topics showing the similarities and differences in opinions. In one of her entries, Merve addressed the process of learning to write an argumentative essay and how this process contributed to her own development as a writer. In her entry, she discusses specific skills and practices she learned to parse academic texts, reflecting a variation of the Toulmin (1958/2003) model of writing:

> *This week we learnt about finding some elements of an argumentative essay like finding evidence, claim, reason, evaluation. We have started to analyze essays. I didn't know about analysing essays in this way before. It is really useful for me because by this knowledge I will be able to separate parts and I will see differences more clearly. When writing argumentative essays, I will now make sure that my writing has important elements like evidence and a strong conclusion.*

In our classes, students read a wide range of texts from English, History, and Philosophy so that they are exposed to different ways of reasoning, and arguing as well as different ideas in the disciplines. Merve's entry about "separating parts" in linguistically dense readings and understanding the linguistic and rhetorical elements emphasizes the importance of coupling personal opinions and evaluations with evidence and warrants when it comes to building effective arguments in her writing.

Similarly, Cemile's entry reports her evolving awareness and commitment to understanding and synthesizing textual evidence to construct her own arguments:

> *From the last courses we have focused on the subject of combining sources which is used in reviews. It is more like synthesizing and comparing two or more than two texts, and it is different from summaries. We use paraphrasing and quoting while synthesizing as we do while summarizing. A summary is putting the information together and reproducing almost 25% of the text. But synthesizing is more than reproducing information. First of all, you have your own ideas, you interpret critically, discover relationships between sources, compare and contrast. Also, the words and links directing the original text is very important. Before I would just summarize the texts I was about to combine. Now, I see I need to do more than that, like evaluating them.*

Part of our argumentative writing instruction in this course included teaching how to summarize and synthesize various texts from different disciplinary traditions. In class, we often explained that the ability to synthesize information we collect from outside resources is an important part of assessing arguments. We observed important learning moments in Cemile's entry with regard to key differences between summarizing and synthesizing sources, which are important skills students needed for the kinds of academic writing they were asked to do in their teacher education program. Cemile's words about discovering relationships between sources without diverting from the arguments presented in the original text while also evaluating them indicate her developing reading awareness. Students like Cemile have long experienced producing decontextualized five-paragraph essays based on descriptive writing, and this entry reveals her increased awareness of the importance of building connections and links between sources.

In addition to learning specific practices such as synthesizing sources, students also pointed out that certain linguistic features made their arguments flow better. For instance, Gizem underlined the importance of coherence for the development of her arguments and emphasizes the discoursal elements of academic writing:

> *I cannot underestimate the importance of the term* coherence *for my arguments. Even if it seems basic and simple, sometimes you can see ones that are total work of madness. Your words make sentences meaningful; your sentences make paragraphs meaningful and in the end your paragraphs are your ultimate heroes that make your arguments in your essay meaningful.*

By saying that "in the end your paragraphs are your ultimate heroes that make your arguments in your essay meaningful," Gizem shares with us that as a writer she needs to pay attention to issues around cohesion and coherence through the use of explicit moves that will help her connect her words and paragraphs. Hyland (2005, p. 4) states that "English differs from a number of languages by placing responsibility for coherence and clarity on the writer rather than on the reader." Many students reported in our class conversations that when writing in Turkish, they did not feel the need to make specific moves to generate coherence in their writing. Rather, several of them mentioned the importance of using metaphors and flowery language in making their writing appealing. For many, grabbing the attention of readers with such moves seemed more important than coherent writing. Here, Gizem reports on the responsibility that she wants to take in making her sentences and paragraphs meaningful to the readers while writing in English.

The results of our content analysis demonstrate that WWJs provided students a space to discuss their increased awareness and intentionality regarding the kinds of linguistic and rhetorical responsibilities they needed to take on and specific rhetorical moves they needed to perform, including in argumentative writing. The documentation in the WWJs is an indication that these pre-service teacher writers were recognizing writing as a context-specific practice and engaging in learning to argue rather than memorizing universal rules about how to write. The value can be the reinforcement or deeper awareness of acquired knowledge that arises through such reflection. In our experience, WWJs provided an informal platform for consciousness-raising and functioned as a helpful instructional activity that enabled us to trace students' reflections and learning processes about L2 writing, including argumentative writing. Thus, both the students and we as their teachers benefited from the WWJ activity.

Pedagogical Implications and Closing Thoughts

This study illustrated the importance of incorporating WWJs as a reflective tool for learning to argue as L2 writers are acclimated to different forms of critical thinking and gain new academic writing practices. While inclusion of the journals may not offer a perfect solution to trace students' development of argumentation, we believe that they can give pre-service teachers a chance to document and understand their journey into and through academic writing and us, as their teachers, a chance to trace their learning moments. As Bangert-Downs, Hurley, and Maniee (2004) state, such "self-reflective monitoring of comprehension" (p. 32) strengthens the learning process by drawing more attention to what has been learned. Taking a closer look at the pre-service teachers' documentation of their learning showed us what enhances their learning-to-argue abilities. As Yigitoglu and Belcher (2014) also argued, both L1 and L2 writing experiences may play varying roles in instructional decision-making, and they suggested that teachers should see "self-reflection—on themselves as L2 learners and writers, not just as teachers—as a routine part of their professional practice" (p. 123). Such reflective practices concerning learning about argumentation could be useful in understanding the thought processes that new teachers undergo as they gain new skills and practices in L2 writing, and give writing instructors insider knowledge on the difficulties that L2 writers go through as they add new skills to their academic repertoires in the L2. Thus, we argue that writing-about-writing tasks such as the one used in this study can be a meaningful tool to engage pre-service teachers with reflective writing, which in turn could help them trace their own understanding and involvement with different kinds of academic writing practices, including the important skill of argumentative writing.

The teacher candidates we worked with utilized journal writing as a metacognitive thinking tool where they evaluated and reflected on their learning. In addition to their increased metacognitive awareness, this informal writing space helped us carefully consider students' understanding of the class content and trace any ambiguities or uncertainties they had about in-class writing tasks. As the data we shared has illustrated, teacher candidates' comprehension of certain academic writing practices can be influenced by their mental frameworks (their cultural schemata that help them make sense of the new knowledge) and prior experiences about that particular writing practice (e.g., Nil's writing experience with a complaint letter). Many of them appeared willing to assume a newcomer writer and learner role and were ready to utilize and re-envision their prior genre knowledge. Sommers and Saltz (2004) coined the term "novices as experts" to indicate how newcomers could effectively draw on various writing resources and prior experiences at their disposal, and how they are changed by what they learn. As they state, first-year students "build authority not by writing from a position of expertise but by writing into expertise. As apprentices they learn to write by first repeating the ideas they encounter in the sources they read and the teachers they admire, using the materials and methods of a course or discipline in demonstrated ways before making them their own" (p. 134).

In this study, language teacher candidates also assumed this "novice as expert" role by productively repeating what they learned and reflecting on the new knowledge they gained concerning argumentative writing in their weekly journals. The WWJ entries provided us a window into these students' thought processes about argumentation while also showing that the students displayed differences in the way they approached argumentative writing. While some emphasized the importance of structural elements of argumentative writing (e.g., the use of thesis statements, making the paragraph flow with transitional words), some saw value behind successful use of composing strategies and seeing the relationships between different texts.

It is also important to note that while we incorporated writing-about-writing journals during pre-pandemic times in a face-to-face teaching context, our current experience with online teaching affirms the benefits of writing for teaching and learning complex concepts and helping students to think through them in a virtual space. Incorporating various online tools, such as google docs or even podcasts, can facilitate the use of writing-about-writing journals, and even move its use to a collective space where pre-service teachers can respond to peers' entries. Such online writing practices could also create low-stakes grading of students' contributions and provide accountability.

We believe that future research can benefit from a focus on the use of writing-about-writing journals in various disciplines of education (e.g. pre-service teacher education, educational sciences) and even other content-area classes that do not focus on teacher education (e.g., history, sociology, economics, etc.), in languages beyond English (e.g. Basque, Greek), and, in diverse under-reported EFL settings. Finally, systematic and longitudinal ethnographic inquiries into writing journals could help us (1) track the changes in EFL teacher candidates' learning-to-argue processes during their undergraduate teacher education and (2) investigate possible transfer of learning over time. Taking a close look at these cognitive processes that pre-service teachers undergo could help us better understand the relationship between their new writing experiences and current knowledge about various writing skills and strategies, as well as their emerging ability to teach argumentative writing as in-service teachers.

REFERENCES

Bangert-Drowns, R., Hurley, M. & Maniee, Z. (2004). The effects of school-based writing-to-learn interventions on academic achievement: A Meta-Analysis. *Review of Educational Research, 74*, 29–58.

Casanave, C. P. (2011). *Journal writing in second language education.* Ann Arbor: University of Michigan Press.

Connolly, S. K. (2006). *Peer-to-peer dialogue journal writing by Japanese junior high school EFL students.* Unpublished doctoral dissertation, Temple University.

Downs, D., & Wardle, E. (2007). Teaching about writing, righting misconceptions: (Re) envisioning "first-year composition" as "Introduction to Writing Studies." *College composition and communication,* 552–584.

Duppenthaler, P. M. (2004). The effect of three types of feedback on journal writing of Japanese EFL students. *JANET Bulletin, 38,* 1–17.

Durst, R. K., & Newell, G. E. (1989). The uses of function: James Britton's category system and research on writing. *Review of Educational Research, 59(4),* 375–394.

Hirvela, A. (2017). Argumentation & second language writing: Are we missing the boat? *Journal of Second Language Writing, 36,* 69–74.

Hirvela, A., & Belcher, D. (2007). Writing scholars as teacher educators: Exploring writing teacher education (Introduction for special issue titled *Writing Scholars as Teacher Educators: Exploring Writing Teacher Education). Journal of Second Language Writing, 16,* 125–128.

Hyland, K. (2005). *Metadiscourse: Exploring interaction in writing.* London: Continuum.

Kabilan, M. K. (2007). English language teachers reflecting on reflections: A Malasian experience. *TESOL Quarterly, 41*(4), 681–705.

Kibler, A. (2017). Pursuing second language argumentative writing scholarship as a synergistic endeavor (Disciplinary Dialogues). *Journal of Second Language Writing, 36,* 75–76.

Langer, J. A., & Applebee, A. N. (1987). *How writing shapes thinking.* Urbana, IL: National Council of Teachers of English.

Manchón, R. (2009) (Ed.). *Writing in foreign language contexts: Learning, teaching, and research.* Buffalo, NY: Multilingual Matters.

Miller, R. T., & Pessoa, S. (2016) Where's your thesis statement and what happened to your topic sentences? Identifying organizational challenges in undergraduate student argumentative writing. *TESOL Journal,* 847–873.

Newell, G. E. (1984). Learning from writing in two content areas: A case study/protocol analysis of writing to learn. *Research in the Teaching of English, 18*(3), 265–287.

Seloni, L. & Henderson-Lee, S. (2020). (Eds.). *Second Language Writing Instruction in Global Contexts: English Language Teacher Preparation and Development.* Bristol, England: Multilingual Matters.

Sommers, N., & Saltz, L. (2004). The novice as expert: Writing the freshman year. *College Composition and Communication, 56*(1), 124–149.

Toulmin, S. (1958/2003). *The uses of argument.* Cambridge, England: Cambridge University Press.

Trites, L. (2001). Journals as self-evaluative, reflective classroom tolls with advanced ESL graduate students. In J. Burton & M. Carroll (Eds.), *Journal Writing* (pp. 59–70). Alexandria, VA: Teachers of English to Speakers of Other Languages.

Unaldi, A., Seloni, L., Yalcin, S., & Yigitoglu Aptoula, N. (2020). The role of writing in an EFL teacher preparation program in Turkey: Institutional demands, pedagogical practices, and student needs. In L. Seloni & S. Henderson Lee (Eds.), *Second language writing instruction in global contexts: English language teacher preparation and development* (pp, 173–195). Bristol, England: Multilingual Matters.

Yi, Y. (2005). *Immigrant students' out-of-school literacy practices: A qualitative study of Korean students' experiences.* Unpublished doctoral dissertation, The Ohio State University.

Yigitoglu, N., & Belcher, D. (2014). Exploring L2 writing teacher cognition from an experiential perspective: The role learning to write may play in professional beliefs and practices. *System, 47(1),* 116–124.

■ Contributors

Diane D. Belcher is a professor of applied linguistics at Georgia State University. Former co-editor of the journals *English for Specific Purposes* and *TESOL Quarterly,* she has also guest edited three special issues of the *Journal of Second Language Writing* and currently serves as co-editor of a teacher reference series titled *Michigan Series on Teaching Multilingual Writers.* Her publications include eight edited volumes, chapters in a number of books, and articles in such journals as the *Applied Linguistics Review* and *Journal of English for Academic Purposes.* Her research interests mainly focus on advanced academic literacy.

Joel Bloch, who recently retired after 30 years of teaching multilingual composition courses at Ohio State University, has published four books and 35 articles on academic writing, technological literacy, plagiarism, and intellectual property law. He lives in a small town outside Columbus, Ohio, with his wife, daughter, cat, and five turtles.

Zehang Chen, PhD in language education and teacher education, is currently a professor in the School of Foreign Languages and Literature at Beijing Normal University. She has published journal articles and books on English language teaching and learning, teacher education, and e-learning. She has also been involved in many important projects as well as national and provincial teacher training programs and workshops in China. In addition, she has been involved in writing textbooks that are widely used across China.

Natalia Verónica Dalla Costa holds a degree in English Language Teaching and a Licentiate degree in English Language and Literature. She also holds an MA degree in English and Applied Linguistics, and a PhD in Language Sciences from the School of Languages, National University of Córdoba, Argentina. She lectures in English Language I, II, and IV and teaches postgraduate courses in EFL reading and writing. Her research interests include feedback on EFL writing and genre-based instruction in summary and argumentative essay writing.

Frankie Har is an instructor in the English Language Centre, The Hong Kong Polytechnic University. His research interests are in the areas of second language acquisition, applied linguistics, gamification in ELT, translanguaging, and bilingualism.

Christine Hardigree is an assistant professor of adolescent literacy in the education department at Iona College. Her research considers how literacy practices can engage or dismiss the language resources students bring to the classroom, which includes both specialized dual language programs as well as general education contexts within literacy-focused and content-area classrooms. Her publications can be found in the *International Journal of Bilingual Education and Bilingualism, Language and Education, Language Learning, Teachers College Record,* and the *Springer International Handbook on English Language Teaching.* She is also co-author of the book *Teaching Disciplinary Literacy in Grades 6–12: Infusing Content with Reading, Writing, and Language.*

Alan Hirvela is a professor of foreign and second language education at Ohio State University. He taught previously at the Chinese University of Hong Kong. His primary areas of scholarship have been reading-writing connections and the teaching and learning of argumentative writing. His most recent work in argumentation includes the books *Teaching and Learning Argumentative Writing in High School English Language Arts Classrooms* (Newell, Bloome, & Hirvela, 2015) and *Dialogic Literary Argumentation in High School Language Arts Classrooms* (Bloome, Newell, Hirvela, & Lin, 2020).

Ann Johns is Professor Emerita, Linguistics & Writing Studies, at San Diego State University (CA/USA). She has devoted her teaching and research careers to multilingual students from across the curriculum both in the United States and abroad. Her publications include six books and more than one hundred articles and book chapters. In recent years, she and Nigel Caplan, from the University of Delaware, have been co-creating guides for teachers and their students. These include an edited volume, *Changing Practices for the L2 Writing Classroom: Moving Beyond the Five-Paragraph Essay* (2019), and a textbook, *Essential Actions in Academic Writing* (in press), both from the University of Michigan Press.

Fares J. Karam is an assistant professor in the College of Education and Human Development at the University of Nevada, Reno. His research focuses on the language and literacy development of immigrant and refugee-background multilingual learners. His publications can be found in *Applied Linguistics, Journal of Language, Identity, & Education, International Journal of Adolescent & Adult Literacy,* and *TESOL Quarterly,* among others.

Amanda K. Kibler is an associate professor in the College of Education at Oregon State University. Her research draws upon sociocultural and ecological perspectives to explore immigrant-origin multilingual children and adolescents' language and literacy development and the implications of these processes for teaching and learning, with a particular focus on second language writing. Her recent books include *Longitudinal Interactional Histories: Bilingual and Biliterate Journeys of Mexican Immigrant-Origin Youth* (2019) and *Reconceptualizing the Role of Critical Dialogue in American Classrooms* (2020). Her work can also be found in *Applied Linguistics, Journal of Second Language Writing, Language Learning, Literacy Research Journal, The Modern Language Journal,* and *TESOL Quarterly,* among others.

Dr. Lucas Kohnke is a Senior Lecturer in the Department of English Language Education, The Education University of Hong Kong. His main research interest lies in EAP/ESP course design, technology-supported teaching and learning, professional development using information communication technologies, and language provision in English-Medium context. His research has been published in journals such as *Asia-Pacific Education Researcher, RELC Journal, Journal of Education for Teaching,* and *TESOL Journal.*

Icy Lee is a professor in the Faculty of Education at The Chinese University of Hong Kong, where she is currently serving as Chair of the Department of Curriculum and Instruction. Her publications have appeared in international journals such as the *Journal of Second Language Writing, TESOL Quarterly, Language Teaching, System,* and *Language Teaching Research.* She was previously Co-Editor of the *Journal of Second Language Writing* and is Principal Associate Editor of *The Asia-Pacific Education Researcher.*

Xiaohui Li is an associate professor in the School of Foreign Languages and Cultures at Chongqing University in China, where she is currently serving as Vice Dean. She has been teaching EFL writing courses for more than 20 years and developed more than 20 textbooks for different levels of EFL learners. Her research focuses on inquiry-based learning, argumentative writing, ad EFL teacher development.

Thomas D. Mitchell is an associate teaching professor of English at Carnegie Mellon University in Qatar, where he teaches courses in academic reading and writing, technical writing, and discourse studies. His research focuses on scaffolding academic literacy development through interdisciplinary collaboration.

Renka Ohta earned her PhD in Foreign Language and ESL Education at the University of Iowa. She taught English as a foreign language at the high school level in Japan, and her research interests include integrated writing assessment and teacher development.

Parva Panahi is a doctoral student in the Second Language Studies program at Purdue University. Her doctoral studies at Purdue are mostly focused on writing, and her particular areas of interest include second language writing, the internalization of U.S. writing programs, and writing teacher education in the era of superdiversity. Her dissertation explores ways in which U.S. writing programs respond to the increasing diversity in first-year writing classes and infuse attention to linguistically and culturally responsive teachers in their teacher preparation programs. Before coming to Purdue, she was a college writing instructor in her home country, Iran.

Silvia Pessoa is an associate teaching professor of English at Carnegie Mellon University in Qatar. Through interdisciplinary collaborations, Pessoa supports academic writing development using genre-based pedagogy and systemic functional linguistics.

Lia Plakans is a professor in Teaching and Learning in the College of Education at the University of Iowa. She has written several books with the University of Michigan Press on reading and writing for academic purposes and on language assessment. She has taught English as a second and additional language in Iowa, Texas, Ohio, and Latvia.

Lisya Seloni is a professor of Applied Linguistics and TESOL in the Department of English at Illinois State University. Her research explores ethnographic approaches to L2 writing, L2 teacher education, and issues related to the sociopolitical context of English language teaching. Her publications have appeared in the *Journal of Second Language Writing, Language Policy, English for Specific Purposes, Journal of Excellence in College Teaching, Journal of Language and Politics* and several edited collections. Her edited book (with Sarah Henderson Lee), *Second Language Writing Instruction in Global Contexts* (Multilingual Matters, 2020), considers second language writing teacher education in non-English dominant contexts.

Lan Wang-Hiles, PhD, is an associate professor of English at West Virginia State University where she also directs the ESL Program. Her research interests include L2 writing, writing center theory and practice, multilingual tutoring, and SLA.

Qiling Wu is a graduate student in the School of Foreign Languages and Literature at BeijingNormal University. Her work focuses on second language studies and language education. She has also developed an interest in investigating how community in a social context may account for children's language learning identity.

Weier Ye, PhD, is an associate professor in the English Department at Queensborough Community College of the City University of New York, where he teaches English Composition 101, BE102 Composition Workshop, and English developmental reading and writing courses. He is particularly interested in researching the effect of various cultural factors on native Chinese speakers' studying English as well as their learning processes with the intention of addressing methods writing teachers may employ to acculturate second language writers into an American style of written discourse.

Nur Yiğitoğlu Aptoula is an associate professor of Applied Linguistics at Boğaziçi University, Turkey. Her current research focuses on the interface between second language (L2) writing and L2 acquisition, genre-based approaches to teaching of L2 writing, and L2 writing teacher education. Her work appears in journals such as *Journal of Second Language Writing*, *Language Awareness*, and *System*.

Nugrahenny T. Zacharias (Henny) is an assistant teaching professor at Penn State University, Abington. Her research interests lie in the interface between multimodality, second language writing, and multilingual identities. Her writing has been published in *TESOL Journal*, *RELC Journal*, and the *Journal of Asian Pacific Communication*.

Min Zou is currently a lecturer and researcher in the School of Foreign Languages at Beijing Institute of Technology in China. She received her PhD from The Chinese University of Hong Kong in 2019, and her research interests include critical thinking and EFL writing.

■ Author Index

■ Subject Index

Printed and bound by CPI Group (UK) Ltd, Croydon, CR0 4YY

09/06/2025

14686122-0001